Windows from the Keyboard

Nicholas Baran

John Wiley & Sons, Inc.

New York • Chichester • Brisbane • Toronto • Singapore

Dedication

For my parents, Elena Baran Baskin and Jack Baskin

Trademarks

Excel, Microsoft Word, and Microsoft are registered trademarks and Windows is a trademark of Microsoft Corporation. WordPerfect is a registered trademark of WordPerfect Corporation. Lotus, 1-2-3, and Ami Pro are registered trademarks of Lotus Development Corp. Quattro Pro is a registered trademark of Borland International, Inc. Other words in this publication in which the Author and Publisher believe trademark or other proprietary rights may exist have been designated as such by use of Initial Capital Letters. However, in so designating or failing to designate such words, neither the Author nor the Publisher intends to express any judgment on the validity or legal status of any proprietary right that may be claimed in the words.

Associate Publisher: Katherine Schowalter
Editor: Paul Farrell
Managing Editor: Frank Grazioli
Editorial Production and Design: Electric Ink, Ltd.

It is a policy of John Wiley & Sons, Inc. to have books of enduring value published in the United States printed on acid-free paper, and we exert our best efforts to that end.

Library of Congress Cataloging-in-Publication Data

Baran, Nicholas.
    Windows from the Keyboard/Nicholas Baran.
      p. cm.
    Includes index.
    ISBN 0-471-59093-2 (paper: acid-free paper)
    1. Windows (Computer programs) 2. Microsoft Windows (Computer file) I. Title.
    QA76.76.W56B355 1993
    005.4'3--dc20   92-43497
                       CIP

Printed in the United States of America

10 9 8 7 6 5 4 3 2 1

Contents

CHAPTER 2

CHAPTER 3

CHAPTER 4

Microsoft Word 87

CHAPTER 5

Lotus Ami Pro 119

CHAPTER 6

Microsoft Excel 149

CHAPTER 7

Borland Quattro Pro 181

CHAPTER 8

Lotus 1-2-3 211

Foreword

This book is about using Microsoft Windows strictly from the keyboard. When you have finished reading this book, you will be proficient at using keyboard commands for virtually every task in Windows and in six major applications.

This is *not* necessarily a book for mouse haters. You may like using a mouse but prefer to keep your hands on the keyboard more of the time. Or you may be a veteran keyboard user, particularly someone from the MS-DOS world, who just can't stand using a mouse. Or perhaps you're a traveller who finds it awkward to ask the passenger next to you if you can use his or her leg as a mouse pad. Or maybe your laptop has a trackball and you find it clumsy and difficult to use. Or you may have found that it's hard to see the mouse cursor on your laptop's LCD screen. (That alone might prompt you to switch to strictly keyboard use.) Or perhaps you do word processing for a living and find that the mouse really slows you down: it can be a real annoyance when you're rapidly typing to have to stop and remove one hand from the keyboard.

Whatever your reasons, this *is* a book about going mouseless. It's about learning to use a keyboard to work with a graphical user interface that was basically designed for use with a mouse. At first, it might seem like we're paddling upstream or going backwards against the relentless force of technological progress. But I think you'll be pleasantly surprised.

When I first sat down to write this book, I was a committed mouse user. After years at the DOS keyboard, I had made the switch to Windows and then the Macintosh and then to NeXT computers. I now use them all. In recent years, I'd become totally accustomed to the point-and-click interaction of the mouse. The problem was, I hated my laptop's "snap-on" trackball: it was a pain to drag around, I found it hard to manipulate the cursor, and of course it was one more thing I'd have to remember to pack. So with some trepidation I permanently disconnected it from my 386SX laptop and set out to find what it would be like to work strictly from the keyboard. After several months of mouseless Windows, I am happy to report that not only have I become thoroughly proficient with Windows from the keyboard, I also find the mouse to be more of a nuisance than a benefit. In fact, I've even started using more keyboard shortcuts on my NeXT and Macintosh systems.

The point here is not to wage a religious battle between keyboards and mice in order to prove the superiority of the keyboard. On the contrary, there is no question that the mouse has not only revolutionized computer interfaces, but has some powerful utility as well. There are certain situations where a mouse simply works better than the keyboard. Working with graphics and drawing programs in particular is generally more efficient with a mouse. As we shall see in this book, most Windows applications now have "tool boxes" of icons on the screen which represent all kinds of tasks you can perform by simply pointing and clicking with the mouse. (The only problem is trying to memorize what all those icons stand for.) The real crux of the mouse-keyboard controversy is that operations that involve visualization are generally easier to perform using a mouse. For example, moving windows or changing margins in a word processing document is very easy if you can simply drag the window or margin to its new location. You can visually see the change as it occurs. With the keyboard, you may not have this luxury. You may have to enter some coordinates and then execute the command before seeing the results. But what about all the other day-to-day tasks? Does the mouse really make operations faster and easier? I've come to believe the opposite is true.

Regardless of your sentiments or your intentions with respect to mice and keyboards, this book will prove useful in making you a better Windows user. The more proficient you are with the keyboard, the more versatile and efficient you will be.

Why a Graphical Interface?

As you consider the topic of this book, you might wonder why you should even bother with a graphical user interface (GUI). After all, if the GUI is designed for use with a mouse, why not stick with MS-DOS? There are several answers to this question. To begin with, the DOS world is moving to Windows. Whether you like it or not, Windows is becoming the standard user interface in the DOS world. That means that more and more offices are switching to Windows and that more and more computers are running Windows. And, most importantly, more and more applications require Windows to run. For this reason alone, it's in your best interest to at least know how to use Windows.

But there are more compelling reasons to learn Windows. Whether you're a mouse or keyboard user, graphical user interfaces such as Windows offer major advantages over so-called command-line interfaces such as MS-DOS. The biggest advantage lies in the very concept of a window. In a command line interface like DOS, there is only one window—namely, the entire screen. A windowing system like Microsoft Windows allows you to view several windows on the screen at the same time. It's like having several separate but smaller screens in which you can view different information. It also means that you can switch from one window to another without having to quit applications. (DOS users will recall having to close one application before opening another.)

For me, the creation of this book was a dramatic illustration of the advantages of Windows over DOS. I prepared all the screen shots using Microsoft Paintbrush, a standard graphics and drawing program which comes with Windows. I had one window running Paintbrush and another window running the application that I was writing about. To create a screen shot, I would hit the Print Screen key and then switch to the Paintbrush window simply by pressing Alt+Tab. I would paste the captured screen into Paintbrush and then switch back to the application. Look at all the screen shots in this book, and imagine creating this book on an MS-DOS system!

Another major advantage of graphical interfaces is that you can see graphical elements in your documents. For example, you can change fonts and see what they look like right on the screen. This is called "WYSIWIG," or "What You See Is What You Get."

In character-based interfaces such as DOS, you have to print the document to see what it will actually look like. The mouse is something I'm willing to live without. Windows is not.

A Consistent Interface

Regardless of the "operating environment" you use, you'll work most efficiently if the way you execute commands and perform operations is consistent throughout the various applications you work with. Interface consistency was and remains the great strength of the Macintosh. Every application in the Macintosh environment obeys certain rules set forth by Apple for software developers. (Software developers can break the rules, but only at the risk of losing compatibility with future releases of the Macintosh operating software.) For example, you open and close all applications the same way. You use the same command key sequences to cut, copy, and paste, in every Macintosh application.

It's been much more difficult to establish user interface consistency in the DOS/Windows world simply because there were no standard user interface guidelines for DOS applications. Therefore, thousands of applications, many of which are still in use today, were developed with unique methods for performing quite standard operations. For example, one DOS application might require the user to press Ctrl+X to exit the application, while another uses Ctrl+X to delete text. One word processor might use Ctrl+Y to delete a line; another might use Ctrl+Y to change to italics. Obviously, this kind of inconsistency makes it difficult for the user. Each application requires a different set of keystrokes to memorize, a different set of conventions to follow. Consistency has become a major goal of Microsoft Windows, and, as you'll see in this book, major progress has been made, although some applications, including several covered in this book, still have some work to do.

The Windows Interface Standard

The Windows interface standard is a set of guidelines that prescribes how applications should behave in a manner consistent with other applications in the Windows environment. Consistent behavior includes the behavior of both mouse and keyboard. The objective according to Microsoft is to provide "visual and functional consistency within and across Windows-based applications." This means, for example, that dialog boxes should behave the same way in any Windows application. Methods for closing and opening files, accessing menu options, opening the Help utility, switching between multiple documents, and selecting text and data, to name a few, should work the same way whether you're working with Microsoft Word or WordPerfect or a business accounting program.

Much of the interface standard was developed together with IBM, when Microsoft and IBM were cooperating on the development of OS/2. The result of this development was an interface guideline, published by IBM, called *Common User Access* (CUA). The objective of CUA was to provide "visual and functional consistency" throughout all of IBM's operating systems and interfaces, from mainframes to PCs. The CUA specification, version 2.0 , is contained in the IBM publication *IBM Common User Access: Advanced Interface Design Guide* (IBM, Boca Raton, FL, 1989).

When Microsoft and IBM went in different directions (IBM with OS/2, Microsoft with Windows), the CUA standard was already in place. And although Microsoft officially calls its guidelines "Windows interface guidelines," they are essentially the same as the guidelines specified by IBM's Common User Access. In other words, if an application supports Common User Access guidelines, it will also support Windows interface guidelines.

This does *not* mean, however, that any CUA-compatible application will run under Windows or that any Windows application will run under other CUA-compatible operating environments such as OS/2. What it *does* mean is that a CUA-compatible application will look familiar to a user of any CUA-based interface and will function in a manner consistent with other CUA applications. In other words, CUA compatibility does not insure operating system level compatibility. Interface compatibility and operating system compatibility are two different things entirely. Interface compatibility means that the interface looks, feels, and functions in a manner consistent with a particular standard. Operating system compatibility has to do more with underlying layers of the environment—layers such as file and data structures, hardware and peripheral interfaces, and so forth—which should not be readily apparent to the user.

Microsoft's interface guidelines are published in a book entitled *The Windows Interface: An Application Design Guide,* (Microsoft Press, Redmond, WA, 1992). While primarily of interest to programmers and developers of Windows applications, the book is of importance to users because it clearly defines and describes the criteria for designing a Windows-compatible application. The guideline specifies both mouse and keyboard actions: how navigation keys should function, what the Enter and Esc keys should do, what functions the Alt, Shift, and Ctrl keys should perform, how the Del and Backspace keys should work, what the function keys should do, and so forth.

The Microsoft guidelines are "recommendations." There is no requirement for software developers to follow them, but it is clearly in the best interests of all developers to produce consistent applications. At the same time, the guidelines leave a great deal of flexibility, so that developers can easily include unique functions that will distinguish their applications from those of their competitors.

A good example of the implementation of a consistent interface is the Cut, Copy, Paste, and Undo functions. These functions appear in virtually every type of business productivity application, from databases to spreadsheets to word processors. The recommended keystrokes in the Windows interface guidelines are Ctrl+X for Cut, Ctrl+C for Copy, Ctrl+V for Paste, and Ctrl+Z for Undo. These keystrokes have become almost universally adopted to perform this function. (They are used on Macintosh, NeXT, IBM, and many UNIX environments as the standard keystrokes for performing these functions.) But not all Windows applications support these keystrokes. Surprisingly, both Borland's Quattro Pro and Lotus 1-2-3 do not support these combinations, using instead the old DOS keystrokes (Shift+Del, Ctrl+Ins, Shift+Ins). We expect that both these applications will support the CUA or Microsoft standards in future releases.

One of the problems with computer books is that they are often obsolete soon after they appear on the bookstore shelves. We think that this book can claim substantial longevity because the keyboard functions described in this book are here to stay. Future releases of Windows and the applications described in this book will certainly continue to support the currently defined standard functions. If anything, future releases of applications will become more consistent with the keystrokes described in this book.

Choosing Applications for Keyboard Use

Although Microsoft is actively encouraging developers to produce consistent applications, you will notice that the degree of consistency varies tremendously among applications. Also, some applications are more capable from the keyboard than others. If you are planning to do a lot of your work strictly from the keyboard, it is well worth investigating how well your prospective software application supports the keyboard. Unfortunately, most magazine product reviews emphasize the use of the mouse with Windows products, not giving much attention to keyboard usage.

The best way to evaluate the keyboard support of a product is to try it out. Does the product support the standard Windows keystrokes described in Chapters 1 and 2 of this book? Does the application include a keyboard template that shows the function of keystroke combinations? Does the Help facility routinely include keystroke equivalents? Does the manual include keyboard equivalents for most operations? Is there an Appendix with a complete listing of key equivalents?

This book provides brief chapters on using three major word processing and three spreadsheet applications with the keyboard—Lotus Ami Pro, Microsoft Word, WordPerfect, Microsoft Excel, Lotus 1-2-3, and Quattro Pro. As we mentioned earlier, the keystrokes in these applications will almost certainly remain the same in future releases of these products. Although some functions and menu items may change in future product releases, these changes should not affect your ability to use the product comfortably from the keyboard. Again, the trend is toward more consistent and uniform application of keyboard functions.

Finally, it must be emphasized that the chapters on the six applications are in no way a substitute for the applications' user manuals and documentation. In the brief chapters in this book, we have focused on using the product with the keyboard and not on the detailed functionality of the product. There is simply not enough space in this book to treat each of these applications in exhaustive detail. We have provided enough information to get you started with the product and feeling comfortable operating the product from the keyboard. In the Appendix, we list the most common keystroke equivalents for Windows and each application, along with space for you to enter the keystrokes you use most frequently.

A Word about Notation

Simultaneous key combinations are shown with the keystrokes separated by a plus (+). For example, Ctrl+B means: press down the Ctrl key, and while holding it down, press the B key, then release both keys. Keystrokes to be pressed in sequence are separated by a comma, although you can press them virtually simultaneously (e.g., Alt+F,C should be interpreted: Press the Alt key, and while holding it down, press the F key, followed by the C key, then release).

How to Use this Book

For each program discussed in this book, a list in the Appendix (beginning on page 237) shows the most frequently used keystrokes. As you read the thumbnail discussions of each application, you should refer to and annotate the corresponding keystroke summary chart at the back of the book.

Acknowledgments

I would like to thank my editor at John Wiley & Sons, Paul Farrell, for his excellent suggestions and remarkable patience in dealing with this project. I would also like to thank my long-standing colleague and associate, Jonathan Erickson, for helping to make this book possible. And finally, I would like to thank my wife, Esther, and my children, Paul and Nicole, for putting up with me during these past months of endless screen shots and keystroke equivalents.

Navigating Windows and Program Manager

1

A concise list of Program Manager keystrokes begins on page 238.

This chapter covers the basic functions of Windows and Program Manager. Using only the keyboard, we first navigate through the Windows interface, then through the Program Manager, since it is such an integral part of Windows. We then look specifically at the capabilities of Program Manager. The keystrokes discussed in this chapter are summarized in Table 1.3, located at the end of the chapter, and in the Appendix.

The PC Keyboard

For our purposes, the IBM PC compatible keyboard is the exclusive input device for Microsoft Windows. A typical keyboard layout is shown in Figure 1.1. The primary keys that operate Windows are the Arrow keys, the Enter key, the Control (Ctrl) key, the Alternate (Alt) key, the Tab key, the Escape (Esc) key, and the Function keys (F1 through F12).

The Enter key is the "decisive" key. When you hit the Enter key, Windows will usually attempt to perform an operation. Hitting Enter when an application or file icon is highlighted will execute the application or open the file. If you hit Enter when a dialog box is waiting for a response, Windows will execute the action or settings represented by the current status of the dialog box (see Fig. 1.2). Note in the example that the OK field is highlighted, which is usually the default action in a dialog box. (The term *default* in computer lingo means "the operation or function automatically provided by the system.") Similarly, if you hit Enter when a menu item is highlighted, Windows will execute the action represented by that item.

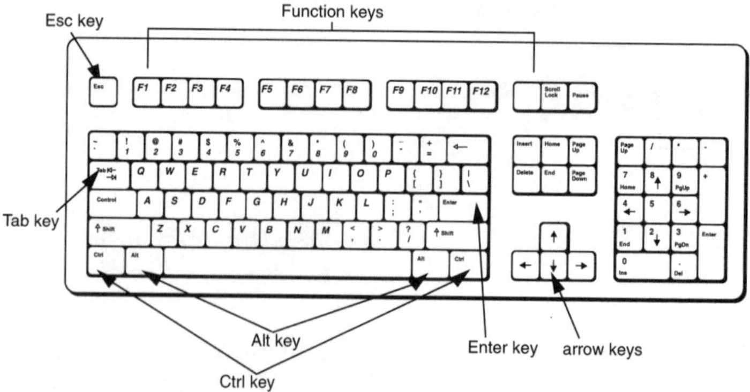

Figure 1.1 A typical IBM PC keyboard.

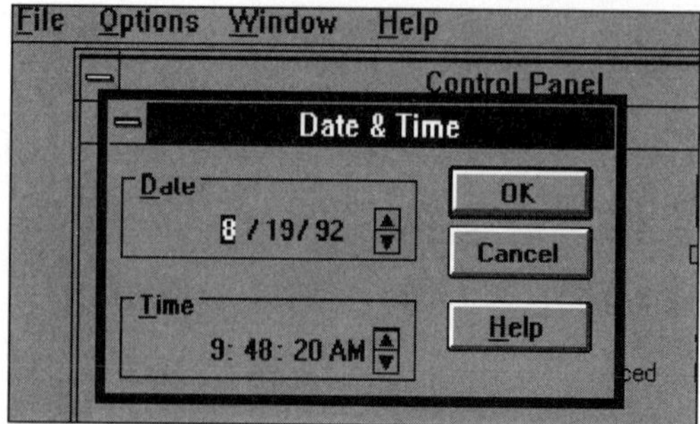

Figure 1.2 A typical Windows dialog box.

The Escape (Esc) key could be characterized as the "indecisive" key. In the above example of the dialog box, hitting the Esc key would cancel the operation of the dialog box. Similarly, hitting Esc when a menu is displayed will cancel the menu, causing it to "roll up" or disappear.

The Enter key is the "decisive" key: by pressing it, you open a selected document, start a highlighted application, or activate the settings in a dialog box. The Esc key, on the other hand, is "indecisive": by pressing it, you will close a menu, cancel a dialog box, and in general "back out" of whatever action you have started to take.

Pressing the Alt or F10 key activates the menu bar at the top of an active window. (For more details on the components of windows, see the next section, "Windows Basics.") For example, Figure 1.3 shows the File menu of Program Manager, selected with Alt+F. You can also press Alt+ the first letter of the other menu options (O, W, or H, in this example) to open a menu. For example, pressing Alt+H would open the Help menu. (Note that the F1 key automatically opens the Help contents in most Windows applications.) Pressing the Esc key cancels the menu but leaves you in the menu bar. Pressing Alt or F10 with an open menu cancels the menu and returns you to the active application (Program Manager, in this example).

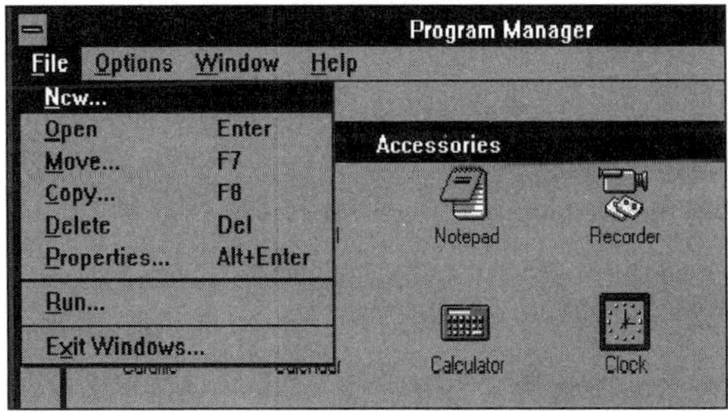

Figure 1.3 The File menu in Program Manager.

Note that the keystrokes listed in the right column of the File menu (Enter for Open, F7 for Move, etc.) are keystrokes that may be pressed to perform those actions *without opening* the File menu. For example, if you highlight a program item in the Main window (File Manager, for example), pressing Enter will execute the File Manager, pressing F7 presents you with a Move dialog box (allowing you to move File Manager to another group window), pressing F8 executes the Copy command, and so forth.

The Arrow keys are the primary navigation keys. The Tab key navigates through dialog boxes, as discussed later in this chapter. The Arrow keys allow you to move from menu to menu in the menu bar or from icon to icon in a window. For example, pressing Alt or F10 activates the menu bar. You can then press the horizontal Arrow keys to move from one menu to another. Pressing the Enter or Down Arrow key opens the menu. Notice that once you've opened a menu on the menu bar, moving horizontally to another menu automatically opens the selected menu.

After opening a menu, use the Down and Up Arrow keys to move from item to item. You can also select menu items by typing the underlined letter of the menu item. Using the File menu in Figure 1.3 as an example, typing the letter O will execute the File Open command, and typing the letter C will execute the File Copy command. As you become familiar with running Windows from the keyboard, you'll see how quickly the program responds to commands such as Alt+F,O and Alt+F,C.

The Alt key or F10 key activates and deactivates the menu bar of a window. If the menu bar is activated, pressing Enter will open the currently highlighted menu. Once a menu is opened, you can move to other opened menus with the Arrow keys. And, after a menu is opened, selecting the underlined letter of a listed action will execute that action.

Windows Basics

Windows allows you to perform three basic tasks: to manipulate windows, dialog boxes, and icons, to execute and close applications, and to perform file operations such as Copy and Delete. All of these tasks can be accomplished easily from the keyboard.

Before we plunge into the details, let's review Microsoft Windows' two primary components: Program Manager and File Manager. These two components do exactly what their names suggest. Program Manager manages the applications or programs on your system, while File Manager manages the data or files. (File Manager can also be used to run programs and applications, but has fewer tools for organizing and managing them.)

In virtually all Windows setups, Program Manager automatically starts up when you start Windows and is always running either in the background or as your main interface. (See Chapter 2 for more on starting Windows without Program Manager.) Therefore, when we discuss the first tasks of manipulating windows, dialog boxes, and icons, we must discuss Program Manager. Later in this chapter, we will cover the primary functions of Program Manager and how you can manage your applications with it. (File Manager is a separate application and does not necessarily have to be running to operate Windows, so we will treat it separately in the next chapter.)

Manipulating Windows and Icons

The first screen you see when you start up Windows will vary, depending on how you've customized Windows or whether you've specified applications that automatically run at start-up. The screen shown in Figure 1.4(a) is a typical start-up screen (with no automatic start-up applications) and will serve as our sample screen for working with general Windows keyboard commands. Note that the large background window is the Program Manager, while the smaller foreground window is entitled "Main." Main is a group, containing the set of Windows' system applications, each represented by its own icon. (Applications are also called *program items.*) The icons at the bottom represent groups of other applications. (These icons are called *group icons.*) We will look at groups and program items later in this chapter.

You navigate from one window to another or to a group icon by pressing Ctrl+Tab or Ctrl+F6 repeatedly until you reach the desired window or icon. You can tell where you are by whether the icon or window title bar is highlighted. If a window or icon is highlighted, pressing Enter will open the icon or open an application or file within the highlighted window. You might want to experiment with Ctrl+F6 or Ctrl+Tab to see how this works. If these keystrokes don't work, check if a menu in the Program Manager menu bar is highlighted, and press F10, Alt, or Esc to deactivate the menu bar. (An activated menu bar will override the Ctrl+Tab function.)

You can also move from one window or icon to another from Program Manager's Windows menu. Pressing Alt+W (or Alt and then moving the Arrow key to the Window option) opens this menu, which is shown in Figure 1.4(b). The currently active window is checked (in this case, the Main window). You can move the Down or Up Arrow keys or press the underlined number to select another group, then press Enter to open it. The Windows menu is especially useful if you can't see all the icons on the screen (if they're covered up by another window or if you're working with a smaller sized Program Manager window, for example).

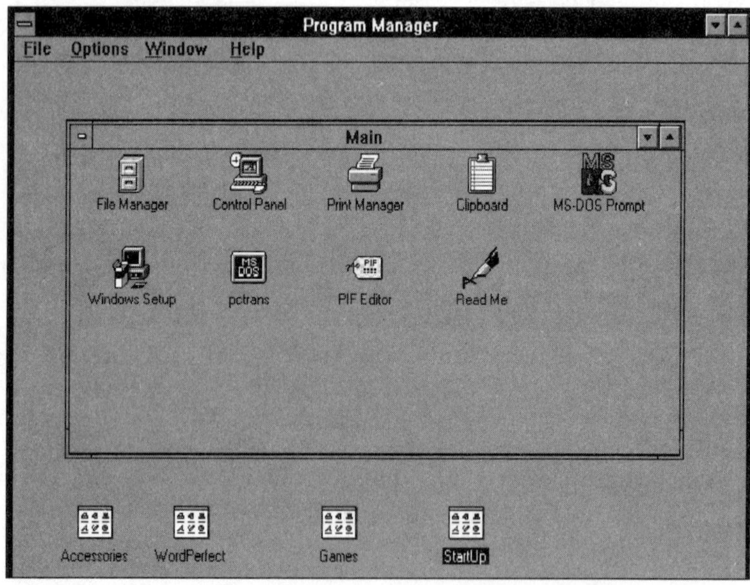

(a)

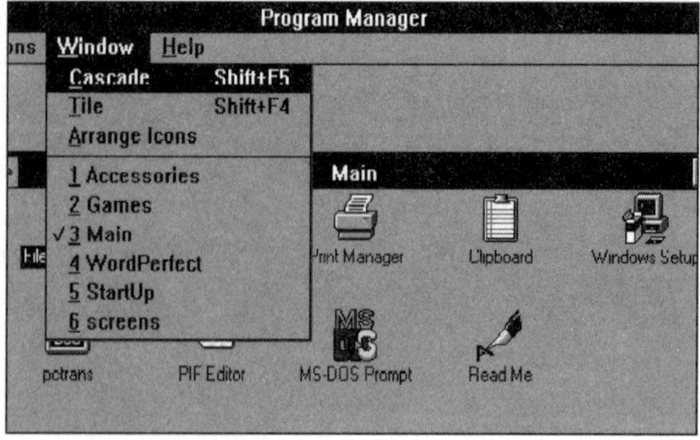

(b)

Figure 1.4(a) A typical screen when you start Windows. (b) The Window menu in Program Manager.

The Control Menus

Figure 1.5 shows the components of a window. The maximize and minimize buttons, the scroll bars, and the window corner (used by the mouse to resize the window), *cannot be operated using the keyboard.* However, you can perform the same functions by means of the *Control menu.*

The Control menu is the most important means of controlling Windows from the keyboard. With a mouse, you would perform operations such as moving and resizing windows by clicking on the window and dragging it to the desired location or size. The Control menu lets you perform these operations using the Arrow keys. Table 1.1 summarizes the commands available from the

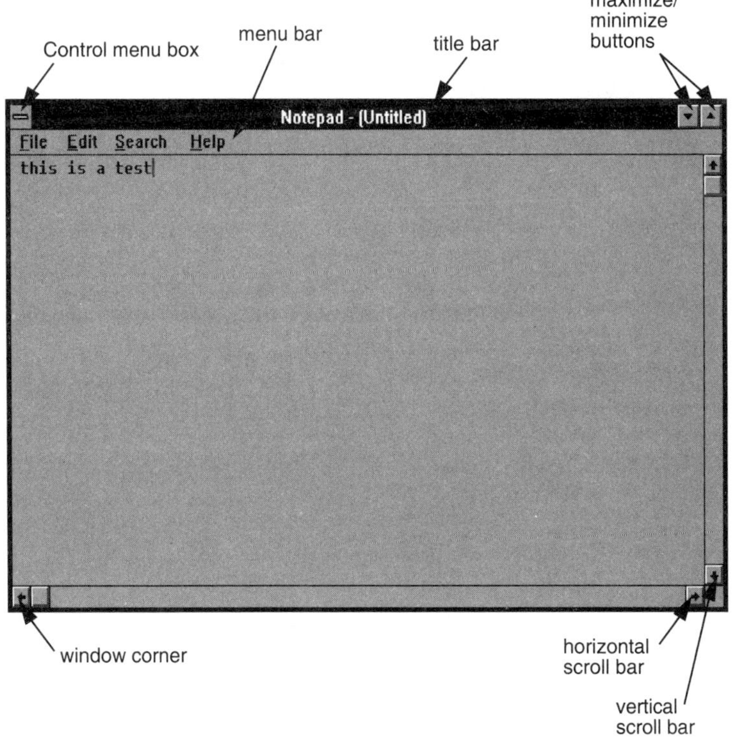

Figure 1.5 The maximize/minimize buttons, scroll bars, and window corner cannot be operated from the keyboard.

Control menu. Each window and icon has a control menu associated with it. Dialog boxes also have control menus, but it is usually easier to select Cancel (Esc key) or OK (Enter key) when working with dialog boxes.

Table 1.1 Control Menu Commands

Once a Control menu is opened, you select one of the listed actions by pressing the key of the underlined letter.

Function	*Command*
Restores window to its original size after being maximized (enlarged to full-screen size) or minimized (reduced to an icon)	Restore
Allows you to move the window or icon to another position on the screen using the Arrow keys	Move
Allows you to change the size of a window using the Arrow keys	Size
Reduces a window to an icon	Minimize
Enlarges window or icon to full size	Maximize
Closes window or dialog box	Close

A Control menu is represented by a small box with a dash in the upper left corner of a window, as shown in Figure 1.5. With the keyboard, there are two keystroke commands for opening a Control menu: Alt+Spacebar, and Alt+Hyphen. The difference between the two types of Control menu icons, which is sometimes hard to see, is shown in Figure 1.6. You use Alt+Spacebar to open the Control menu of an *active application*. You use Alt+Hyphen to open the Control menu of a window or icon *within* the active application. It is important to understand this distinction. In Figure 1.4, for example, the active application is Program Manager. Pressing Alt+Spacebar will open the Control menu of Program Manager. You can execute Control menu commands by typing the underlined letter of the command. For example, typing Alt+Spacebar,N executes the Minimize command, and Alt+Spacebar,X executes the Maximize command.

There are two basic types of Control menus, and they are easy to confuse because their icons are so similar (see Fig. 1.6). To open the Control menu of an application, press Alt+Spacebar. To open the Control menu of a document or other window within an application, press Alt+Hyphen.

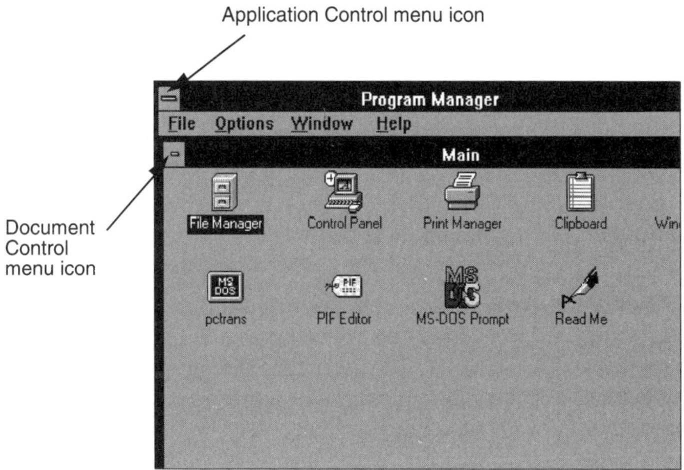

Figure 1.6 Press Alt+Spacebar to open the Control menu of an *application*. Press Alt + Hyphen to open a *document's* Control menu.

Now, let's say you want to open the Control menu of the window entitled Main. Main is not an application window. It is a *document window* that contains a group of applications. If the title bar of the Main window is not highlighted, press Ctrl+Tab until Main is highlighted. Then press Alt+Hyphen to open Main's Control menu. You can also open the control menu of group icons by moving to the desired icon using Ctrl+Tab, then pressing Alt+Hyphen to open that icon's Control menu, as shown in Figure 1.7.

To go one step further, let's open the Control Panel application inside the Main window. Highlight the Control Panel icon using the Arrow keys and press Enter to open the application. Press Alt+Spacebar to open the Control menu. The reason you press Alt+Spacebar rather than Alt+Hyphen is because the Control Panel is now the *active application.*

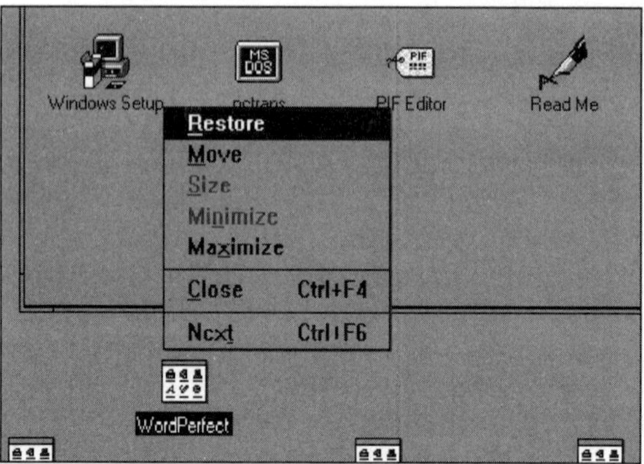

Figure 1.7 The Control menu of the minimized WordPerfect application is open.

Now let's pick one of the options within the Control Panel. Highlight the Fonts icon and press Enter to open the Fonts dialog box. Press Alt+Spacebar to open the Dialog Box Control menu. Note that Alt+Spacebar operates the control menu within a dialog box. Most dialog box control menus only have two options: closing the dialog box or moving the dialog box. As mentioned earlier, if you want to close the dialog box, hitting the Esc key or Alt+F4 is easier than opening the Control menu. However, if you want to move the dialog box, you will have to use the Control menu.

Navigating through Dialog Boxes

Working with dialog boxes is a matter of moving to the desired field and entering the appropriate data, either from a list of options provided in the dialog box, or by typing in the data. To move from one field to the next, you can use the Tab key to move forward, or Shift+Tab to move backwards. Many dialog box fields have an underlined letter, in which case you can press Alt+ the underlined letter to move directly to that field. For example, in Figure 1.8, pressing Alt+S moves you to the Icons Spacing field. Pressing Alt+R moves you to the Cursor Blink Rate field. Press Enter to execute the desired action or setting of the dialog box. Press Esc or Alt+F4 to cancel.

Figures 1.8(a), (b), and (c) show the various types of fields that can appear in Windows dialog boxes. Most of these are self-explanatory. Command buttons are operated with the Enter key. Check boxes are toggled on and off with the Spacebar. Option buttons (such as Center and Tile in Fig. 1.8a) are operated with the horizontal Arrow keys. Text boxes usually provide a default value. When the value is highlighted, you can type new text over the highlighted text if you need to change the value, or you can use the Arrow keys to move through a list of options if one is provided.

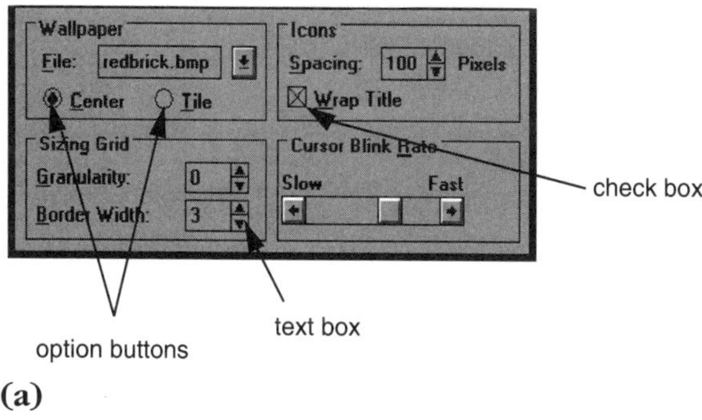

(a)

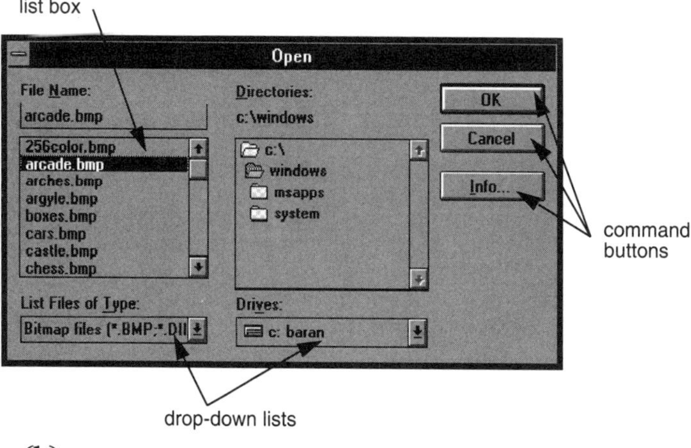

(b)

Figure 1.8(a–b) Typical dialog boxes. Note the underlined letters in many of the dialog box fields.

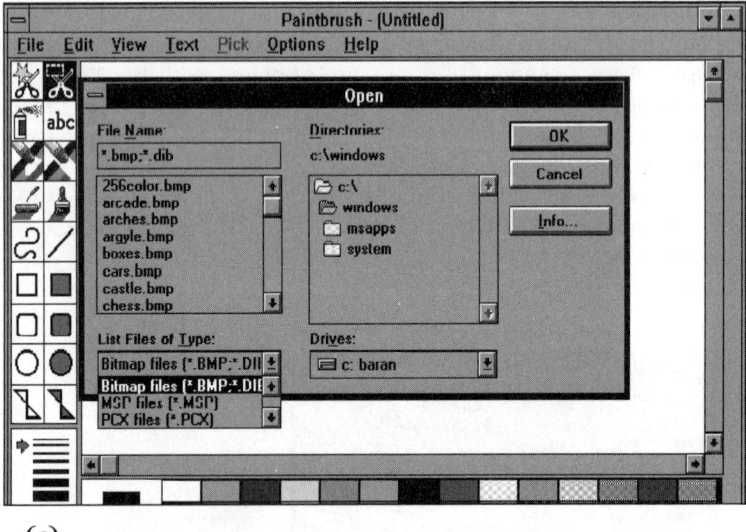

(c)

Figure 1.8(c) Typical dialog box (continued).

The File Name field in Figure 1.8(b) is a list box. The currently selected option from the list box is placed in the File Name field. To select from options in a list, first press the Tab key (or Shift+Tab) to move to the list box, and then use the Up and Down Arrow keys and press Enter to select the desired option.

The List Files of Type field in Figure 1.8(b) is a *drop down list*. Drop down lists are identified by the down arrow in the right corner of the field. Figure 1.8(c) shows the contents of the drop down list. To open a drop down list, move with the Tab or Shift+Tab key to the drop down list field, and press Alt+Down Arrow to open the list. You can also press the Down and Up Arrow keys to scroll through the list. Press Enter to select the desired item in the list.

Switching Applications

One valuable feature of Windows is its ability to have several applications running at one time. For example, you could have WordPerfect, a game of Solitaire, and Paintbrush all running simultaneously, as shown in Figure 1.9. In this example, the three applications have been reduced to their icons, or minimized. (Actually, there are *four* applications running in Figure 1.9. The fourth is Program Manager, which is running in its window.)

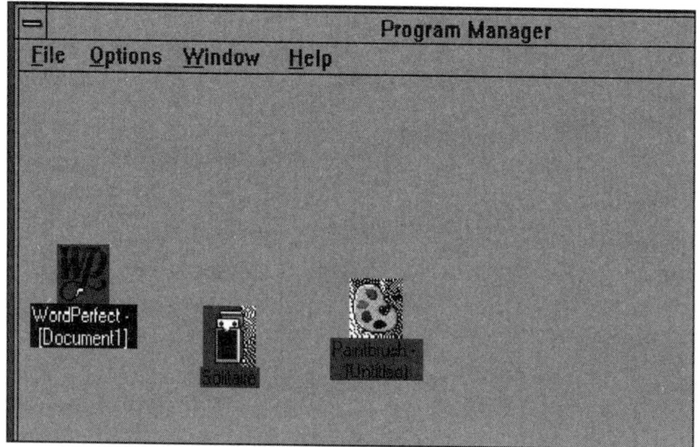

Figure 1.9 Three applications plus Program Manager running simultaneously.

The keyboard offers a very convenient way to switch from one application to the next: press Alt+Esc. This switches you from one application to the next, leaving the application in its current state (running as an icon or in a window, for example). If you want to open the currently highlighted icon, press the Enter key.

Alt+Tab switches you to the application you last used. Holding down Alt and pressing Tab repeatedly switches you to the next application, but only displays the title bar. (Releasing the Tab key opens the application window.) This is faster than using Alt+Esc, which draws the entire application window rather than just the title bar on the screen (assuming the application is running in a window).

The Task List

Another method of switching applications is to press Ctrl+Esc to bring up the Task List or Task Switching menu (also accessible from the Control menu), as shown in Figure 1.10. The Task List is an important feature of Windows because it enables you to see immediately what programs are running. From the Task List, you can also arrange open application windows in a *tile* or *cascade* configuration, as shown in Figures 1.11 and 1.12. Note that open windows in Program Manager can be tiled or cascaded either from the Windows option on the menu bar or by pressing Shift+F4 (tile) or Shift+F5 (cascade).

One of the best features of Windows is that it lets you run several applications at once, but doing this can be confusing because one application window may hide others. The Task List is a useful tool because it displays a list of all applications that are currently running and lets you switch from one application to another. You access the Task List by opening the Control menu and choosing Switch To or by pressing Ctrl+Esc.

To try these methods of switching applications, open a few applications, minimizing each one by pressing Alt+Spacebar,N. (Minimize the document window from which the application executed by pressing Alt+Hyphen,N.) Then press Alt+Esc, Alt+Tab, and Ctrl+Esc.

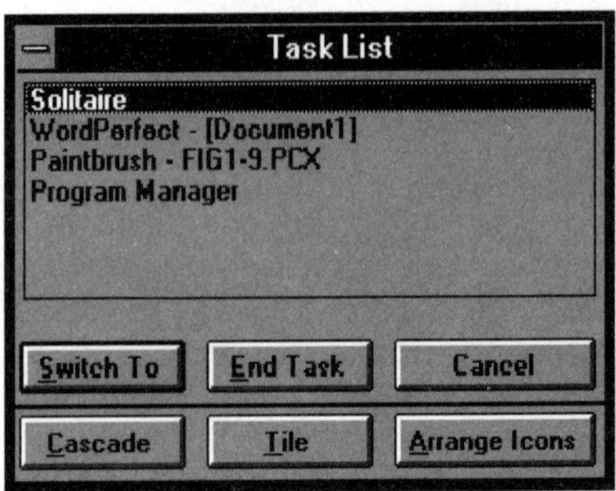

Figure 1.10 The Task List can be activated with Ctrl+Esc, allowing you to switch or to terminate tasks.

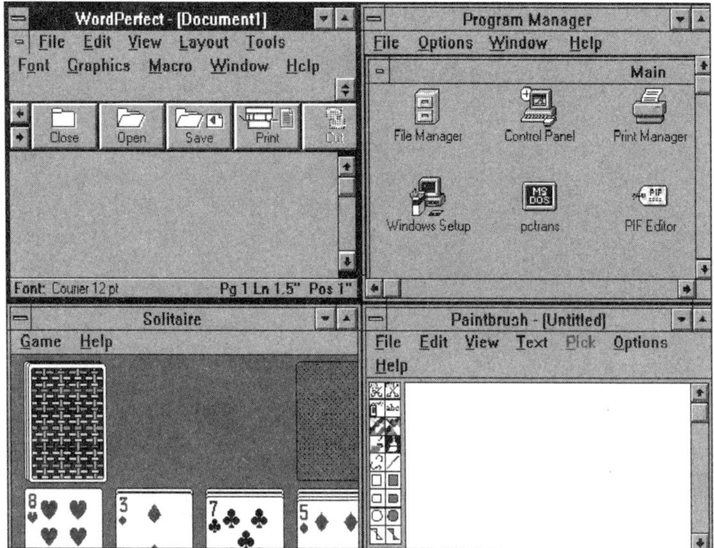

Figure 1.11 A tiled layout of four concurrently running applications (using the Tile command in the Task List window).

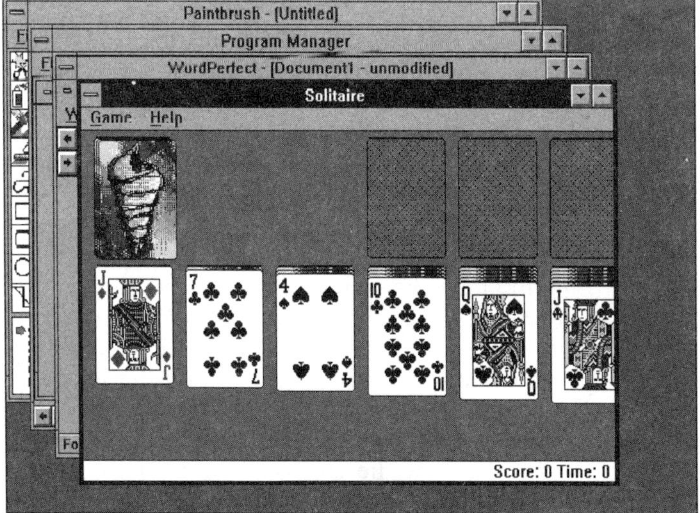

Figure 1.12 A cascaded layout.

Keystrokes for non-Windows Applications

It is possible to run non-Windows (MS-DOS) applications from Windows. MS-DOS applications are assigned icons with a rectangle entitled "MS-DOS." (See the icon entitled "pctrans" in Figure 1.4. You must use the Windows setup program and PIF Editor to set up icons for non-Windows applications, as described in the Windows documentation.) You can open MS-DOS applications just like any other Windows application.

When you first start an MS-DOS application, it takes over the full screen. Pressing Alt+Enter will switch the application to a smaller window. Pressing Alt+Enter again switches back to full-screen mode. You can also press Alt+Spacebar to open the control menu for an MS-DOS application. (You cannot usually close MS-DOS applications from the Control menu, however.) In 386 enhanced mode, the Control menu does provide options for transferring data between the Windows clipboard and the non-Windows application, as well as options for changing fonts and setting multi-tasking options.

The Clipboard

The *clipboard* is the repository of text or graphics cut or copied from Windows applications. The contents of the clipboard can be pasted into other documents or saved as a file. Clipboard files have the extension .CLP and can be opened from the clipboard. As has become standard in other graphical interfaces, Cut, Copy, and Paste are executed from the keyboard by Ctrl+X, Ctrl+C, and Ctrl+V, respectively. Shift+Del, Ctrl+Ins, and Shift+Ins may also be used for Cut, Copy, and Paste, but it is recommended to get in the habit of using the more standard Cut, Copy, and Paste functions. (You may have to use a Macintosh one day.) You can use these functions to copy text from a word processor or data from a spreadsheet to the clipboard and then paste this information into another application. You can clear the contents of the clipboard by selecting the Delete option from the Clipboard Edit menu.

As an example of how the clipboard works, let's copy some text from the README.WRI file which appears in the Main window in Program Manager, as shown in Figure 1.13. You select text in Write documents by pressing Shift+Up Arrow or

Shift+Down Arrow. You can select entire pages using Shift+PgDn or Shift+PgUp. Ctrl+Shift+Home and Ctrl+Shift+End select all text from the current position to the top or bottom of the document, respectively.

In Figure 1.13, we have selected the first few lines of the document. To copy this text to the clipboard, type Ctrl+C. Figure 1.14 shows the copied text in the clipboard viewer, which is opened from the Main window in Program Manager. We could then take this text and paste it into another document by opening that document and typing Ctrl+V at the insertion point.

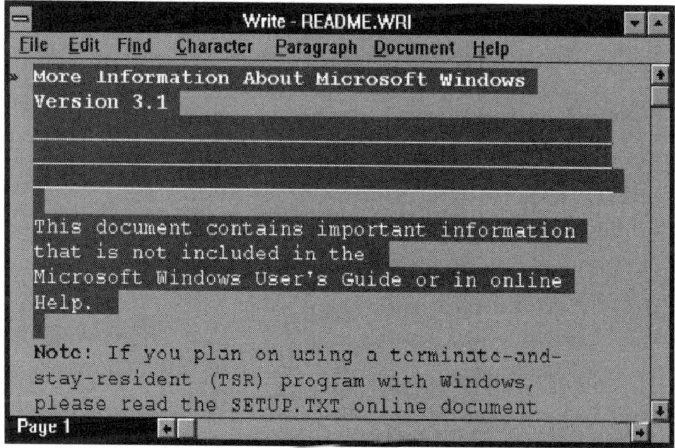

Figure 1.13 Selected text to be copied or cut in a Write document.

Printing the Screen

Windows provides the Print Screen function for capturing an image of the full screen and copying it to the Windows clipboard. Alt+Print Screen captures an image of only the active window, rather than the full screen. You can paste the image from the clipboard into other applications such as Paintbrush, or save the image directly from the clipboard.

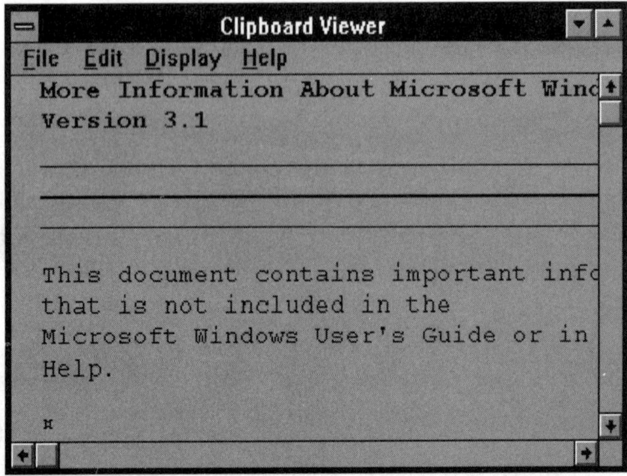

Figure 1.14 The clipboard viewer containing the text copied from the Write document in Figure 1.13.

Working with Text

Microsoft Window provides two text editors called *Windows Notepad* and *Write*. While these applications do not have capabilities comparable to full-featured word processors such as Microsoft Word, they can be very useful for writing simple notes, letters, or other basic documents. Therefore, we briefly review in the following paragraphs the keystrokes used to manipulate text in Windows. Fortunately, these basic keystrokes are the same ones used in other Windows word processing applications.

The Arrow keys move one character at a time horizontally (Left and Right Arrows) and one line at a time vertically (Up and Down Arrows). To move one word at a time, press Ctrl+Right Arrow or Ctrl+Left Arrow. To move one paragraph at a time, press Ctrl+Up Arrow or Ctrl+Down Arrow.

The Home and End keys move the cursor to the beginning and end of the current line, respectively. PgUp and PgDn move the cursor to the top and bottom of the screen, respectively. If pressed repeatedly, these keys move the cursor up or down one screen of text at a time. To move the cursor up or down one page (the equivalent of one printed page of the document), press

Alt+PgUp or Alt+PgDn. To move to the beginning or end of the document, press Ctrl+Home or Ctrl+End, respectively.

Selecting Text

Next to entering text, selecting text is probably the operation performed most frequently. You select text for cut, copy, and paste operations, for example. To select text, you use the cursor movement keystrokes described above but add the Shift key.

For example, to select one line of text at a time, press Shift+Up Arrow or Shift+Down Arrow. To select the word to the right of the cursor, press Shift+Ctrl+Right Arrow. To select the next paragraph of text, press Shift+Ctrl+Down Arrow. (Press the Up Arrow to select the previous paragraph.) To select the text in the entire document, position the cursor at the top of the document (Ctrl+Home), and then press Shift+Ctrl+End. To deselect text, simply press an Arrow key.

Getting Organized with Program Manager

So far, we have concentrated on the basic navigational tools in the Program Manager and Windows. But Program Manager is also a powerful tool for organizing your applications. We'll look at the Program Manager's primary capabilities and how they can be accessed from the keyboard.

The Program Manager File Menu

The primary purpose of Program Manager is to enable you to organize your applications into groups. You can access these capabilities from the File menu, shown in Figure 1.15. When you use the Program Manager File menu, you are working with applications (program files or program items). For more general file-management capabilities, you must use File Manager, which is covered in Chapter 2. Table 1.2 summarizes the Program Manager File menu commands.

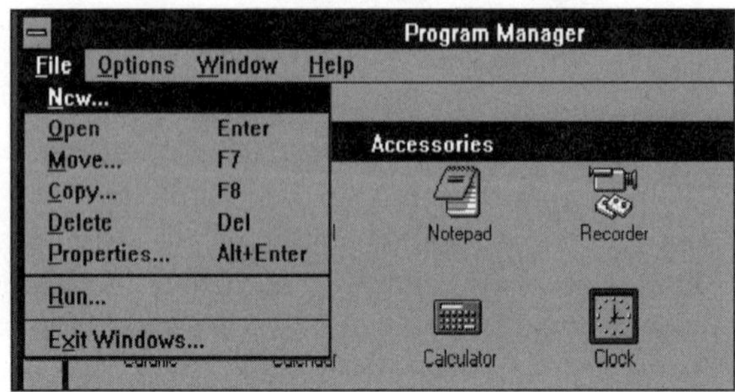

Figure 1.15 The Program Manager File menu.

Table 1.2 Program Manager File Menu Commands. (Keyboard equivalents are shown in parentheses.)

Function	Command
Create a new program group or program item by specifying properties	New
Open a group window or program item (execute the program item)	Open (Enter)
Copy a program item from one program group to another	Copy (F7)
Move a program item from one program group to another	Move (F8)
Delete a program group or item	Delete (Del)
View or edit properties of program groups or items	Properties (Alt+Enter)
Run an executable program (normally used for programs not represented by program items)	Run
Exit Program Manager (You will also exit Windows unless you have specified File Manager as the shell setting in your system initialization file. See Chapter 2.)	Exit

Program Groups and Items

A *program group* is simply a window for storing a set of program items. Program items are applications represented by an icon in the program group. Every progam item represents an executable program file (a file with an extension .COM, .EXE, .BAT, or .PIF). For example, the File Manager is a program item in the Main group. (Its executable program file is called WINFILE.EXE and is located in the Windows directory.)

You can see this relationship by selecting the Properties command from the File menu (Alt+F,P or Alt+Enter). Figure 1.16 shows the properties of File Manager. The Description field contains the description that appears in the program item icon.

Figure 1.16 The Program Item Properties window.

The *Command Line field* contains the DOS command which executes the program file. In this example, the command is simply WINFILE.EXE. Of course, this command can include directory paths as in DOS or you can append a filename that is always opened with the command.

The *Working directory field* gives you the option to specify a directory for saving files generated by the application or for retrieving files for use in the application.

The *Shortcut Key field* allows you to specify a keyboard sequence that automatically switches you to that program when it is running. For example, you could specify Ctrl+Alt+F as the shortcut key for the File Manager. (You must use Ctrl+Alt or Ctrl+Shift as the first two keystrokes of keyboard shortcuts.)

The *Run Minimized box* allows to you to run a program as an icon when you start it up rather than opening its application window. This feature is handy if you always run certain programs in the background (an electronic mail program, for example).

The *Change Icon option* allows you to select a different icon to represent the program. (Windows provides a set of icons to choose from.) The *Browse option* allows you to browse through the available executable program files on disk. This function is mainly for creating new program items, which will be discussed shortly.

Program groups also have properties, which consist simply of the group name and the file created by Windows for storing this description (see Fig. 1.17). This file always has the extension .GRP.

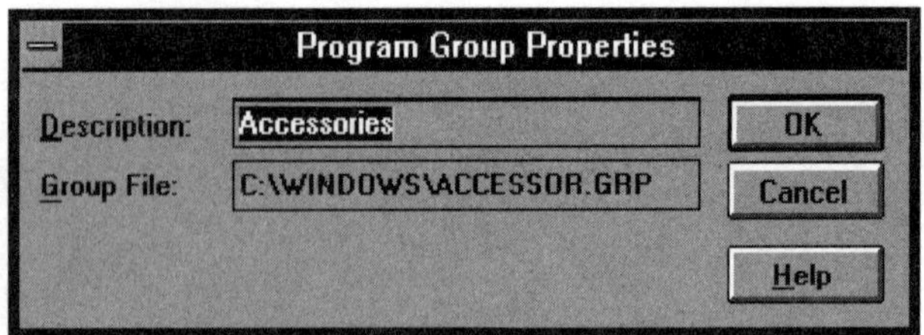

Figure 1.17 The Program Group Properties window.

Creating Your Own Program Groups and Items

The idea behind program items and program groups is to store related programs in a single group. Windows provides a set of groups such as Main, Accessories, Games, and Startup. (Note that the Startup group is used for running applications automatically when you start Windows. Any program item that you copy to the Startup group automatically executes when you start Windows). Most applications that you install in Windows automatically create their own program groups, and with few exceptions create their own program items.

However, there will be situations in which you want to create your own program groups and items. You may wish to group a favorite set of applications in a single window. Or you may use an MS-DOS application frequently and would like to create a program item so that the application appears as an icon on your Windows desktop. Finally, you may always use a specific file (say, a particular spreadsheet) and would like to set up the spreadsheet as a program item. (Remember that you can append a particular filename to the DOS command in the Program Item window shown in Fig. 1.16.)

If you want to create a new program group or item, select New from the Program Manager File menu. You are then presented with the New Program Object window shown in Figure 1.18. You can then choose either to create a new program group or a new program item. If you choose program group, Program Manager will open a blank Program Group window as shown in Figure 1.17. If you choose program item, a blank window like the one shown in Figure 1.16 will appear.

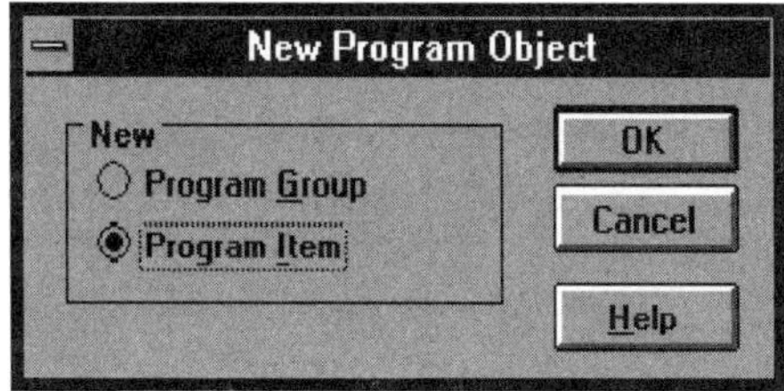

Figure 1.18 The New Program Object window.

Other File Menu Commands

The other File menu commands described in Table 1.2 are straightforward. The Open command works just like the Enter key as we discussed earlier. The Move command moves a program item from one group to another (no copy is left in the original window), whereas the Copy command duplicates the item, copying it to another window. Figure 1.19 shows the Move command. (The Copy command window is exactly the same.)

The Delete command deletes a program group or item. As with all delete commands, it should be used with caution. The Delete dialog box checks with you before deleting the specified group or item.

The Run command allows you to execute programs not available on the Windows desktop (programs that are not program items). The Run window is shown in Figure 1.20. This works the same way as setting up a program item. You type in the DOS command in the Command Line field. You can use the Browse option to find available executable files.

Figure 1.19 The Move Program Item window.

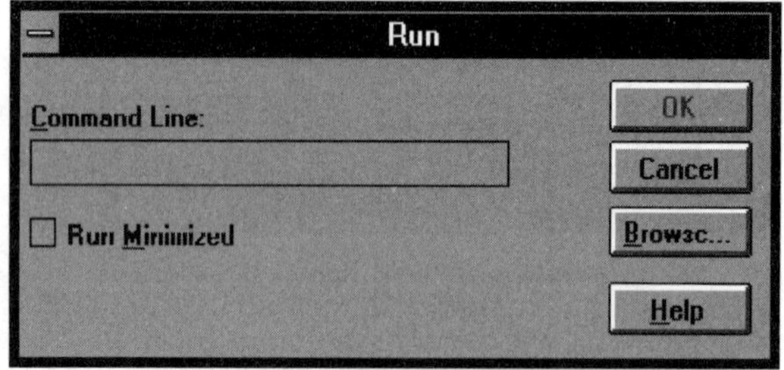

Figure 1.20 The Run command window.

The Windows Help Menu

Microsoft Windows provides a Help utility that is consistent in most Windows applications. In other words, if you are familiar with the Help function in Program Manager, you'll be able to quickly use the Help function in other Windows applications.

The standard method to open the Help menu is to press the F1 key. You can also press Alt+H to open the menu. The opening screen of Program Manager Help is shown in Figure 1.21. The primary keys for navigating Help are Tab and the Arrow keys. The Tab key moves you from one topic to another. Some topics will have lists of subtopics, which you can navigate with the Up and Down Arrow keys. Press the Enter key to open a topic.

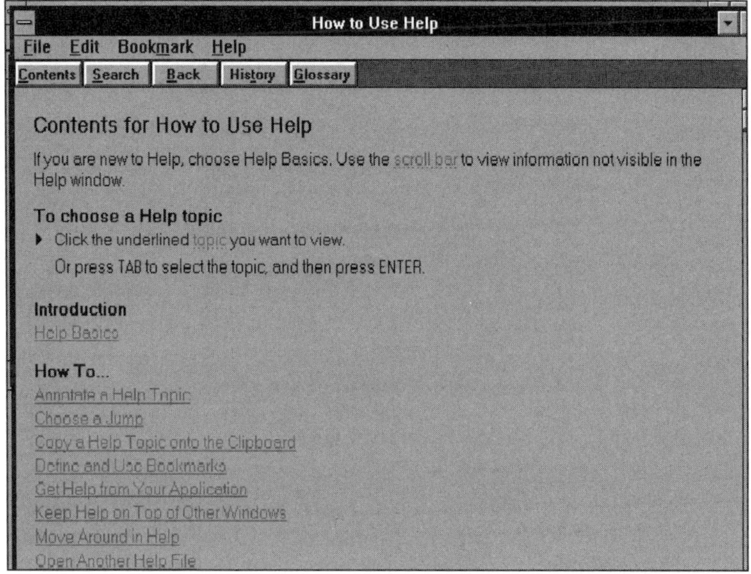

Figure 1.21 The Windows Help utility.

The Contents, Search, Back, History, and Glossary functions are accessible by typing the underlined letter of each function, as shown in Figure 1.21. For example, when you have finished reading a topic and want to return to the opening contents window, type C for the Contents screen or B (Back) to retrace your steps back to the opening Contents window.

The Glossary function provides an index (some applications call it an index rather than a glossary) of topics covered, as shown in Figure 1.22. Use the Arrow keys to scroll through the Glossary window.

The Search function allows you to search for a specific topic. The History function lists sequentially the topics you have viewed in the current Help session, allowing you to quickly find and return to a recently selected topic.

The main menu bar in the Help window provides functions for printing help files (the File menu), copying or annotating help topics (the Edit menu), marking specific topics so that they can be accessed directly from the Bookmark menu, and, of course, getting Help on using Help.

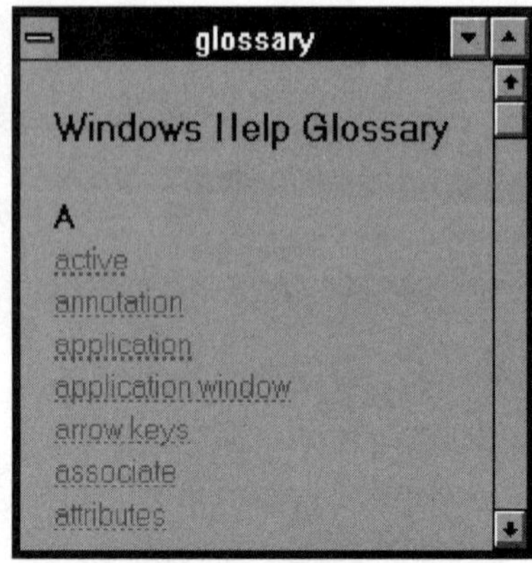

Figure 1.22 The Windows Help Glossary.

The Help function is a useful tool and is well supported in most Windows applications. It will be worth your while to learn to use it and take advantage of it.

Table 1.3 General Windows Keyboard Commands

Program Manager Keys

Function	Keystroke
Move between icons within a group or document window	Arrow keys
Move between group windows or icons	Ctrl+F6 or Ctrl+Tab
Start application or open file	Enter
Arrange open windows in tile or cascade format, respectively	Shift+F4, Shift+F5
Close active group window	Ctrl+F4
Exit Windows	Alt+F4

General System Keys

Function	Keystroke
Select (highlight) or cancel first menu selection on menu bar (Pressing Alt+ the first character of menu selection opens that menu.)	Alt or F10
Close dialog boxes and menus	Esc

Table 1.3 General Windows Keyboard Commands *(continued)*

Function	*Keystroke*
Move forward and backward through fields in dialog boxes	Tab, Shift+Tab
Move to field in dialog box designated by pressed character	Alt+character
Open the Control menu of the active application	Alt+Spacebar
Open document window's Control menu	Alt+Hyphen
Quit application or close a window	Alt+F4
Switch non-Windows DOS application between running in a full screen or in a window	Alt+Enter
Close active window	Ctrl+F4
Open Help if available in active application	F1
Switch to Task List (also available from Control menu)	Ctrl+Esc
Switch to next application, running as icon or window	Alt+Esc
Switch to application last used (opens application window), or by pressing Tab repeatedly, cycle through title bars of open applications	Alt+Tab
Switch to previous applications (reverse of Alt+Tab)	Shift+Alt+Tab

Other Dialog Box Keystrokes

Move to first item or character in a list or text box	Home
Move to last item or character in a list or text box	End
Scroll up or down a list, one screen at a time	PgUp, PgDn
Open a list	Alt+Down Arrow
Select an item in a list or cancel selection. Select or clear check box	Spacebar

Table 1.3 General Windows Keyboard Commands *(continued)*

Function	*Keystroke*
Select all items in a list	Ctrl+Slash (/)
Cancel all selections except current selection	Ctrl+Backslash (\\)
Execute dialog box command	Enter
Extend or cancel the selection to the first character in a text box	Shift+Home
Extend or cancel the selection to the last character in a text box	Shift+End
Closes dialog box without executing command (same as Esc key)	Alt+F4

Clipboard and Text Selection Keys

Copy full-screen image into clipboard	Print Screen
Copy image of active window into clipboard	Alt+Print Screen
Copy selected text to Clipboard	Ctrl+C, Ctrl+Ins
Cut (delete) selected text and copy it to the clipboard	Ctrl+X, Shift+Del
Paste text from Clipboard into active document or window	Ctrl+V, Shift+Ins
Undo most recent editing action (Cut, Copy, Paste)	Ctrl+Z, Alt+Backspace
Select one line of text at a time	Shift+Up Arrow or Shift+Down Arrow
Select one page of text at a time	Shift+PgUp or Shift+PgDn
Select text from current position to beginning or end of line	Shift+Home or Shift+End
Select text from current position to beginning or end of document	Ctrl+Shift+Home or Ctrl+Shift+End

Cursor Movement Keys

Move the cursor up or down one line or one character to the left or right	Arrow keys (Up, Down, Left, Right)

Table 1.3 General Windows Keyboard Commands *(continued)*

Function	*Keystroke*
Move cursor right one word	Ctrl+Right Arrow
Move cursor left one word	Ctrl+Left Arrow
Move cursor to beginning of line	Home
Move cursor to end of line	End
Move cursor up one screen	PgUp
Move cursor down one screen	PgDn
Move cursor to beginning of document	Ctrl+Home
Move cursor to end of document	Ctrl+End

Text Selection

Use the above Cursor Movement Keys in addition to the Shift key. For example, press Shift+Ctrl+Right Arrow to select the word to the right.

Running File Manager

2

A concise list of File Manager keystrokes begins on page 242.

This chapter covers the keyboard operation of the Windows File Manager. The basic concepts of files and directories are reviewed and then the file-management options available in File Manager are discussed.

Overview of File Manager

If Program Manager is the heart of Windows, then File Manager is the brain. In fact, File Manager is more versatile than Program Manager because you can execute applications (run programs) as well as manage your files and directories from it. The main function provided by Program Manager that is missing in File Manager is the ability to incorporate programs into the Windows graphical interface and to organize them into logical groups represented by icons. Another way to look at the difference between the two: File Manager manages the *structure of your files and directories,* while Program Manager manages the *structure and layout of your Windows interface,* which is often called the *desktop.*

File Manager provides you with the basic capabilities of the operating system: creating and removing directories and subdirectories, copying and deleting files, formatting floppy disks, running applications, printing documents, and, if applicable, connecting to networks.

Although Program Manager is a useful tool, some users prefer to operate Windows exclusively from File Manager. In fact, you can change the shell setting in the SYSTEM.INI file to SHELL=WINFILE.EXE in order to make File Manager rather than Program Manager the primary application that is always running. (The procedure for doing this is described in the SYSINI.WRI file located in the Windows directory and readable using the Windows Write application.)

But whether you prefer Program or File Manager as your main operating mode in Windows, a thorough knowledge of File Manager is indispensible.

Before we plunge into the details, note that many of the keystrokes and operations covered in Chapter 1 also apply to File Manager (for example, the Control menu, or using Alt+Tab to switch between applications). File Manager is just another application in Windows and is controlled just like any other application.

Directories and Files

When you open File Manager, you are presented with a directory window, an example of which is shown Figure 2.1. The title bar of a directory window shows the current path or location of the current directory. In Figure 2.1, the current path is C:\WINDOWS. Below the menu bar are the drive icons (in this case, drives A and C) and the volume label (in this case, C:BARAN). Other available storage devices such as tape drives or CD-ROM players would also be shown in this area, as well as any network connections.

Note that the WINDOWS directory is also highlighted in the left-hand column of the window. The icon that looks like a file folder to the left of each name in the left-hand column of the directory is called a *directory icon.* Notice that the folder representing the WINDOWS directory icon is open, indicating that the WINDOWS directory is currently open.

The split window (separated by what is called the *split bar*) shows the *directory tree* on the left-hand side, and the files and subdirectories of the currently selected directory on the right-hand side (also called the *contents list*). Use the Tab or F6 key to move from the directory tree to the contents list, then to the drive icons, and then back to the directory tree. (Shift+Tab moves in the opposite direction.)

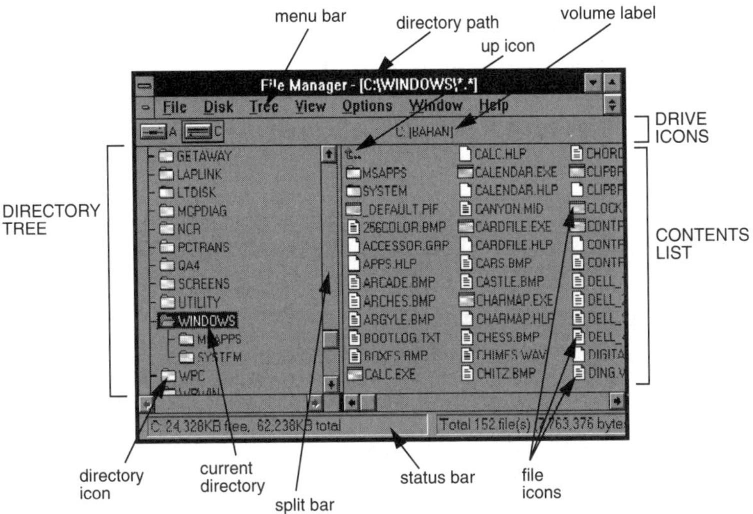

Figure 2.1 The File Manager directory window.

In Figure 2.1, the subdirectories MSAPPS and SYSTEM are also displayed on the right side, because they are subdirectories of the WINDOWS directory. The other items on the right side are files in the WINDOWS directory. The arrow icon (also called the "up icon") in the upper left corner of the right side indicates that there is a higher level directory (in this case, C:\, which is the root directory). Selecting the arrow icon and pressing Enter makes the higher level directory the current directory.

The three key elements of a directory window are the drive icons, the directory tree, and the contents list. To move from one to the other, use the Tab key.

Note that files have different types of icons depending on their type. Executable files, such as programs and batch files, have an icon with a horizontal bar across the top. (All files with the extensions .EXE, .COM, .BAT, or .PIF have this type of icon.) For example, in Figure 2.1, the files CALC.EXE and CALENDAR.EXE (the Windows calculator and calendar applications, respectively,) are executable files, and therefore have the program file icon.

Files that are associated with an application have an icon representing a document with horizontal lines running across the page (for example, the file ARCADE.BMP in Fig. 2.1). When you open this type of file, the application with which the file is associated is automatically executed and used to display the contents of the file. For example, opening ARCADE.BMP also opens Paintbrush, which then displays the file ARCADE.BMP, as shown in Figure 2.2.

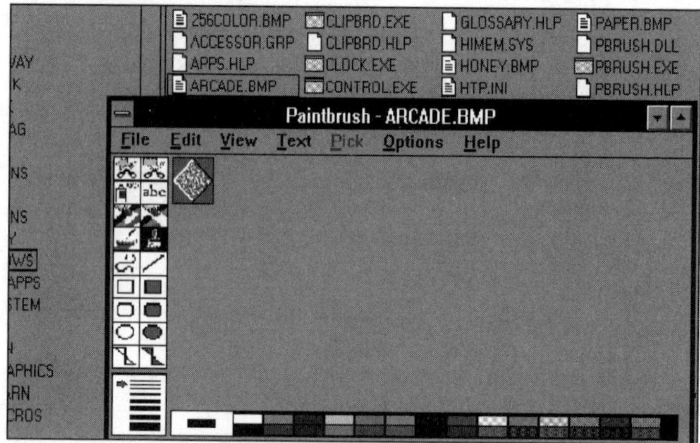

Figure 2.2 Opening ARCADE.BMP also opens Paintbrush, because this is an associated file.

Blank document icons (such as APPS.HLP in Fig. 2.1) represent miscellaneous files that are neither associated nor executable. Such files are usually opened from within an application rather than directly from File Manager.

The remaining type of file icon represents system or hidden files as shown in Figure 2.3. In this example, the files IBMDOS.COM and IBMBIO.COM are system files, which are normally hidden and not displayed in File Manager. The system/hidden files icon is distinguished by an oversized exclamation point. You can display hidden files by selecting the By File Type option in the File Manager View menu (Alt+V) and selecting the Hidden/System Files check box. (File Manager menus will be discussed in more detail later in this chapter.)

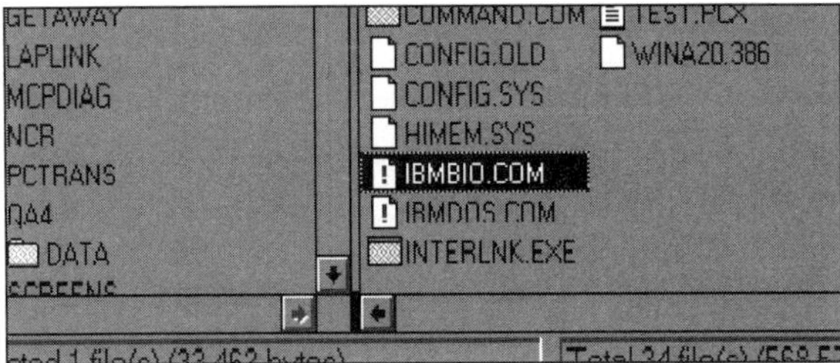

Figure 2.3 The icons with the exclamation point are hidden system files. Tampering with these files can disable your computer.

The Directory Tree Structure

As mentioned earlier, the left-hand side of the directory window shows the directory tree on the current disk. You can view the directories only (the first level) or include subdirectories in the tree. The various options are shown in Figure 2.4, Figure 2.5, and Figure 2.6. In Figure 2.4, only the first directory level is shown. The Tree menu is open (Alt+T), which allows you to expand the displayed directory levels and to collapse them. In Figure 2.5, we have expanded the WINDOWS directory one level. In Figure 2.6, we have expanded all branches (note the additional subdirectories shown in the WINDOWS directory and in the QA4 and WPWIN directories). The Expand Branch option expands the current directory to all its levels, but does not affect other expandable directories.

Notice in Figure 2.4 that we have checked the Indicate Expandable Branches option. (The check indicates that this option has been activated. You can activate or deactivate checked options simply by selecting them and pressing Enter to toggle the check on and off.) With this option activated, all directories that have subdirectories have either a minus (-) or plus (+) sign in their folder icons, depending on whether the directory is expanded or not. In Figure 2.4, all the directories are collapsed so that the expandable directories display the plus sign (indicating that they can be expanded). In Figure 2.5, the WINDOWS directory has been expanded, so the icon displays a minus sign, indicating that it can be collapsed.

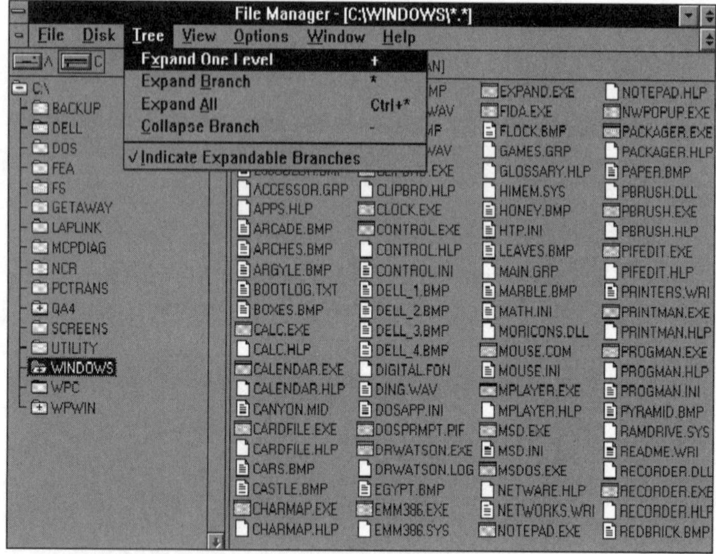

Figure 2.4 Directories are collapsed.

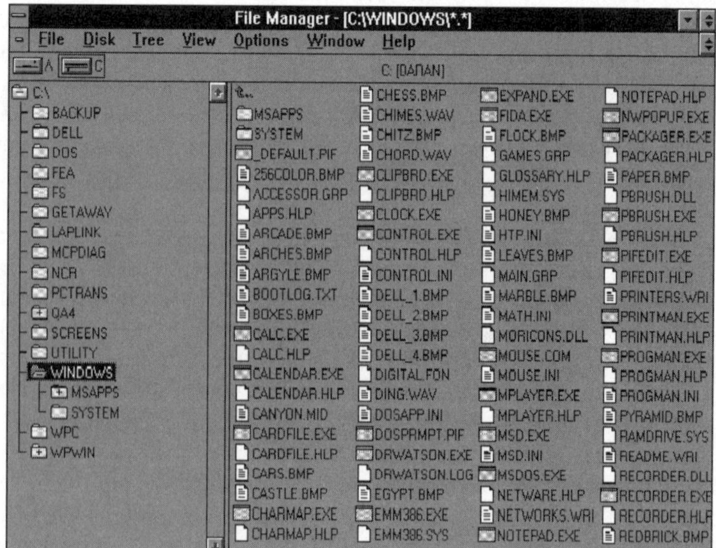

Figure 2.5 The WINDOWS directory is expanded.

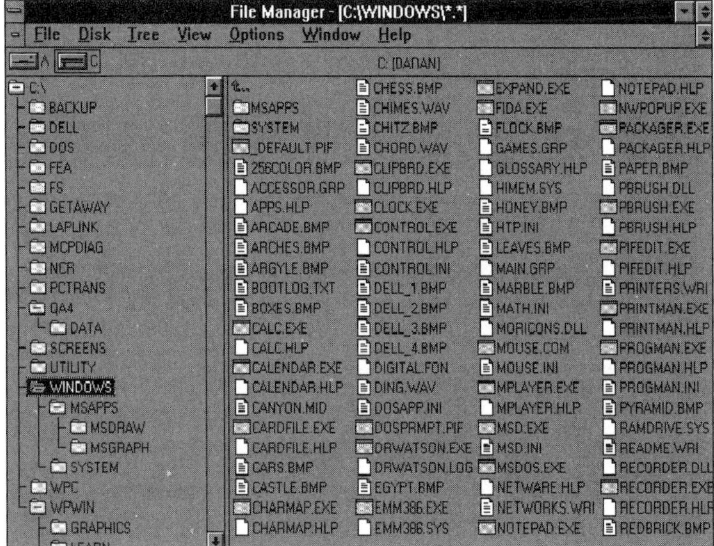

Figure 2.6 **All directories are expanded.**

You can expand and collapse directories without opening the Tree menu by using the keystroke equivalents shown in the right-hand column of the Tree menu (see Fig. 2.4). The minus and plus signs collapse and expand the current directory, respectively. The asterisk key (*) expands the current directory branch, and pressing Ctrl+* performs the Expand All function.

Different Points of View

The directory window, with the directories on the left side and the files on the right, is the default window when you first start File Manager. You can also view your directories and files in a variety of different ways by selecting the options in the View menu (Alt+V), shown in Figure 2.7. The default window uses Tree and Directory, Name, and Sort By Name as its display options. You can also view just the directory tree (Tree Only) or just the contents of the current directory (Directory Only). Note that pressing Shift+Enter opens a new window displaying the contents of the currently selected directory in Directory Only mode.

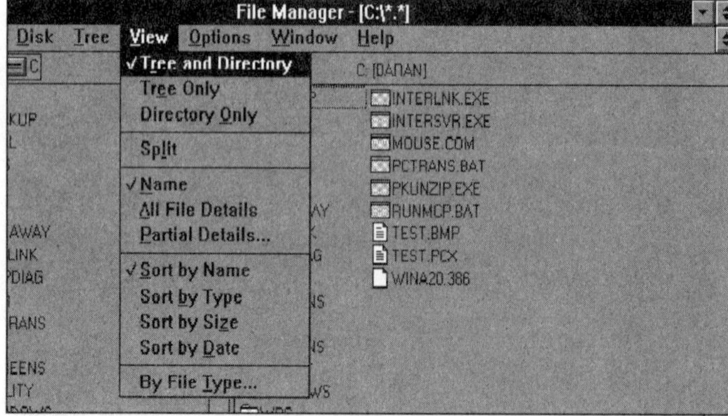

Figure 2.7 The File Manager View menu, which enables you to view the directory window in a variety of ways.

The Split option lets you move the split bar to the right or left to increase the viewing size of either side of the directory window.

Name, All File Details, and Partial Details provide varying degrees of file detail. The All File Details option provides the file-name, file size, date last modified (saved), and the file's attributes, as shown in Figure 2.8. The Partial Details option allows you to specify what details you want included in the file listing (Fig. 2.9).

Figure 2.8 The directory window shown displaying All File Details.

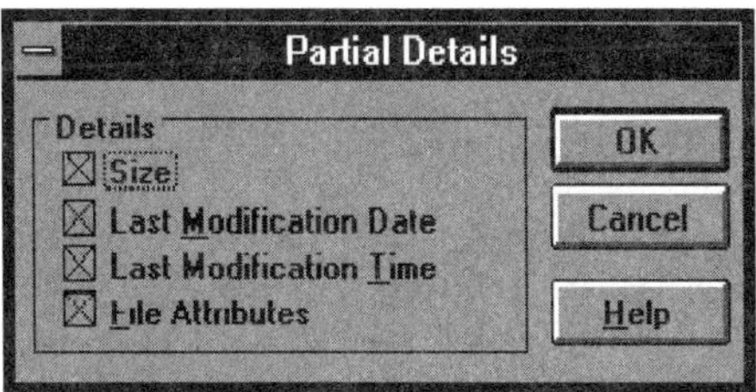

**Figure 2.9 The options if you wish to view
only partial file details.**

The Sort options allow you to sort filenames by Name, Type,
Size, and Date. Name, Size, and Date, are self-explanatory, but
File Type is best explained by looking at the next option, View
(Alt+V) By File Type, which we briefly discussed earlier in this
chapter in relation to the types of file icons. By selecting the By
File Type option, you can specify what types of files should be
displayed in the current directory window. In most cases, you
will want to display all file types, but if the directory is particularly large and you just want to see the executable files in that
directory, for example, you can mark only the Programs box in
the By File Type dialog box, as shown in Figure 2.10.

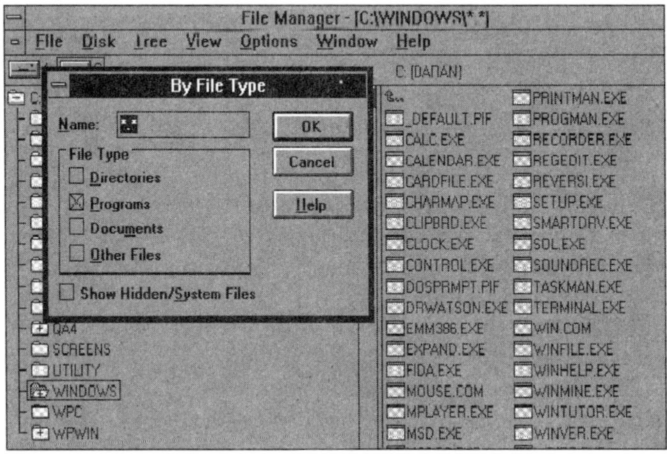

Figure 2.10 Viewing files by file type.

You can check and un-check check boxes by pressing the Spacebar. Note that the filename field shows *.*, meaning all files in the current directory which meet the specified file type criteria. The right-hand window shows only the executable files in the WINDOWS directory. (Compare this screen to Fig. 2.1, which shows all the files in the WINDOWS directory.)

The Show Hidden/System Files option allows you to display hidden files, but should be used with caution. Certain files are hidden so they cannot be altered or modified by the user. If you tamper with these files, you can corrupt the system files, causing the computer not to run.

Navigating through Directories and Files

The easiest way to move from one directory to another is by using the Arrow keys. You can also press the first character of a file or directory's name to move to or near to that file or directory. For example, suppose you have a long list of directories sorted by name, and that at the end of that list are the directories ZAP, ZING, and ZIP. Rather than scrolling through the list with the Down Arrow, you could type the letter Z, which would move you to the first directory beginning with the letter Z. Pressing the Tab key moves you from the directory to the directory's contents on the right side of the directory window. Pressing Shift+Tab moves you back to the directory tree. The selected file is highlighted by the *selection cursor*. You can perform file operations from the File Manager File menu (Open, Move, Copy, Delete, etc.) on the selected file.

When a file is highlighted, pressing Enter will cause Windows to try to open the file (the same operation as the Open command in the File Manager File menu). If it is an associated or program file, the file will open with its associated application or as a self-contained program, as we described earlier. If it's a miscellaneous file (represented by a document icon with a blank page), most likely you'll get a message that looks something like Figure 2.11. In this case, you either have to associate the file with a particular application using the Associate option in the File menu, or you have to first open the application with which you intend to use the file, and then open the file from within that application.

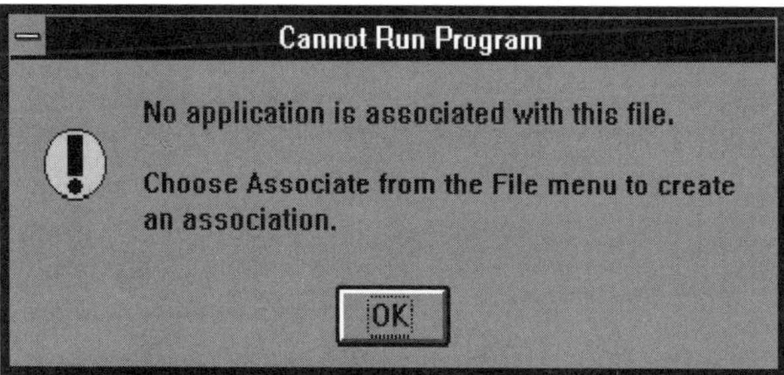

Figure 2.11 This is what happens if you attempt to open a non-associated file from the File Manager.

You can use the Arrow keys to move through the drive icons, the directory tree, and the contents list. However, if you have large numbers of drives (as on a network) or files or directories, you can also type a letter to "scroll" quickly through the list. For example, if you are in the directory tree, typing P will highlight the first directory that begins with the letter P; and typing P again will highlight the next directory that begins with the letter P.

Selecting Multiple Files

You can select multiple files whether or not they are adjacent. Figure 2.12 shows several files selected. To select a group of adjacent files, select the first file in the sequence, then hold down the Shift key as you move the Arrow key (Up or Down) to select the remaining files. To select non-adjacent files, place the cursor at the first file you want to select and press and release Shift+F8. The selection cursor will become a blinking dotted line. Move the cursor to the desired file and press the spacebar to select the file. You can then move the cursor to another file and select it or press Shift+F8 again to end the operation. You can use the Slash and Backslash keys to select and deselect all the files in a directory: pressing Ctrl+/ selects all files, and pressing Ctrl+\ deselects the files.

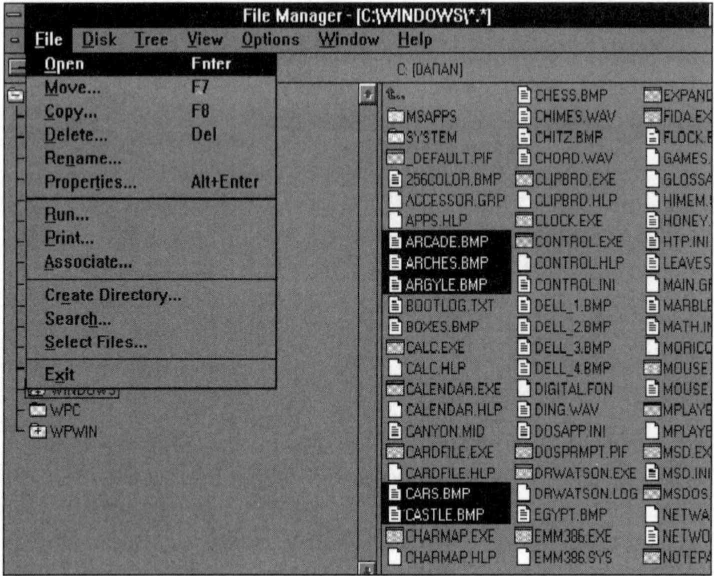

Figure 2.12 Multiple files are selected, both adjacent and non-adjacent.

To select all the files in a directory, press Ctrl+/. To deselect them, press Ctrl+\. To select adjacent files, select the first file you want, and hold down the Shift key as you use the Up or Down Arrow to select the adjacent files. To select non-adjacent files, move the selection cursor to the first file you want to select, then press and release Shift+F8; then move to the other files you want to select, pressing the Spacebar for each.

Switching Drives

The drive icons in the upper left-hand corner of the File Manager window indicate which drives are available on your system (see Fig. 2.1). In this example, there is one hard disk (drive C), and one floppy drive (drive A). From the directory window, the easiest way to switch from one drive to another is to simply press Ctrl+ the letter of the drive. For example, pressing Ctrl+A switches you to drive A. You can also press the Tab or F6 key to move to the drive icons and then use the Arrow keys to switch to the desired drive. (Press Enter to open the directories on that drive.) But the Ctrl+ drive letter method is much more efficient. As we shall see later, you can also switch drives from the Disk menu.

The File Menu

The File menu (see Fig. 2.13) is the main stage of operations in File Manager.

The Open command opens the highlighted file in the directory window. As we mentioned in the discussion of different file types, the Open command will only successfully open program files or associated files.

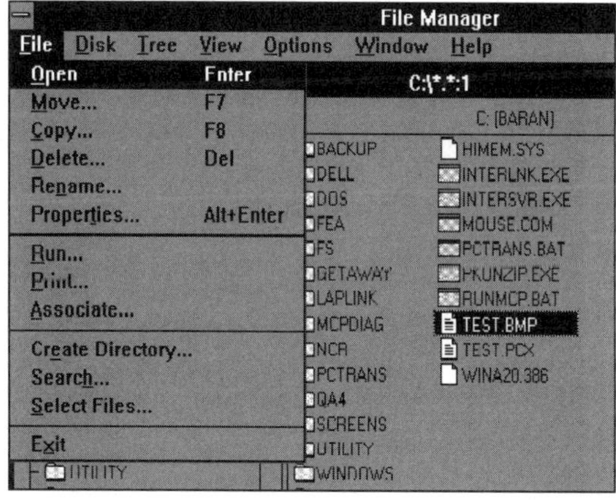

Figure 2.13 The File Manager File menu is the main stage of operations.

Copying, Moving, and Deleting Files

Probably the most frequently used commands in File Manager are the Copy and Move commands. Frequently backing up your files is crucial to ensuring that you don't lose data. The way to back up files in Windows is with the Copy command. Selecting

Copy from the File menu copies the selected file (or files) to the destination that you specify. Figure 2.14 shows the Copy command being used to copy a file to the floppy drive A. You can also type F8 from the directory window without opening the File menu to execute the Copy command.

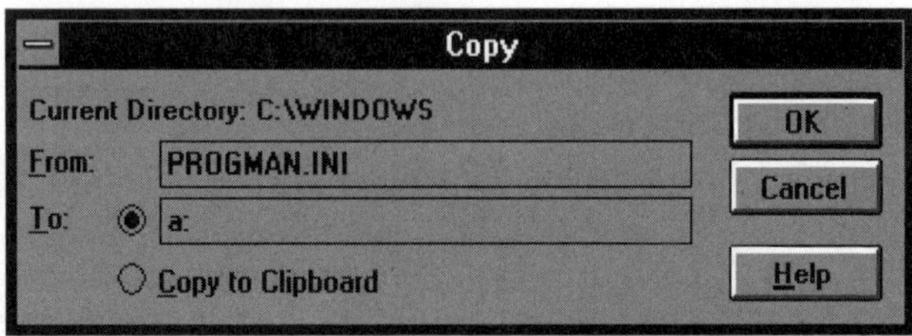

Figure 2.14 The Copy command copies files to other directories or disks or to the clipboard.

For those used to copying files in DOS, File Manager offers the major advantage of being able to copy selected multiple files in a single operation. (In DOS, you have to use wildcards to copy multiple files.) First, select the desired files using the methods described above and then press F8 or open the File menu and select the Copy command.

The option to copy the file to the clipboard may be used if you wish to paste an entire document from the clipboard into another document, or if you wish to establish a link between the copied file and other applications that support object linking and embedding. The procedures for linking or embedding objects are specific to the particular application. Consult the relevant documentation of the applications you intend to use for object linking or embedding.

The Move command (press F7 from the directory window) moves files from one directory to another rather than copying them. In other words, the file is deleted from the source directory and moved to the target directory.

The Delete command deletes the selected file or files. You can also press the Del key from the directory window without opening the File menu. A dialog box appears asking you to confirm the delete operation. (Note that confirmation can be disabled from the Options menu, but this is generally not recommended.) If you are deleting more than one file, you can confirm the deletion of each file individually or select Yes to All from the confirmation box, confirming that all the files should be deleted (see Fig. 2.15).

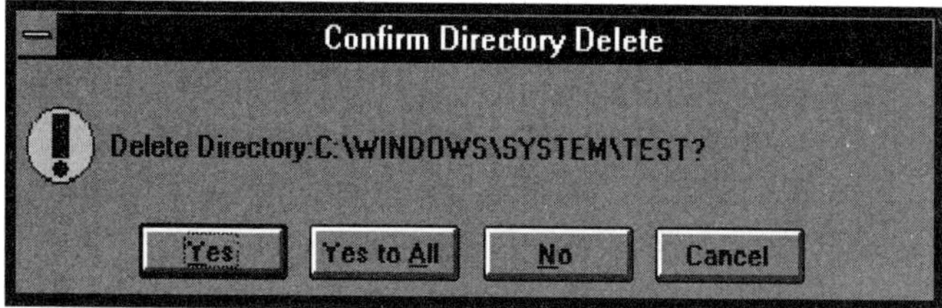

Figure 2.15 The Delete Confirmation window.

Renaming Files

The Rename command enables you to rename DOS files or directories, according to the file naming conventions of DOS. The filename can contain up to eight characters and the extension can have up to three. You may not use periods, commas, quotation marks, back or forward slashes, colons or semicolons, vertical bars, or equal signs in filenames. The following are reserved filenames and cannot be used: CON, AUX, COM1, COM2, COM3, COM4, LPT1, LPT2, LPT3, PRN, and NUL. The extensions .EXE, .COM, and .PIF are normally generated by the system for executable files and should not be used arbitrarily.

Setting File Properties

The Properties command enables you to set or modify the attributes of the selected file or directory as shown in Figure 2.16. You can press Alt+Enter from the directory window to execute the Properties command without opening the File menu. The only file attribute that you are likely to modify is the Read Only attribute. By making the file Read Only, no one can edit or modify the file. This is useful if you share your computer or directories with other users and want to ensure that no one tampers with your file.

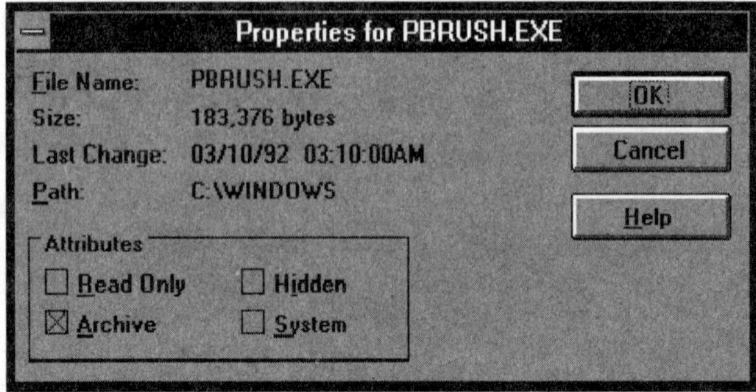

Figure 2.16 The Properties window.

The Archive attribute is set automatically by MS-DOS depending on whether or not the file has been copied (backed up) since it was last modified. This attribute may be useful for checking whether or not you need to back up a file.

The Hidden and System attributes should generally be left alone. In some circumstances, you may want to hide a file, but then you can only access it by turning on the Show Hidden/System Files check box in the By File Type option of the View menu as we discussed earlier.

Run

The Run command is identical to its counterpart in the Program Manager as discussed in the previous chapter. It is useful for running a program when you wish to append a filename. If the file is associated, however, it may be easier to find the file and open it from the directory window.

Print

The Print command prints the selected file on the system's printer. You can only print associated files by this method. You must print non-associated files by first opening the appropriate application and using the application's print capability.

Associate

The Associate command allows you to establish associations between files and applications. Many files are already automatically associated. For example, files with the .BMP extension are automatically associated with Paintbrush, files with the extension .MID are associated with Media Player, .WAV files with Sound Recorder, and so forth. In the event that you must set up the association yourself, the Associate command lets you do so. You enter the extension and then find the appropriate application to associate with that extension. (You can use the Browse option to find the application, as shown in Fig. 2.17.)

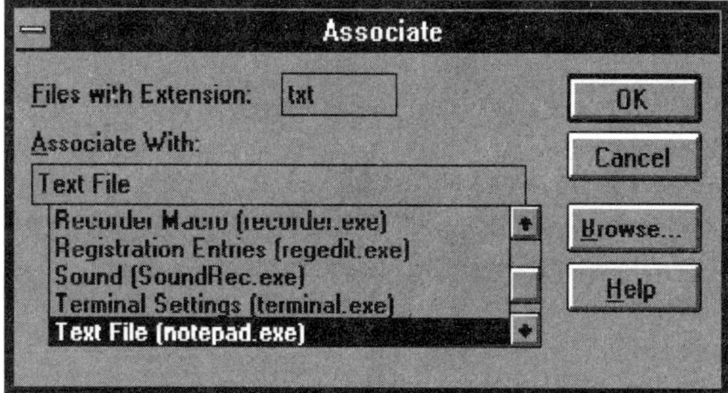

Figure 2.17 The Associate command.

Create Directory

The Create directory enables you to create new directories or subdirectories on your system. Note that the directory will be created as a subdirectory of the current directory shown in the Create Directory window. In other words, if you want the directory to be at the first level, make sure that the current directory is C:\ (see Fig. 2.18). The file conventions discussed in the paragraph on the Rename command also apply to the Create Directory command.

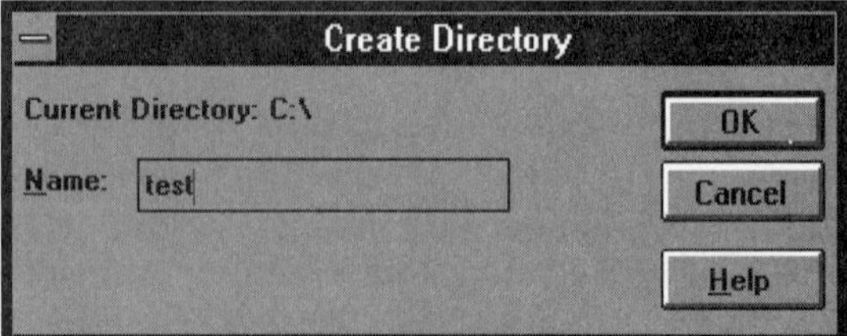

Figure 2.18 The Create command.

Search

The Search command allows you to search the disk for particular files. You can search for a single file or use wildcards to search for multiple files of a specific type. For example, the search in Figure 2.19 is for all files with the extension .TXT. Note that you can specify which directory to start the search from and whether to search subdirectories.

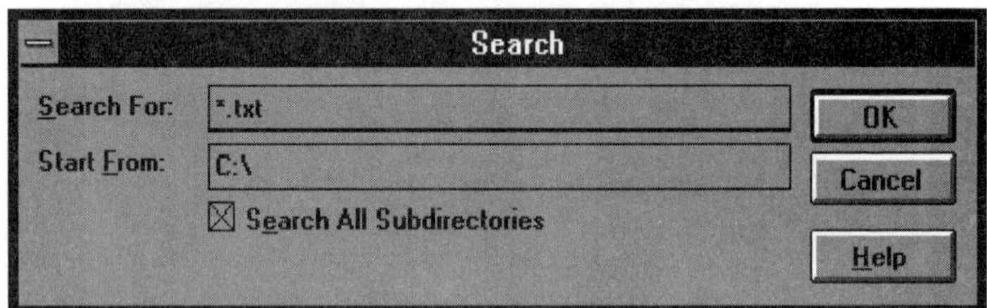

Figure 2.19 The Search command.

Select

The Select command selects the specified files. In most cases, it is easier to select files directly from the directory window as we have discussed earlier. But the Select command is useful for selecting files by means of wild cards or files that are not displayed in the current directory. The Deselect option allows you to void the selection without leaving the Select Files window (see

Fig. 2.20). Typing Ctrl+\ from the directory window also deselects selected files.

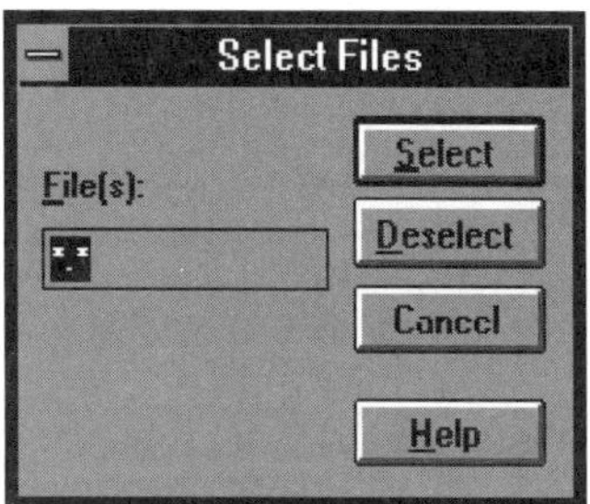

Figure 2.20 The Select Files command.

Disk Operations and Maintenance

The File Manager Disk menu (Fig. 2.21) provides the functions for copying floppy disks, labeling and formatting disks, and creating system disks containing the DOS operating system. You can also switch drives from the Disk menu. Type Alt+D from the directory window to open the Disk menu.

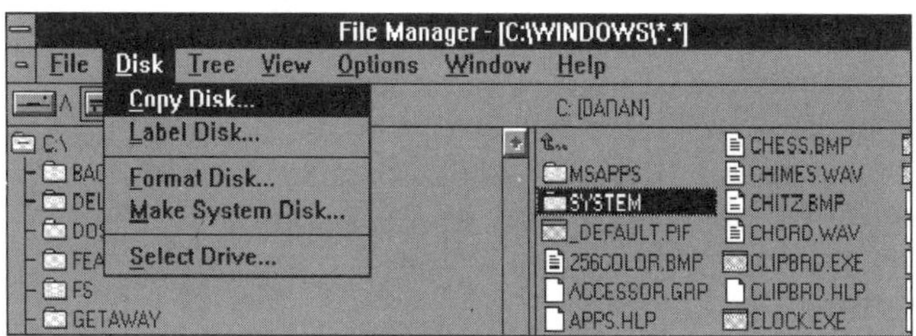

Figure 2.21 The Disk menu.

The Copy Disk command makes copies of floppy disks. In single floppy drive systems, you insert the source disk first and then are prompted to switch to the target disk. In dual drive systems, you insert both source and target disks and specify which drive contains each disk. When using the Copy Disk command, both source and target disks must have the same storage capacity (e.g., if the source disk is a 1.44 MB disk, then the target disk must have the same capacity).

The Label Disk command allows you to change the label of either floppy or hard disks as shown in Figure 2.22. Disk labels are optional, but they do provide a means of identifying disks, which can be useful if you use a lot of different floppy disks or if you are on a network and share hard disks. The label appears in the directory window as described earlier (see Fig. 2.1). Labels can contain up to 11 characters.

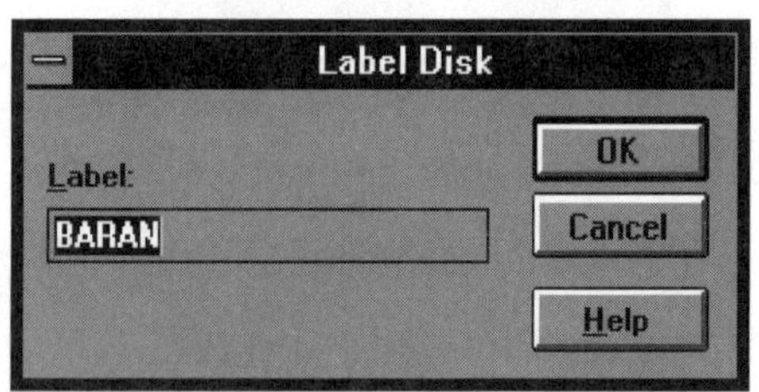

Figure 2.22 The Label Disk command.

The Format Disk command (Fig. 2.23) enables you to format floppy disks or hard disks, if necessary. If you have a single hard disk, you can only format it from a floppy disk running MS-DOS. Formatting disks erases all existing data on the disks. The Format Disk command provides options to label the disk and also to make the disk a system disk, in which case the computer can boot off the disk. If you boot your computer off a hard disk, you will probably not need to create system disks. The Quick Format option may only be used with disks that have been previously formatted. This option skips the bad sector check, which is normally performed during the format operation. (This option is not recommended.)

The Make System Disk command takes an already formatted disk and copies the system files to the disk, making it a bootable disk. Again, if you normally use a hard disk to boot your system, you probably won't have much use for this option.

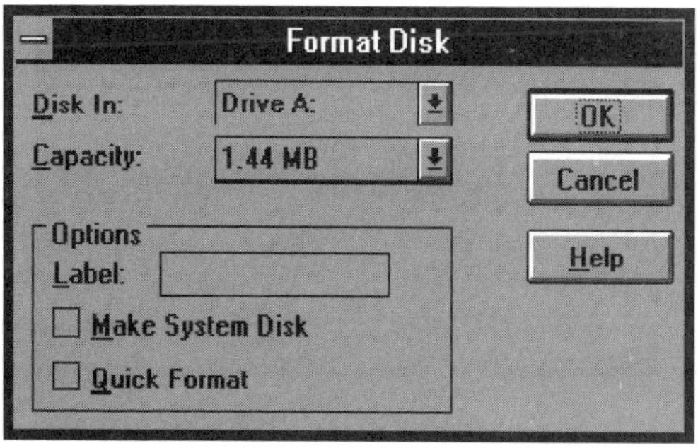

Figure 2.23 The Format command.

Other File Manager Commands

The Options menu provides additional commands for customizing the File Manager interface (Fig. 2.24) and file operations. The Confirmation option allows you to disable File Manager's Confirmation dialog box for deleting files or directories, replacing files, and disk commands such as copying and formatting (Fig. 2.25). It is strongly recommended that you do not disable the confirmation functions, even if you want to save some time. The chance for error is simply too great, and going through the confirmation process proves to be well worth the few additional seconds and keystrokes.

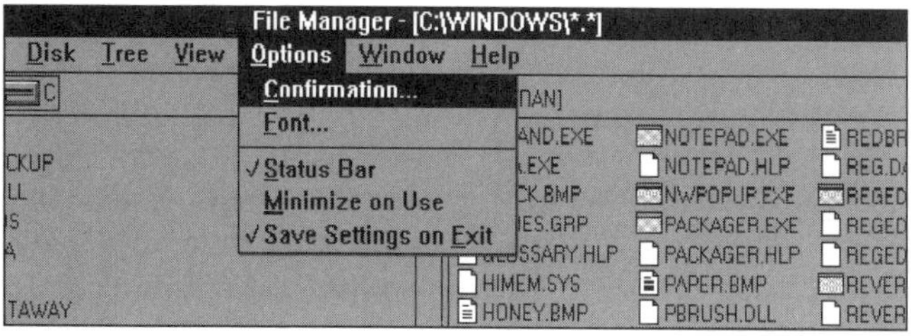

Figure 2.24 The Options menu.

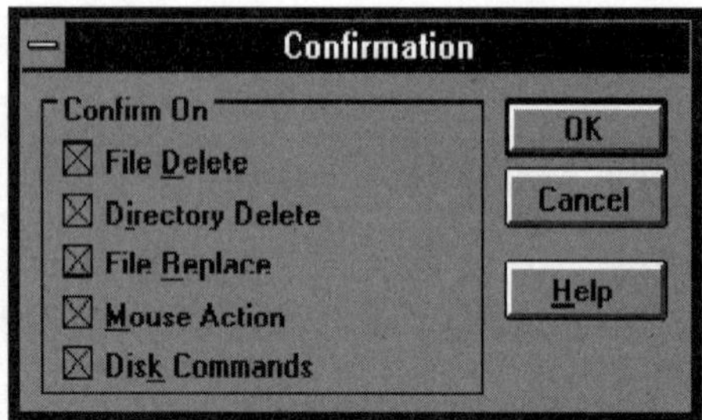

Figure 2.25 It is recommended to leave confirmation enabled.

The other commands in the Option window are straightforward. The Font command allows you to change the font of the file and directory listings in the directory window. (The default font is Sans Serif.)

You can remove the status bar at the bottom of the directory window (thus creating a larger directory window, but also giving up the disk status information) by disabling the Status Bar function. (Press Enter with the Status Bar option selected to remove the check.)

The Minimize on Use setting makes File Manager collapse to an icon when you open a file from File Manager. (In other words, rather than remaining a background window, File Manager automatically becomes an icon when you are in a different application window.)

Finally, the Save Settings command preserves the state of File Manager when you exit Windows.

The Windows menu allows you to open a new window in File Manager, and arrange windows in cascade or tile format, as we discussed in Chapter 1. You can arrange icons in the directory window, although this command is not very useful in strictly keyboard mode, since you can't drag icons around without a mouse (which is what causes icons to require rearrangement). Opening multiple File Manager windows may be useful if you want to look at multiple directories frequently, but the primary function of multiple windows is to be able to drag files from one location to another using the mouse. You can open a new window by pressing Shift+Enter from the directory window without opening the Windows menu.

The most important command in the Windows menu is the Refresh command (see Fig. 2.26). This command refreshes the current directory window. To put it another way, it updates the window to its most current state. Refreshing the window is sometimes necessary if you have just saved or copied some new files to a directory, but these changes are still not reflected in the directory window. The Refresh command causes File Manager to update the directory window to reflect the most recent file changes. It is also very useful if you have just switched floppy disks and the directory is still displaying the previous disk's directory. You can press the F5 key from the directory window to refresh the window without opening the Windows menu.

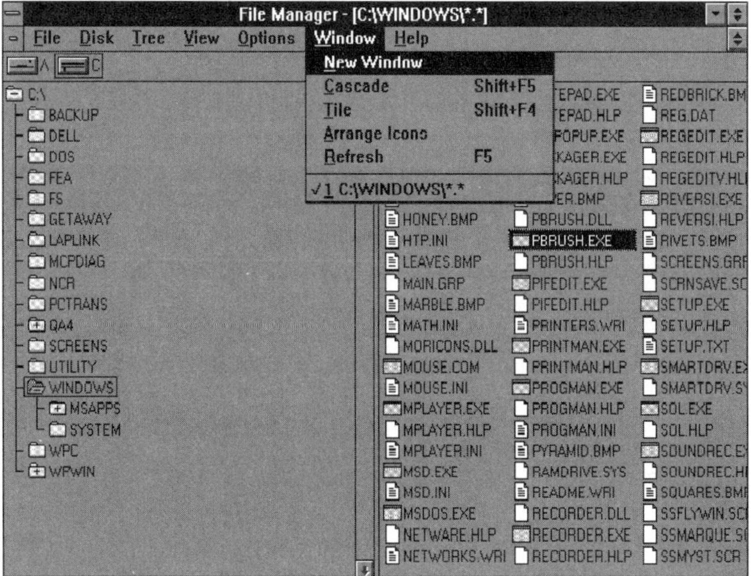

Figure 2.26 The Refresh command.

WordPerfect 3

A concise list of WordPerfect keystrokes begins on page 244.

This chapter covers the basic keystrokes for WordPerfect for Windows.

WordPerfect is one of the most popular word processing applications in the DOS and Windows environments. WordPerfect has traditionally been a character-based, keyboard-oriented word processing package, making heavy use of Shift, Ctrl, Alt, and the function keys for performing editing and file operations. While WordPerfect for Windows retains some of the look and feel of the DOS version, it is a graphical or "WYSIWYG" (What You See Is What You Get) version of the product. This means that graphics and text attributes such as fonts, italics, and boldface are shown on the screen instead of being represented by codes as in the character-based version. (WordPerfect for Windows also uses codes, but they are generally not displayed on the screen.)

WordPerfect for Windows is also a Windows-compliant application. In other words, it is consistent with the Windows interface, using the Windows menu bar and supporting the Windows clipboard and windowing system. Naturally, WordPerfect for Windows is also designed to take advantage of the mouse.

Although the Windows version of WordPerfect includes some new features that work only with the mouse, virtually all of the functionality of the mouse can be duplicated from the keyboard.

But, just to set the record straight, we'll start by reviewing what *can't* be done from the keyboard.

What You Can't Do from the Keyboard

The vertical and horizontal scroll bars (by default, only the vertical scroll bar is displayed) do *not* work with the keyboard. You can remove the scroll bars by changing the display settings under the Preferences option of the File menu. (See the section on Preferences later in this chapter.) From the keyboard, you can duplicate the function of the scroll bars with the Arrow and PgUp and PgDn keys, as discussed later in this chapter.

One of WordPerfect's new features is an optional graphical *button bar* at the top or side of the screen that allows mouse users to point and click on icons representing frequently used commands such as Open, Print, and Close, or to activate the WordPerfect spelling checker. In addition to the main button bar which appears at the top of the active document, as shown in Figure 3.1, optional button bars are also available in the Graphics Figure Editor, the Equation and Table Editors, and with the Print Preview function. The button bar provides customizable buttons so that users can execute frequently used macros or other user-specified commands.

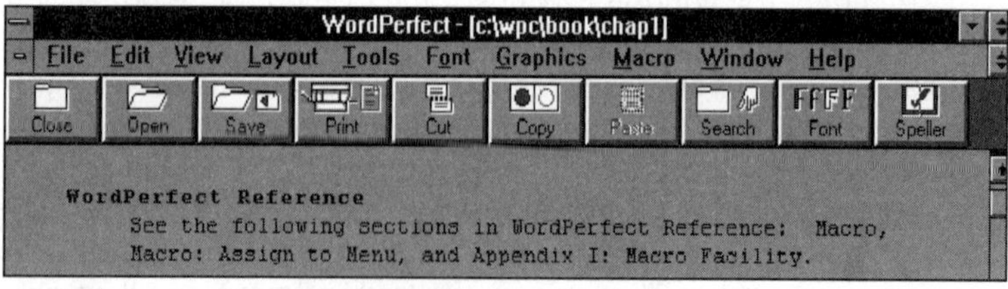

Figure 3.1 The WordPerfect button bar.

In any case, the button bar won't work from the keyboard. However, while the button bar is convenient, it is neither necessary nor does it offer any functionality that can't be duplicated from the keyboard. Fortunately, keyboard users can remove the button bar from the main document window, or from the other editing windows described above, by un-checking the Button Bar option in the View menu (Fig. 3.2). To do this, highlight the Button Bar option, and press Enter to remove the check, thus deactivating the option.

Another new feature that won't work without a mouse is the *ruler* (Fig. 3.3), which is also activated from the View menu. The ruler allows you to visually modify page attributes such as tabs and margins, line spacing, text fonts, and so forth. Here again, keyboard users will find the same functionality in the Layout and Font menus. Similar to the button bar, you disable the ruler by un-checking the Ruler option in the View menu.

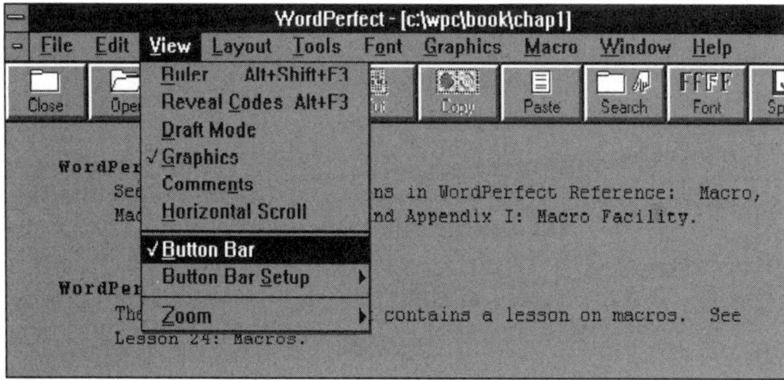

Figure 3.2 You can remove the button bar by un-checking the Button Bar option in the View menu.

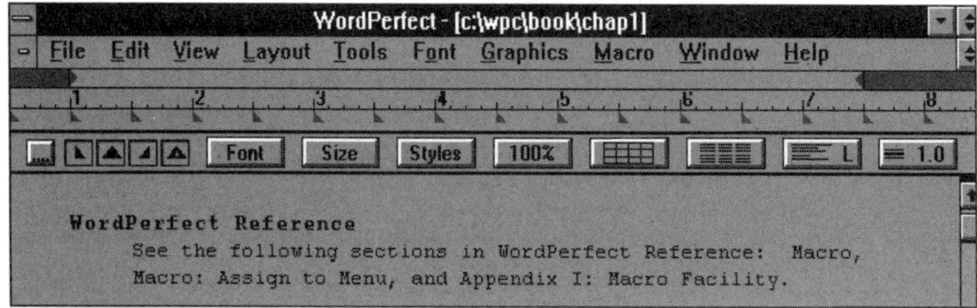

Figure 3.3 The ruler is only accessible with the mouse.

The Drag and Drop feature requires a mouse. This feature allows the user to select text and drag it to another location in the document or to another window. However, the same functionality can be achieved with WordPerfect's standard Cut, Copy, and Paste functions.

WordPerfect Keyboards

WordPerfect for Windows comes with two keyboard configurations which can be selected by the user. The default keyboard configuration is called the CUA keyboard (Common User Access). This configuration complies with the CUA interface guidelines as discussed in the foreword of this book. The alternate keyboard configuration is the WordPerfect DOS keyboard, which adheres to the DOS interface standard established in the DOS version of WordPerfect. WordPerfect provides a keystroke chart for each keyboard configuration on a two-sided keyboard template (one configuration on each side), which can be placed across the top of your keyboard. You choose keyboards using the Keyboard option discussed later in this chapter.

The primary purpose of the DOS keyboard configuration is to appease long-time DOS users of WordPerfect who are making the transition to the Windows version. It is particularly helpful to those users who have developed a lot of macros based on the DOS version of WordPerfect, which uses keystroke sequences for executing macros rather than macro names. (See the section on macros later in this chapter.) While this is certainly a considerate gesture on the part of WordPerfect Corp., most users will be better off in the long run by adopting the CUA keyboard. This is because the CUA keyboard complies with the interface standard used in virtually all Windows applications, and is therefore consistent with other applications.

For example, according to the CUA standard, pressing Alt+F4 closes the window or quits the application. In the WordPerfect DOS keyboard configuration, Alt+F4 selects a block of text. Using CUA, Ctrl+F6 moves you from one window or document to another. Using the DOS keyboard, Ctrl+F6 invokes the decimal tab. Obviously, you can eliminate a lot of confusion by sticking with the CUA keyboard, even if you are a long-time DOS WordPerfect user. In this book, we will focus on using the CUA keyboard with WordPerfect.

Custom Keyboards

In addition to the two keyboard layouts described above, WordPerfect allows you to set up custom keyboard layouts from the Preferences option of the File menu. For more on this topic, see the next section on customizing WordPerfect.

Customizing WordPerfect with Preferences

One of the most important and useful menu options in WordPerfect is the Preferences option in the File menu, shown in Figure 3.4. With this option, you can customize many of the features of WordPerfect to your particular requirements. While there isn't enough space for an exhaustive treatment of all the Preference options, we'll look at some of the most important ones. The reader is encouraged to look at all the options in the Preferences menu and to study their functions in WordPerfect's reference manual.

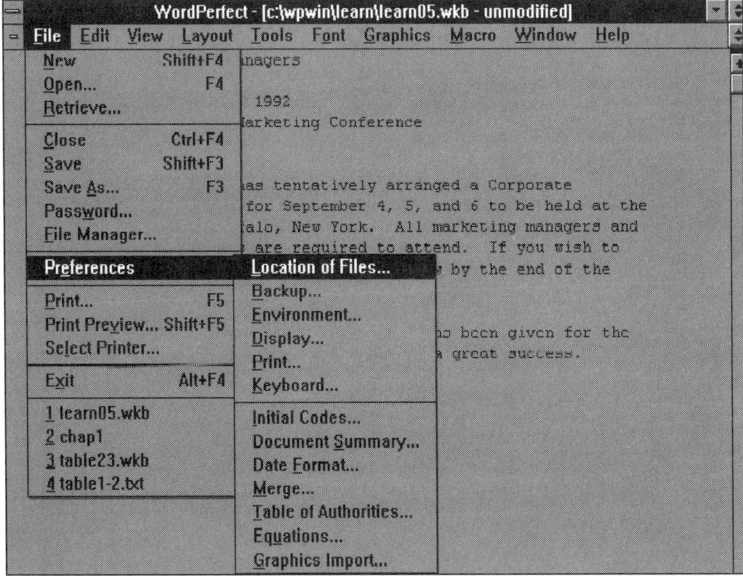

Figure 3.4 The Preferences option in the File menu.

Location of Files

The Location of Files option allows you to specify the directory locations of both WordPerfect system files and any files that you create. A typical dialog box is shown in Figure 3.5. While WordPerfect provides default directories for its system files and there is normally no need to change them, it is useful to create your own directory in which to save your documents and, if you wish, your backup files. (By default, backup files are saved in the WPWIN directory). When you specify a directory for documents, WordPerfect automatically uses this directory as the default directory for retrieving and saving files. (Of course, you can access other directories when executing the various file save and retrieval commands.) In this example, \WPC\BOOK is the directory for saving the user's documents.

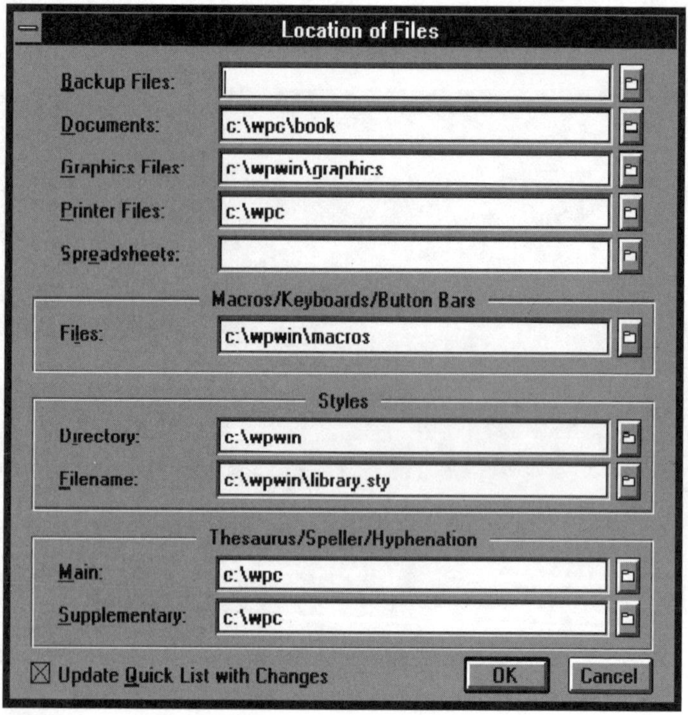

Location of Files

Backup Files:
Documents: c:\wpc\book
Graphics Files: c:\wpwin\graphics
Printer Files: c:\wpc
Spreadsheets:

Macros/Keyboards/Button Bars
Files: c:\wpwin\macros

Styles
Directory: c:\wpwin
Filename: c:\wpwin\library.sty

Thesaurus/Speller/Hyphenation
Main: c:\wpc
Supplementary: c:\wpc

Update Quick List with Changes   OK   Cancel

Figure 3.5 The Location of Files dialog box.

QUICK LISTS

Notice the Update Quick List check box in Figure 3.5. The Quick List is displayed in the Open File or Retrieve File dialog box as shown in Figure 3.6. This list represents common categories of files you use in WordPerfect. By selecting one of the items on the Quick List, WordPerfect automatically opens the directory containing that file category. WordPerfect uses the directories specified in the Location of Files dialog box to establish the Quick List. In the example, documents are stored in the C:\WPC\BOOK directory. You can add items to the Quick List or modify directory locations of the files by selecting the Edit Quick List box in the Open File window or by changing directory locations in the Location of Files window.

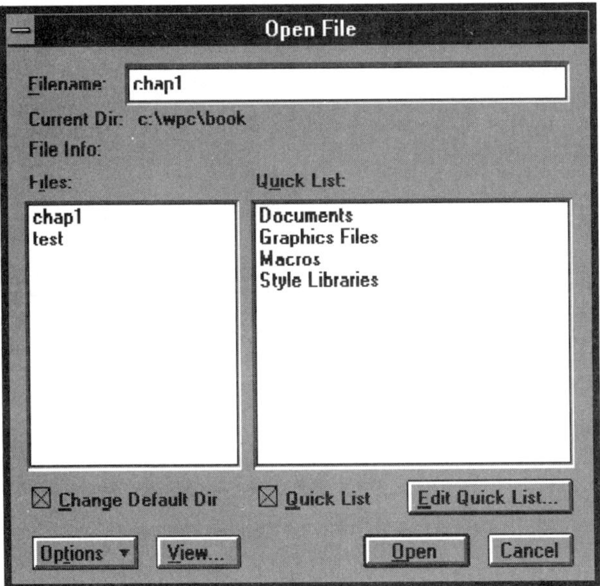

Figure 3.6 The Open File dialog box.

Display Option

The Display option allows you to modify the display settings as shown in Figure 3.7. If you are not using a mouse, you may wish to remove the vertical and horizontal scroll bars, since they cannot be accessed from the keyboard. Another feature that you may wish to change is the size of the window for revealing WordPerfect codes, which we will discuss later in this chapter.

You may also wish to experiment with the color settings depending on the type of monitor you have.

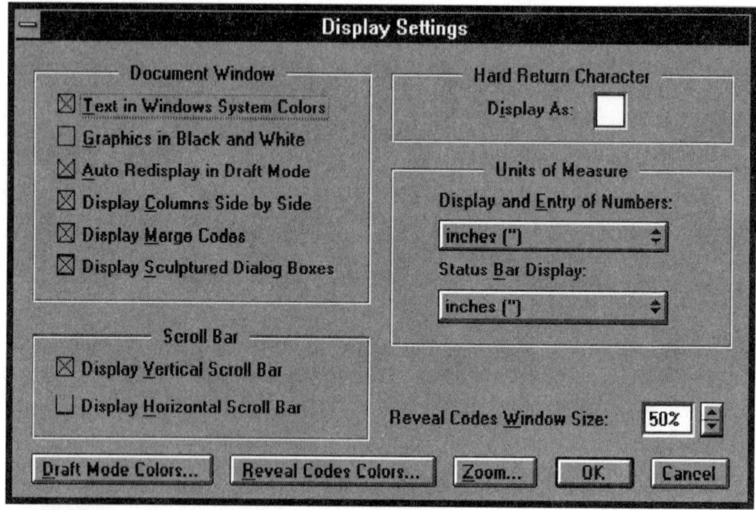

Figure 3.7 The Display Settings dialog box.

Notice the option for specifying draft mode colors. Draft mode displays your document in text mode rather than graphics mode, so that italics, boldface, and other graphic text attributes are represented by colors rather than their actual appearance. The purpose of draft mode is to allow faster typing and editing than is possible in graphics mode. This feature may be of interest to advanced users and to those working on very large documents. Most users, however, will probably find that the performance in graphics mode is adequate.

Keyboard Option

The Keyboard option allows you to select alternate keyboard layouts in addition to the default CUA keyboard layout as shown in Figure 3.8(a). As mentioned earlier, the CUA keyboard is the default setup supplied in WordPerfect, and we strongly recommend sticking with that keyboard layout.

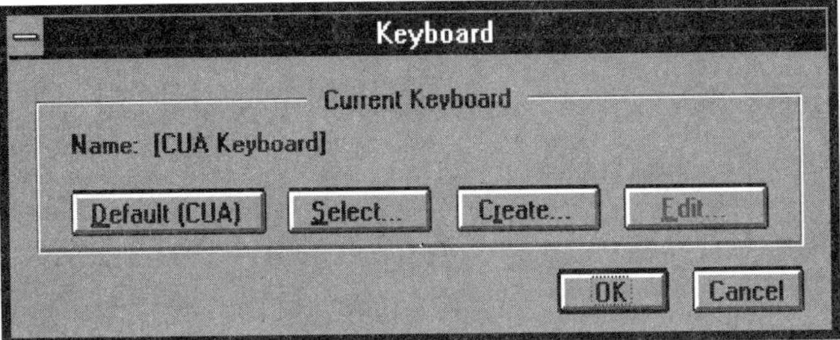

(a)

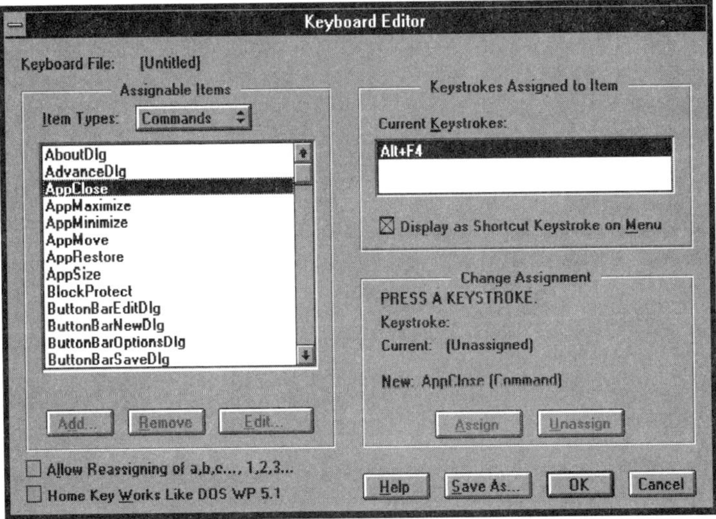

(b)

Figure 3.8(a) The Keyboard option. (b) The Keyboard Editor.

Alternate keyboard layouts are stored as files with the extension .WWK. WordPerfect configures the keyboard according to the specifications of the selected keyboard layout file. With the exception of the DOS keyboard file, custom layout files start out with the CUA layout codes. In other words, when you create a custom keyboard, its initial settings are identical to the CUA keyboard. You can then modify existing settings (not recommended), or add new settings of your own.

The primary purpose of creating a custom keyboard is to add keystroke sequences that execute custom macros or insert special characters into your document. For example, WordPerfect provides a keyboard layout designed for entering equations (EQUATION.WWK).

Unless you are an advanced user, you probably won't need to use custom keyboard layouts. But if you do decide to customize the keyboard layout, you should first select Create from the Keyboard dialog box. This will bring up the Keyboard Editor as shown in Figure 3.8(b). Note that each keystroke sequence is mapped to a particular action in WordPerfect. In the example in Figure 3.8(b), Alt+F4 is mapped to the AppClose command, which exits WordPerfect. Alt+F4 is the standard CUA keystroke for closing an application. After you have modified the keyboard layout, you can save the layout as a file and select it as needed.

Further attention will be given to keyboard layouts in the section on macros later in this chapter.

Navigating WordPerfect

Assuming you are using the CUA keyboard, WordPerfect behaves very much like other Windows applications, and much of WordPerfect will look familiar to you if you have mastered the basic Windows navigational and menu keystrokes.

Figure 3.9 The WordPerfect menu bar can be accessed using standard Windows keystrokes (e.g., Alt+F opens the File menu).

A typical WordPerfect document window is shown in Figure 3.9. You access the WordPerfect menu bar like you would any other Windows menu bar. Pressing Alt activates the menu bar. Alt+Spacebar brings up the Control menu, which we discussed in Chapter 1. Alt+F opens the File menu, Alt+E opens the Edit menu, and so forth. As in other Windows applications, the menu bar must be deactivated for keystrokes to take effect in the main document window. (If one of the menu bar options is highlighted, the menu bar is still active.) Press the Esc key to deactivate the menu bar.

Working with Files

Unless you specify a file, WordPerfect opens with a blank document and is ready for you to begin entering text. As we learned in the first two chapters, you can open files associated with an application directly by selecting the file's icon in Program Manager or the filename in File Manager and pressing Enter. The associated application opens automatically to display the file. If you open WordPerfect without specifying a file (by selecting the WordPerfect icon or the file \WPWIN\WPWIN.EXE and pressing Enter), you start with a blank document.

To open a file in WordPerfect, you can simply press the F4 key to open the Open File dialog box, or you can press Alt+F to open the File menu in the menu bar, as shown in Figure 3.10. One useful feature is the list of most recently opened files at the bottom of the menu. You simply type the number of the desired file to open it. In Figure 3.10, pressing "3" on the keyboard opens the file, LEARN05.WKB.

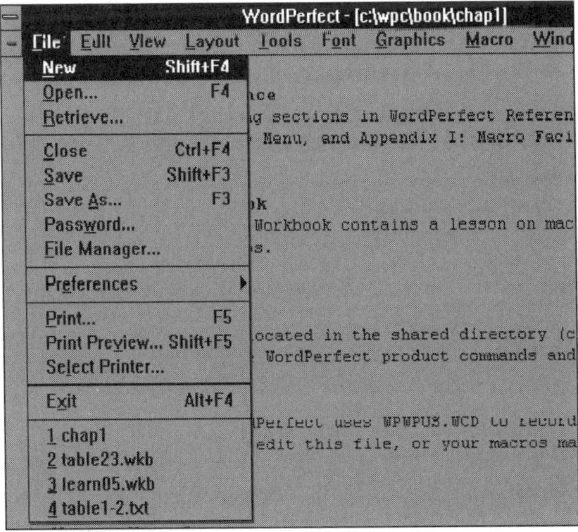

Figure 3.10 The WordPerfect File menu.

Note that the Open command opens an existing file in a new window. If you want the file to appear in the current window, select the Retrieve option from the File menu.

Moving the Insertion Point (Cursor)

The blinking vertical bar which tells you where you are in the document is called the *insertion point* or *cursor.* As we saw in Chapter 1, Windows provides a standard set of keystrokes for cursor movement and text selection. If you are using the CUA keyboard, cursor movement in WordPerfect is the same as it is in Windows Notepad or Write. For that matter, it's virtually the same as in other word processing packages such as Microsoft Word and Lotus AmiPro, both of which are also covered in this book. There are a few minor differences between these packages, but if you're familiar with one of these word processors, you can easily adapt to one of the others.

The Arrow keys move one character at a time horizontally (Left and Right Arrows) and one line at a time vertically (Up and Down Arrows). To move one word at a time, press Ctrl+Right Arrow or Ctrl+Left Arrow. To move one paragraph at a time, press Ctrl+Up Arrow or Ctrl+Down Arrow.

The Home and End keys move the cursor to the beginning and end of the current line, respectively. The PgUp and PgDn keys move the cursor to the top and bottom of the screen, respectively. If pressed repeatedly, these keys move the cursor up or down one screen of text at a time. To move the cursor up or down one page (the equivalent of one printed page of the document), press Alt+PgUp or Alt+PgDn. To move to the beginning or end of the document, press Ctrl+Home, or Ctrl+End, respectively.

Selecting Text

Next to entering text, selecting text is probably the operation performed most frequently. Text is selected for Cut, Copy, and Paste operations and for changing fonts or other text attributes such as italic or boldface. To select text, you use the cursor movement keystrokes described above but add the Shift key. For example, to select one line of text at a time, press Shift+Up Arrow or Shift+Down Arrow. To select the word to the right of the cursor, press Shift+Ctrl+Right Arrow. To select the next paragraph of text, press Shift+Ctrl+Down Arrow. (Press the Up Arrow to select the previous paragraph.) To select the text in the entire document, position the cursor at the top of the document (Ctrl+Home) and then press Shift+Ctrl+End. To deselect text, simply press an Arrow key.

Another method is to press the F8 key to turn on Select mode and then simply move the navigation keys as you would normally (without holding down the Shift key). The text that you traverse with the navigation keys is automatically selected. (Pressing F8 again cancels the selection.)

It is also possible to select text using the Select option in the Edit menu, as shown in Figure 3.11. You can select the sentence or paragraph at the location of the insertion point. The Tabular Column and Rectangle options allow you to select individual columns in a table or a rectangular portion of text. However, these options only work with the mouse. In most cases, it is more efficient to select text directly using the Arrow keys and keystroke sequences rather than from the Select option in the Edit menu.

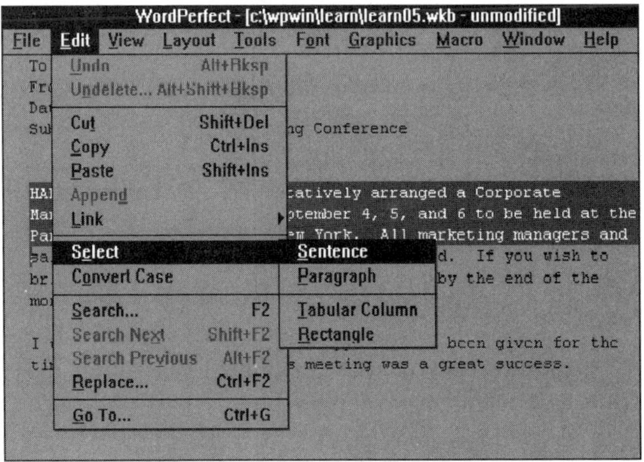

Figure 3.11 You can select text directly from the keyboard using F8 or the Shift and Arrow keys, or you can use the Select command from the Edit menu.

Working with Selected Text

Once you have selected text, you are obviously going to do something with it. You may want to move it, cut or copy it, delete it, save it as a file, change the font, change its margins or tabs, print it, and so on. There are two ways you can work with selected text: by using keystroke combinations or by executing commands from the menu bar. In some cases, you may have to use the menu bar if no keystroke combination is available. In most cases, however, it is much faster and more efficient to use keystroke combinations. The following paragraphs discuss the various ways you can work with selected text.

Cut, Copy, and Paste

There are several methods to cut, copy, or paste selected text. The easiest way is to select the text, and then press Ctrl+X or Ctrl+C to cut or copy the text, respectively. Cutting the text removes it from the document and places it in the Windows clipboard. (See Chapter 1 for more on the Windows clipboard.) Copying the text copies the text to the clipboard while at the same time leaving it in the original document. To paste the text into a different location or into another document, move the cursor to where you wish to paste the text, in either the current document or another one, and press Ctrl+V to paste. Press Ctrl+Z to undo the most recent Cut, Copy, or Paste operation.

Shift+Del, Ctrl+Ins, Shift+Ins, and Alt+Backspace, are alternative keystrokes for Cut, Copy, Paste, and Undo, respectively. However, as mentioned in Chapter 1, we strongly recommend getting in the habit of using the Ctrl combinations, which have become the standard keystroke combinations for Cut, Copy, and Paste in most computer operating systems.

The alternative method for performing Cut, Copy, or Paste is using the Edit menu, as shown in Figure 3.11.

Deleting Text

The Backspace key deletes the character immediately before (to the left of) the current location of the cursor. The Del key deletes the character immediately after (to the right of) the cursor. Pressing Ctrl+Del deletes all characters to the end of the line. Pressing Ctrl+Backspace deletes the word nearest to the insertion point. And, most importantly, pressing Ctrl+Z will undo your deletion. You can also press Alt+Backspace to Undo, or Alt+Shift+Backspace to Undelete, which is slightly different from Undo. Undelete brings up a dialog box allowing you to restore the last three deletions made with the Delete key. The Undelete option does not work with cut text. (You must use Paste or Undo to restore cut text.) The Undelete and Undo options are also available using the Edit menu.

Displaying and Working with Codes

WordPerfect stores document format and text attribute information in the form of codes. It is important to understand how WordPerfect codes work so that you can fully control and, when necessary, use the codes to make changes to your document. While most changes can be made using keystrokes or the menu bar options, some situations require you to work with the WordPerfect codes.

WordPerfect maintains two copies of your document: one that represents how the document will look on the printed page (which is what you normally work with on the screen), and one that contains both the text and the codes that define the document. You can see the codes by selecting Reveal Codes in the View menu (Fig. 3.2) or by pressing Alt+F3 while in the document.

Figure 3.12(a) shows a document with the codes revealed. Notice that the screen is split with the "WYSIWYG" version on the top half and the coded version on the bottom half. If you wish to use a smaller portion of the screen for either version of the document, you can change the screen percentage devoted to codes using the Display option of the Preferences menu described earlier. Pressing Alt+F3 with the codes displayed hides them again.

If you look carefully at Figure 3.12(a), you can see that all the formats and text attributes are specified in the coded version of the document. For example, the text, "Corporate Marketing," has a different font. The word "International" is in italics and is denoted in the coded version by "Italc On" and "Italc Off."

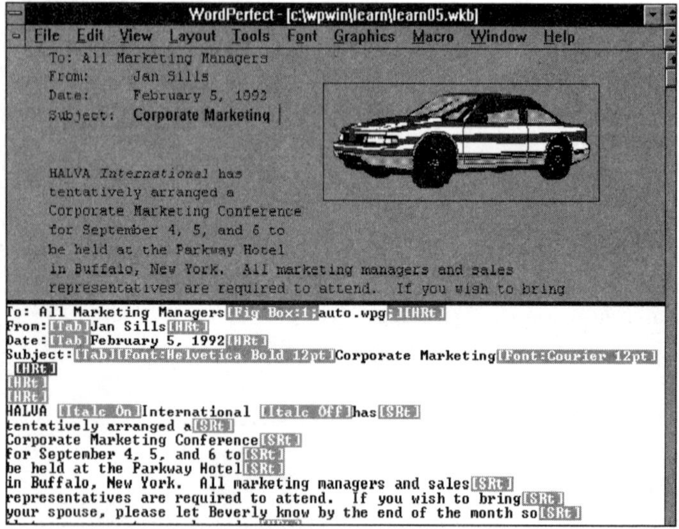

Figure 3.12(a) The Reveal Codes option is in effect in this screen. Note that the first line of the Codes window specifies the AUTO.WPG file representing the figure.

Note that any of these codes can be edited or deleted simply by moving the cursor to the code that you want to change. When the code becomes highlighted it can be changed or removed. If you remove the code, the corresponding attribute in the document is also removed.

Removing Document Features Using Codes

One of the reasons that codes are so important is that they are necessary in order to remove certain attributes from your document. Notice in Figure 3.12(a) that the automobile graphic image is represented in the coded version by "Figure Box:1:auto.wpg." The figure is stored as a file called AUTO.WPG, which is one of the graphic images supplied by WordPerfect. While the Graphics menu provides facilities for creating, retrieving, and editing figures, the only way to delete the figure from the document is to delete the appropriate code. In this example, we would move the cursor to the "Fig Box" field and press the Delete key to remove the figure. Note in Figure 3.12(b) that the figure has been removed.

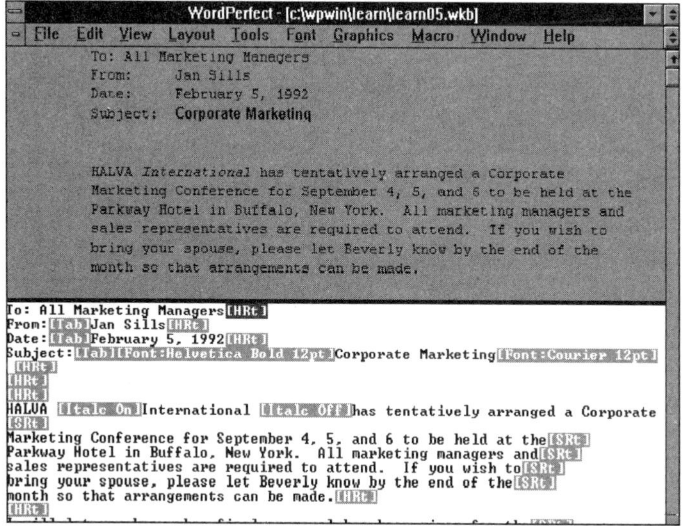

Figure 3.12(b) The figure has been removed by deleting the reference in the first line of the Codes window.

Another attribute that is easiest to remove directly using codes is the *hard page break*. A hard page break is a page break that the user inserts in the document to start a new page. (This is accomplished using the key combination Ctrl+Enter.) To remove a hard page break, find the corresponding code in the document and delete it.

Modifying Attributes of Selected Text

One of the main reasons to select text is to modify the text's attributes. For example, you may want to change some text to boldface or italics, or change from a right justified margin to a ragged margin. Here again, you can use keystroke combinations for many of the text modification commands, or you can access the commands in the menu bar. For example, pressing Ctrl+B changes the selected text to boldface. Pressing Ctrl+I changes it to italics. Or, you can select the Font menu (Alt+O) and select these same attributes from the menu options. Note that the Undo command (Ctrl+Z) will undo the most recent text modification.

Fonts

The Font menu is shown in Figure 3.13. As with other Windows menus, keystroke equivalents for many of the commands are shown on the right-hand side of the menu. Note that certain font characteristics such as Subscript and Superscript are only available from the Font menu.

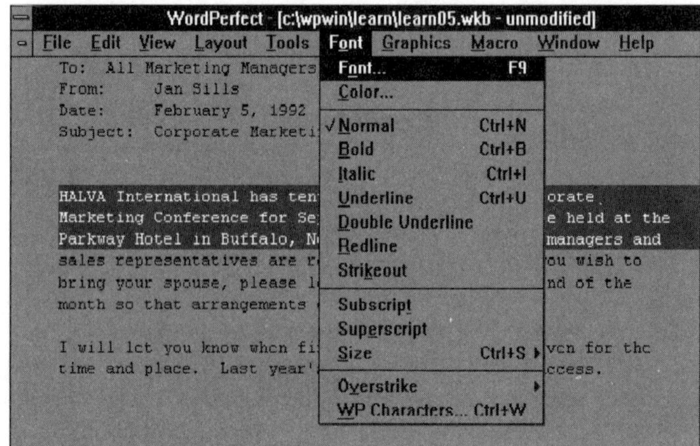

Figure 3.13 The Font menu allows you to change text attributes. Keystroke equivalents are shown on the right side of the menu.

Selecting the Font option opens the Font dialog box, which displays all the fonts and point sizes available on your system, as shown in Figure 3.14. You can change the font of selected text by highlighting the desired font and point size and then pressing Enter.

SPECIAL CHARACTERS

One of WordPerfect's most valuable features is its extensive library of characters, which can be accessed from the WP Characters option in the Font menu or by pressing Ctrl+W from the document window. There are 12 character sets and a user-defined character set. The sets include Japanese, Cyrillic, Greek, mathematical symbols, and typographical symbols, among others.

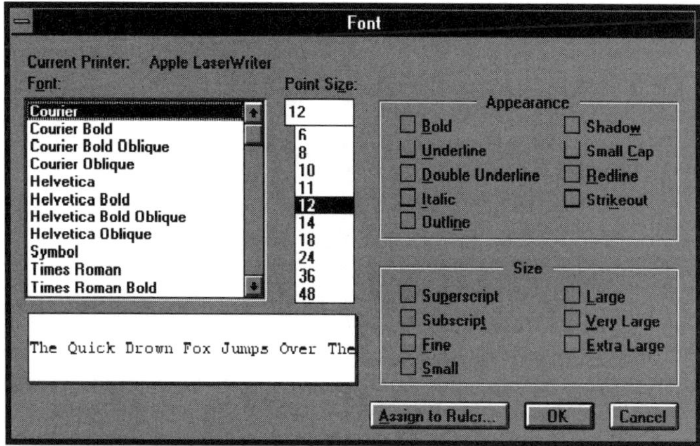

Figure 3.14 The Font dialog box.

The WP Character dialog box is shown in Figure 3.15. You can scroll through the various character sets and then press Alt+C to move the cursor into the window of displayed characters. Use the Arrow keys to move through the Character window. You can insert selected characters into your document.

Layout

The Layout menu (Fig. 3.16) provides the tools for setting margins and tabs, page breaks, line spacing, text justification, columns, footnotes, headers and footers, and other document characteristics. As we mentioned earlier, this menu provides all of the functions (and more) that are contained in the ruler, which is only accessible using a mouse. Admittedly, the ruler offers some advantages over the Layout menu, simply because you can see your modifications as you move the mouse pointer. For example, the ruler may be the better method for dragging the margin or tab setting to a new location. Nevertheless, you can perform efficient page layout directly from the keyboard by mastering the commands in the Layout menu. Note that virtually every Layout command includes a cascading submenu (denoted by the triangle next to the command) as we discussed in Chapter 1. For example, when you select the Line command, the submenu in Figure 3.17 appears.

Note that the keystroke sequence you use from the document window automatically opens the submenu. For example, if you press Shift+F9 from the document window, the Line submenu opens.

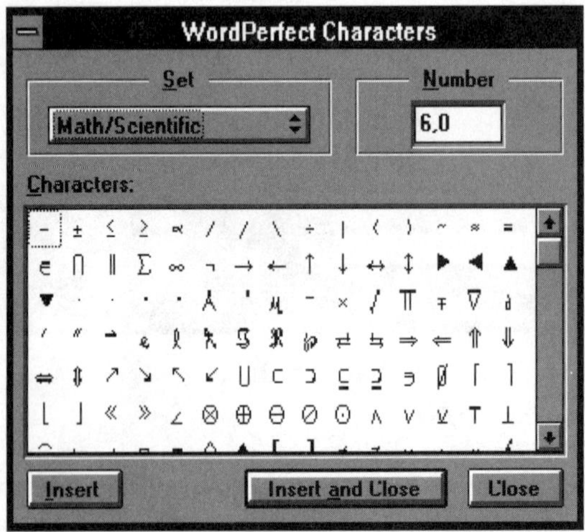

Figure 3.15 There are 12 WordPerfect character sets to choose from.

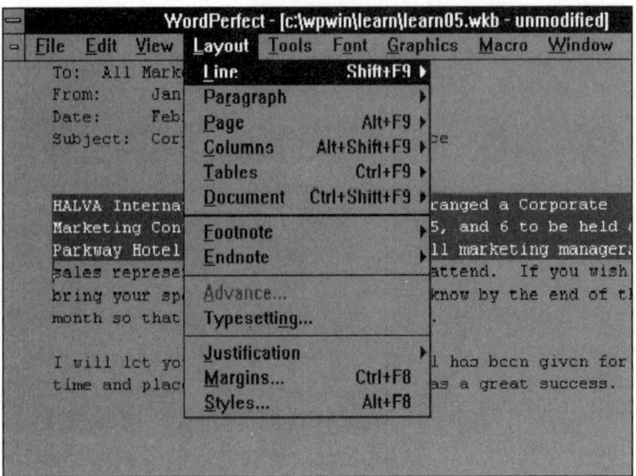

Figure 3.16 The Layout menu.

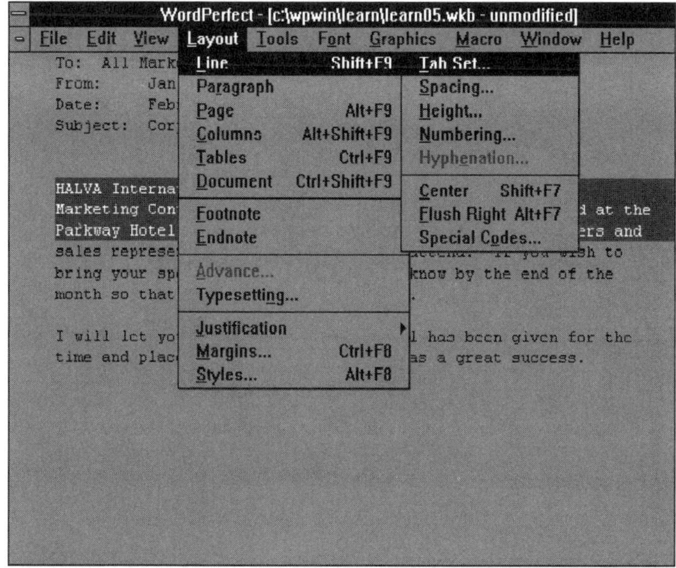

Figure 3.17 The Line submenu.

Many of the Layout commands operate on selected text, or, if no text is selected, on the entire document starting with the current position of the cursor. For example, the Columns command creates columns throughout the whole document unless you select a specific section of text. If you select text, only the selected text will be converted into columns. This is shown in Figure 3.18(a) and 3.18(b). You can use either the Reveal Codes command or the Columns Off command in the Columns menu to delete columns. (Convert the text back to full-page width.)

You can set margins and text justification for either the entire document or selected text. Press Ctrl+F8 to bring up the Margins dialog box shown in Figure 3.19 or select Margins from the Layout menu. From the document window, press Ctrl+R, Ctrl+J, or Ctrl+L to set right, center, or left text justification, respectively, Ctrl+F for full justification (justified on both margins), or select Justification from the Layout menu, as shown in Figure 3.20.

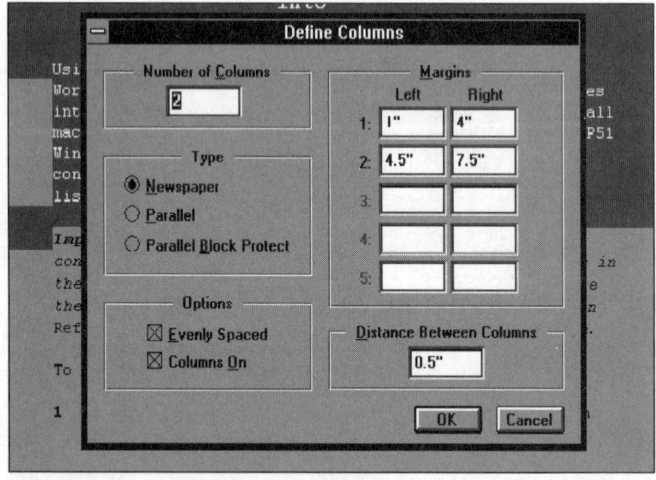

(a)

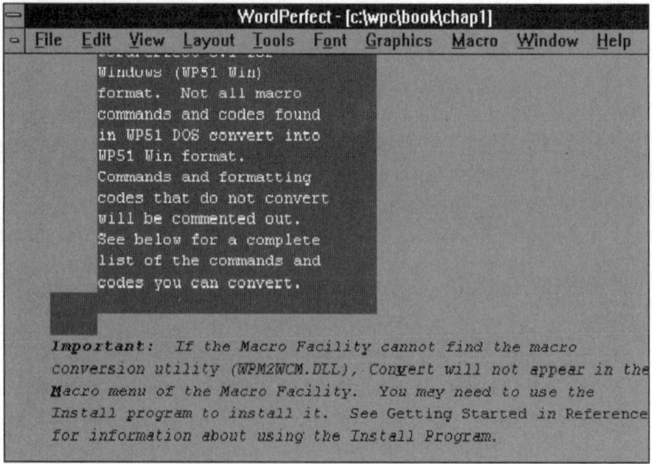

The following is a reproduction of a WordPerfect window:

WordPerfect - [c:\wpc\book\chap1]

File   Edit   View   Layout   Tools   Font   Graphics   Macro   Window   Help

Windows (WP51 Win)
format. Not all macro
commands and codes found
in WP51 DOS convert into
WP51 Win format.
Commands and formatting
codes that do not convert
will be commented out.
See below for a complete
list of the commands and
codes you can convert.

*Important: If the Macro Facility cannot find the macro
conversion utility (WPM2WCM.DLL), Convert will not appear in the
Macro menu of the Macro Facility. You may need to use the
Install program to install it. See Getting Started in Reference
for information about using the Install Program.*

(b)

Figure 3.18(a) Only the selected text is converted to Column format. (b) Columns are easily removed using the Reveal Codes option.

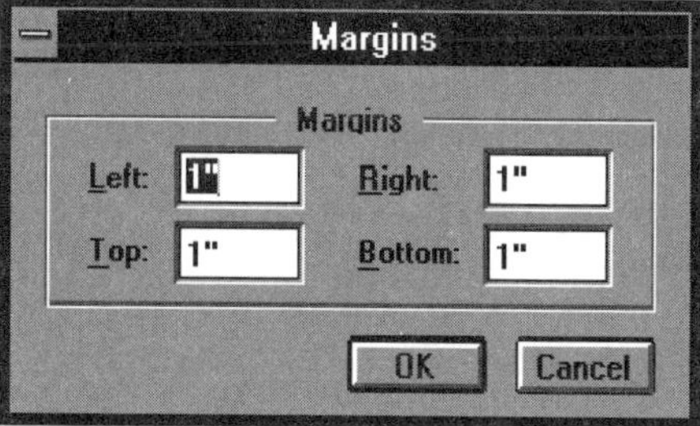

Figure 3.19 The Margins dialog box. (Units of measure are in inches in this example, but you can change units from the Display Settings option in the Preferences menu).

Figure 3.20 The Justification option in the Layout menu. Note the keystroke equivalents.

The Tables option provides a convenient tool for creating tables without the difficulty of setting tabs, lining up text, and so forth. You can also use formulas and calculations similar to a spreadsheet to produce subtotals and totals or other calculated cell values. In the example in Figure 3.21(a), the interest amount is a calculated value.

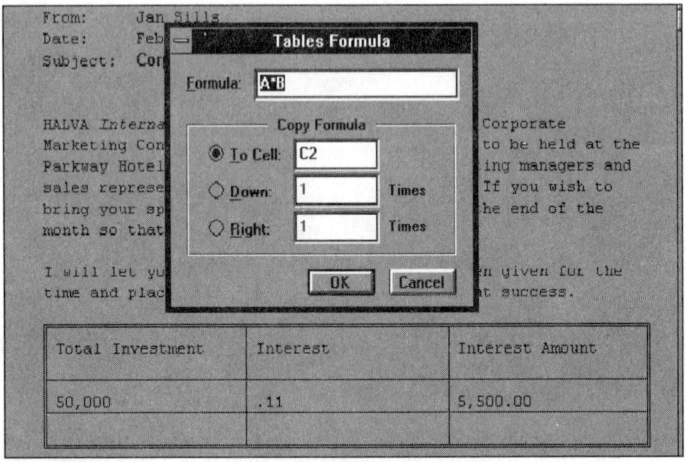

(a)

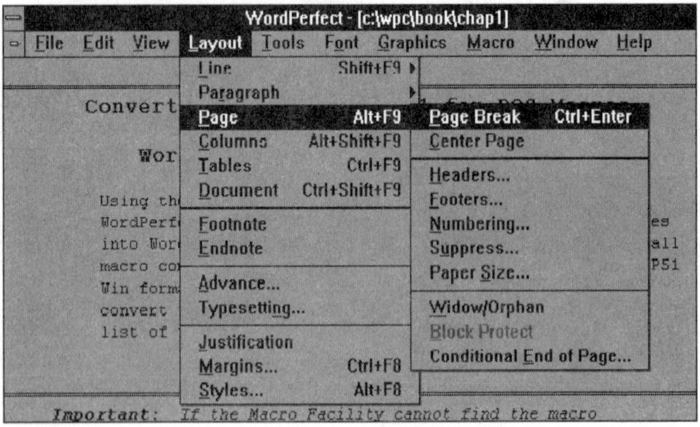

(b)

Figure 3.21(a) The Tables command. In the example, the product of the first two columns is displayed in the third column in cell C2. (b) The Page option in the Layout menu.

The Page command provides the options shown in Figure 3.21(b). You can press Alt+F9 from the document window to open the Page menu. As we mentioned earlier, pressing Ctrl+Enter creates a page break at the current insertion point. The

Page command includes options for creating headers and footers, page numbering, and adjusting the paper size.

The Layout menu provides a comprehensive set of commands for formatting text and pages. We have only touched on some of the capabilities in the Layout menu, so the reader is encouraged to experiment with the features we haven't covered.

Tools

Pressing Alt+T from your document opens the Tools menu shown in Figure 3.22. Whereas the Layout menu provides tools for formatting the appearance of your document, the Tools menu provides tools for working with the text in your document: checking the spelling, using the Thesaurus, counting the number of words in the document, changing the character set to a foreign language, sorting or merging text, creating outlines, linking spreadsheets, and so forth.

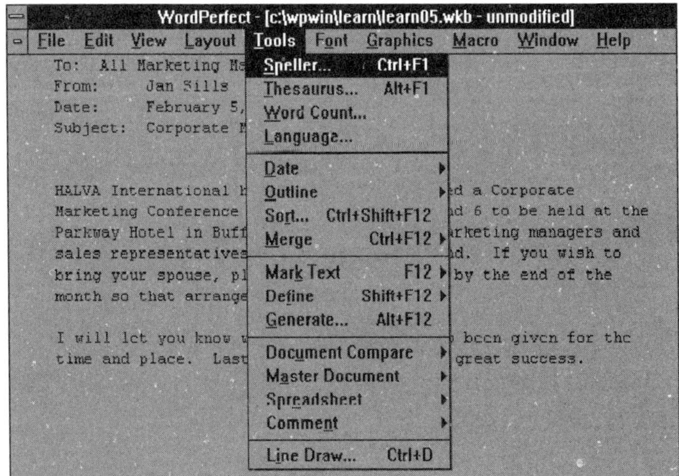

Figure 3.22 The Tools menu.

Most features of the Tools menu work either with the entire document or selected text. For example, you can spell-check the entire document or just selected text. The word count feature also works in this manner. Obviously, you would use the Thesaurus with individual words.

The Mark Text, Define, and Generate options are all related to generating lists, tables of contents, and indexes from the text in your document. The Master Document function provides a means of linking multiple smaller document files together to form a large document such as a book. As an author of several books in which I used WordPerfect to do the writing, I must confess that I never used any of these features. I found them to be simply more trouble than they are worth. However, other users may find them to be of great utility in some situations, particularly the table of contents and index features.

The Sort feature is useful if you are generating mailing lists or other data in a WordPerfect text file. In Figure 3.23(a), we have selected a list of names to be sorted alphabetically. Press Shift+Ctrl+F12 or select Sort from the Tools menu to open the Sort window, shown in Figure 3.23(b). The result is shown in Figure 3.23(c).

Use the Merge feature to merge names and addresses into a form letter, for example. The Merge feature is somewhat complicated to learn, and it is recommended that you go through the lesson on the Merge feature in the WordPerfect tutorial.

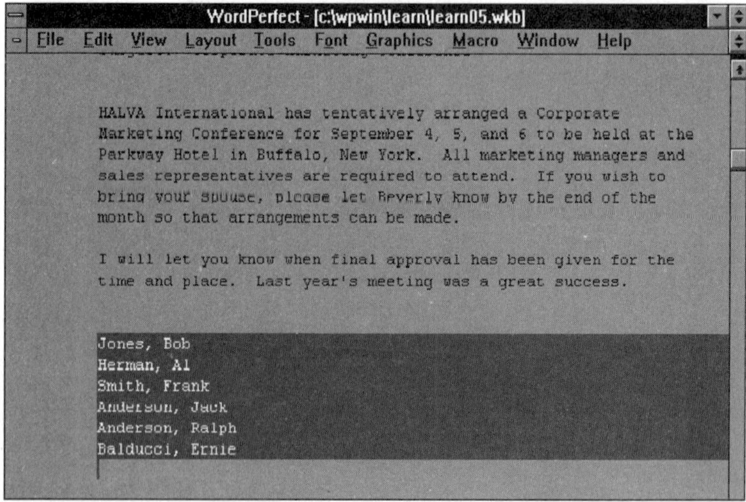

Figure 3.23(a) The Sort option is particularly useful for creating sorted lists.

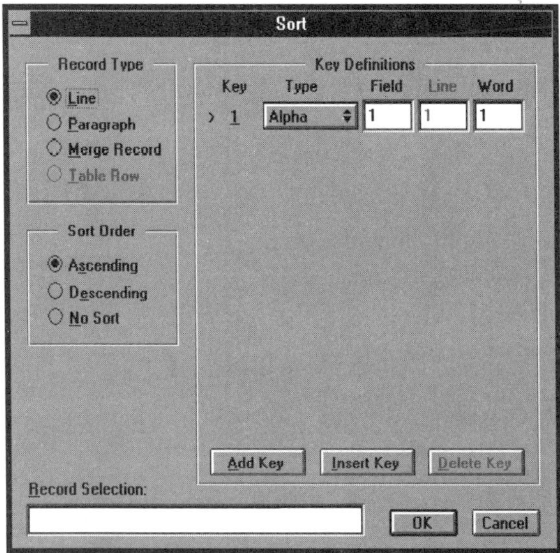

(b)

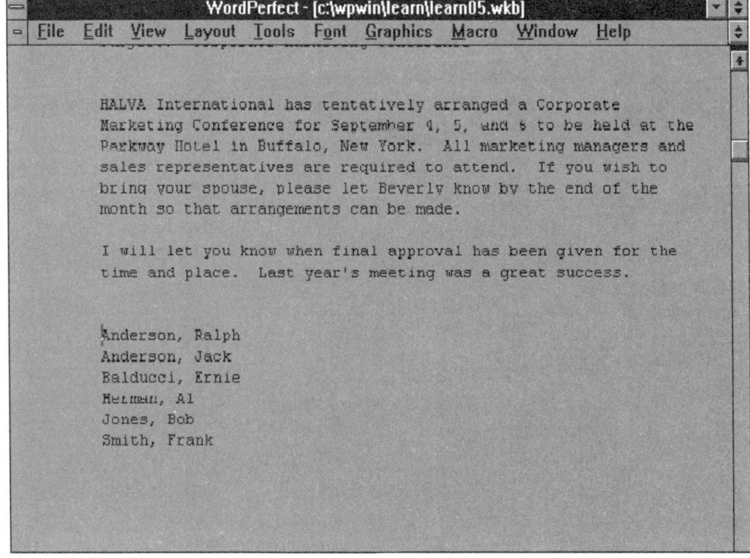

(c)

Figure 3.23(b–c) The Sort option (continued).

Graphics

WordPerfect inserts graphics images as boxes into your document. These boxes can contain graphics, text, equations, tables, or other information contained in a *user box*. Pressing Alt+G brings up the Graphics menu shown in Figure 3.24(a). In the figure, we have opened the Figure submenu. The submenus of each option in the Graphics menu are virtually identical, allowing you to retrieve, create, edit, re-position, and write captions.

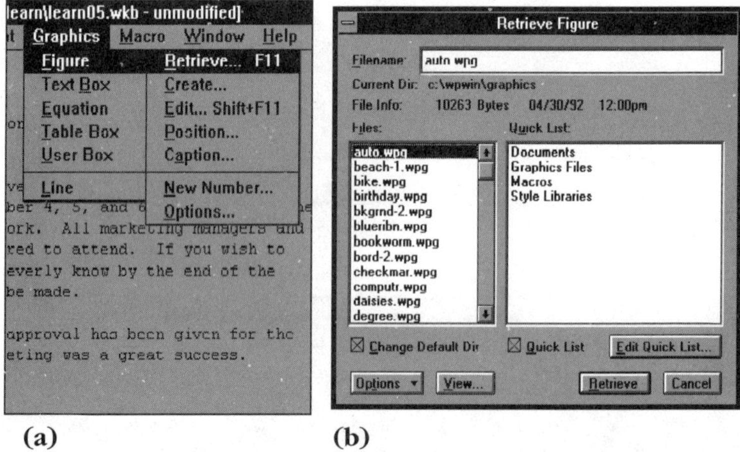

(a)   (b)

Figure 3.24(a–b) The Graphics menu and Retrieve submenu. In the example, WordPerfect file AUTO.WPG has been selected.

WordPerfect provides a set of graphics images in a native WordPerfect format (files with the extension .WPG) for use in your documents as shown in Figure 3.24(b). You can also import graphics images from standard PC formats such as TIFF, BMP, or PCX, by using the Figures Editor accessed from the Create option of the Figures menu. The Figures Editor (Fig. 3.25) is actually a separate application which you can use to import graphics figures and convert them to WordPerfect's graphics format. We saw earlier how you can use the Reveal Codes option from the Layout menu to remove graphics images from your document.

Figure 3.26 shows a text box created using the Create command from the Text Box option of the Graphics menu. Notice that we have opened the Caption Editing dialog box. As with graphics boxes, you can remove text boxes using the Reveal Codes command (Alt+F3).

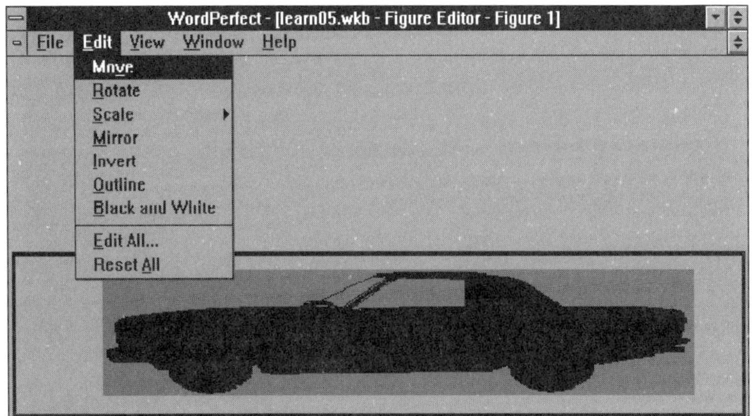

Figure 3.25 You use the Figures Editor to import other image formats to WordPerfect. In the example, we have imported a TIFF file.

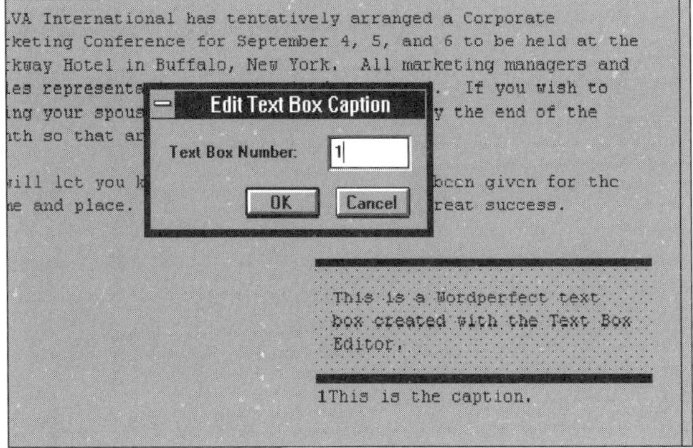

Figure 3.26 Use the Text Box option to create text boxes in your document.

Macros

Macros in WordPerfect for Windows are completely different from their counterparts in the WordPerfect for DOS version of the product. In the Windows version, macros store the *results* of keystrokes or mouse actions rather than the keystrokes themselves. The macro is stored in a compiled file rather than in an editable text file. Macros designed in the DOS version of WordPerfect must be converted to the Windows version, the procedure for which is beyond the scope of this book. WordPerfect provides a lengthy document called MACRO.DOC, which describes in detail procedures for converting WordPerfect for DOS macros. WordPerfect provides an impressive library of built-in macros, which can be accessed from the Macros menu as shown in Figure 3.27. For example, the Envelope macro will take the address from a letter and automatically format the envelope. Simply select the address and then press Alt+M to bring up the Macro menu. Play the Envelope macro to get a screen similar to Figure 3.28.

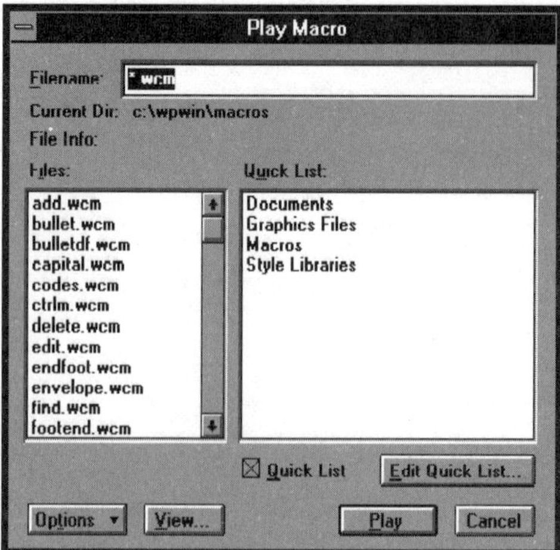

Figure 3.27 The Play Macro dialog box.

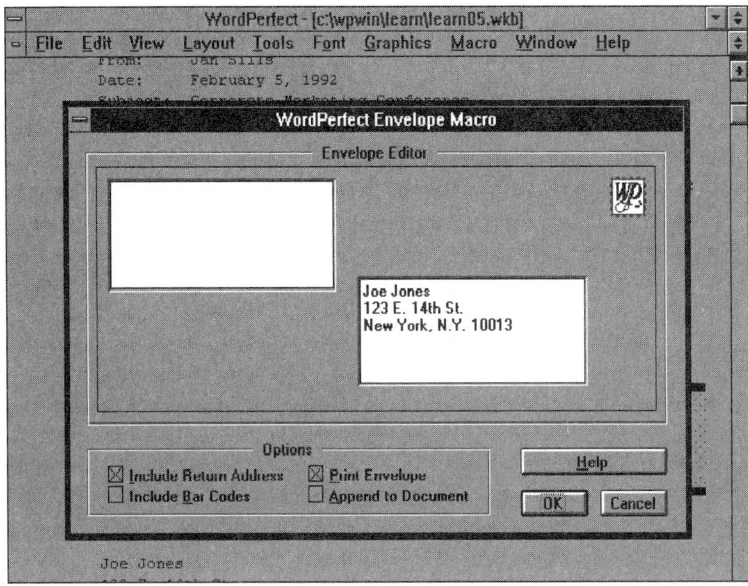

Figure 3.28 The WordPerfect Envelope macro.

Microsoft Word

4

A concise list of Microsoft Word keystrokes begins on page 252.

This chapter covers the basic keystrokes for Microsoft Word for Windows.

Microsoft Word is among Microsoft's oldest and most venerable application software products, popular in both the MS-DOS and Macintosh environments as well as on Microsoft Windows. The product has undergone major revisions and improvements throughout its history, and in its current version offers a wealth of advanced features and capabilities.

Like WordPerfect (covered in the last chapter), Word for Windows is a graphical or "WYSIWYG" (What You See Is What You Get) application. This means that graphics and text attributes such as fonts, italics, and boldface are shown on the screen, although a Draft Mode option allows you to switch to a character-based format for faster editing and display speed.

Not surprisingly, Word for Windows is a fully Windows-compliant application. In other words, it is consistent with the Windows interface, using the Windows menu bar and supporting the Windows clipboard and windowing system. Naturally, Word for Windows is also designed to take advantage of the mouse.

Like WordPerfect, Word has some features that only work with the mouse. These features can be duplicated from the keyboard, but, as in the last chapter, we'll start by reviewing what can't be done from the keyboard.

What You Can't Do from the Keyboard

The vertical and horizontal scroll bars do *not* work with the keyboard and can be removed by changing the display settings using the Options command in the Tools menu. (See the section on the Tools menu later in this chapter.) From the keyboard, you can duplicate the function of the scroll bars with the Arrow and PgUp and PgDn keys, as discussed in greater detail later in this chapter.

Like WordPerfect's button bar, Word for Windows features an optional graphical *toolbar,* which allows mouse users to point and click on icons representing frequently used commands such as Open, Print, and Close, or activate other Word features such as the spelling checker. The toolbar includes customizable buttons so that users can add other commands or macros represented by icons. The toolbar is shown in Figure 4.1.

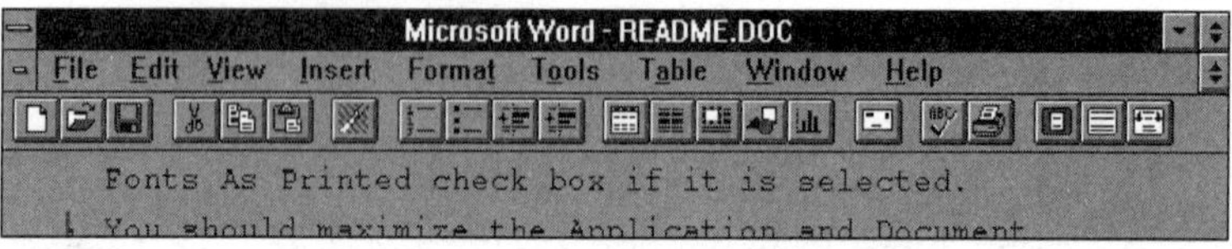

Figure 4.1 The toolbar.

All of the functionality of the toolbar can be duplicated from the keyboard using keystroke sequences or the Word menu options. If you are strictly using the keyboard, you can reclaim some space on the screen by removing the toolbar. This is accomplished by un-checking the Toolbar option in the View menu (Fig. 4.2). To do this, select the Toolbar option in the View menu (Alt+V), and press Enter to remove the check, thus deacitivating the option.

Word also provides a *ribbon* and *ruler* (Fig. 4.3a and 4.3b) for graphically setting tabs, margins, line spacing, text justification, fonts, and so forth. The ribbon only works with the mouse and can be removed by un-checking the Ribbon option in the View menu.

The ruler allows you to visually set margins, paragraph indentation, and tab stops. You can use the ruler from the keyboard to set tab stops but not for setting margins or paragraph indentation. To set tab stops, press Ctrl+Shift+F10. This keystroke combination activates a cursor in the ruler. You can move the cursor with the Arrow keys and then use the Ins and Del keys to insert or remove tab stops. Pressing Enter exits the ruler. If you wish to remove the ruler, you can also deactivate it from the View menu.

The Drag and Drop feature requires a mouse. This feature allows the user to select text and drag it to another location in the document or to another window. However, the same functionality can be achieved with Word's standard Cut, Copy, and Paste functions.

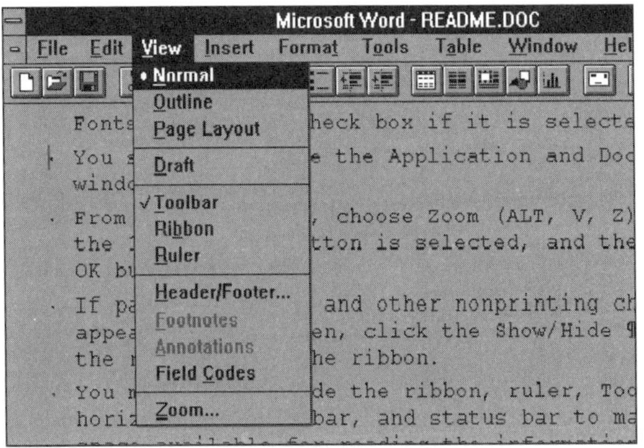

Figure 4.2 Use the View menu to remove the toolbar by "un-checking" the Toolbar option.

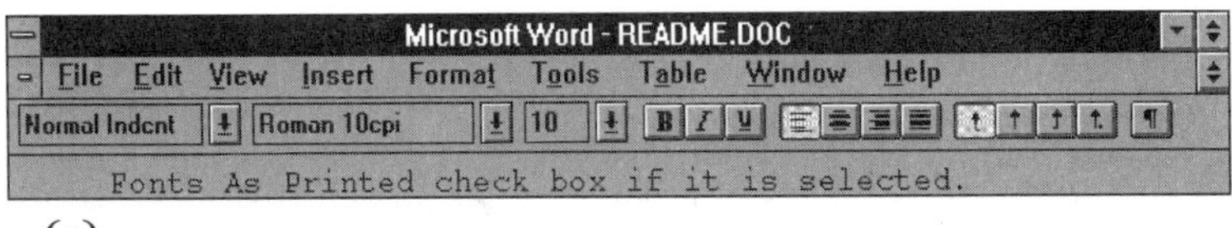

(a)

(b)

Figure 4.3(a) The ribbon and ruler are also mouse-driven graphical tools for formatting your document. (b) The ruler does have limited functionality with the keyboard.

The Word Keyboard

The Microsoft Word keyboard conforms to the Windows keyboard interface standard, which is consistent with the Common User Access (CUA) standard as discussed in the Foreword. As we shall see, navigation keys and menu selection keys are virtually the same as in other Windows text and word processing applications.

The keyboard can be extensively customized using the Options command in the Tools menu. To attract WordPerfect users, Word includes an option to configure the navigation keys according to the WordPerfect keyboard, as well as a special Help option for WordPerfect converts.

Word for Windows also provides a keyboard template listing all major keystrokes, which you can place along the top of the keyboard.

Custom Keyboards and Document Templates

Microsoft Word does not specifically employ custom keyboards, but instead allows you to add custom keystrokes to *document templates*. Document templates are files ending with the .DOT extension. They specify patterns for certain types of documents. Word provides a series of ready-to-use document templates, which can be accessed from the Template option in the File menu. You can add custom keystrokes to templates from the Tools menu as discussed in the next section. (See the section on the File menu for more on document templates.)

Customizing Word from the Tools Menu

One of the most important and useful menu options in Word is the Options command in the Tools menu, shown in Figure 4.4. (Press Alt+O to open the Tools menu.) With this option, you can customize many of the features of Word to your particular requirements. While there isn't enough space for an exhaustive treatment of all the customization options, we'll look at some of the most important and interesting ones. The reader is encouraged to look at all the options in the Options command of the Tools menu and to study their functions in Word's user's guide.

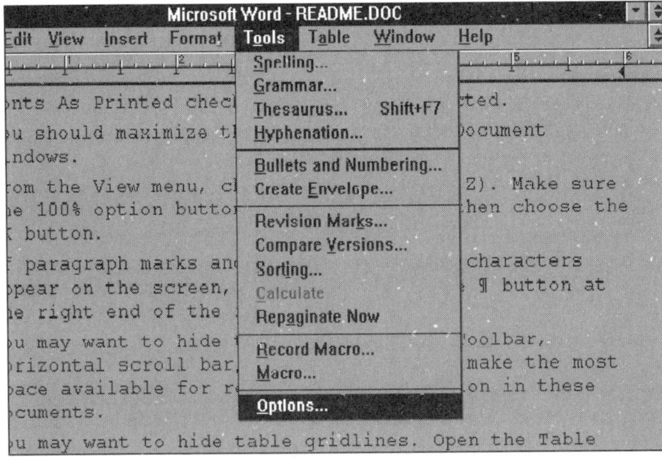

Figure 4.4 The Tool menu.

When you select the Options command, the Options window opens with the various customization categories represented by icons shown in the left-hand panel of the window, as shown in Figure 4.5. In the example, the View category is displayed and three other category icons are visible.

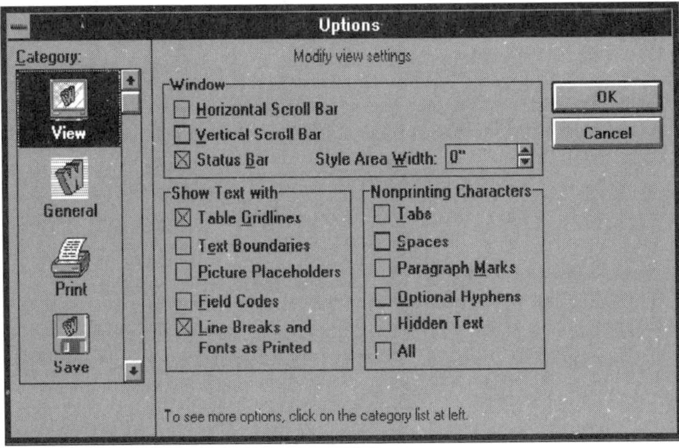

Figure 4.5 The Options window.

There are a total of 11 categories, which you can access by pressing the Up or Down Arrow keys. These include View, General, Print, Save, Spelling, Grammar, User Info, Toolbar, Menus, Keyboard, and WIN.INI. Each of these categories allows you to modify functions or features pertaining to that category. Microsoft provides default settings that are probably satisfactory for most users. Nevertheless, the Option command offers remarkable flexibility for those who want to customize Word.

View

The View category (see Fig. 4.5) allows you to modify display settings. Of particular interest to keyboard users are the Horizontal and Vertical Scroll Bar check boxes, which allow you to remove the scroll bars by un-checking the check boxes. For example, to disable the horizontal scroll bar, press Alt+H to un-check the box.

The View category also includes options for changing how text is displayed on the screen. One useful option is the Picture Placeholder option, which allows you to display a rectangle representing a graphic image in your document instead of the image itself, therefore allowing faster scrolling and editing, since Word does not have to constantly redraw the image on the screen. (See the section on Graphics in this chapter for more on this topic.)

The Nonprinting Characters option allows you to display codes and symbols that Word uses to format your document, such as tab or paragraph markers.

User Info

A useful feature of the User Info option is the ability to enter your own mailing address in the User Info window, which you can then specify as the return address on envelopes printed in Word. This is shown in Figure 4.6.

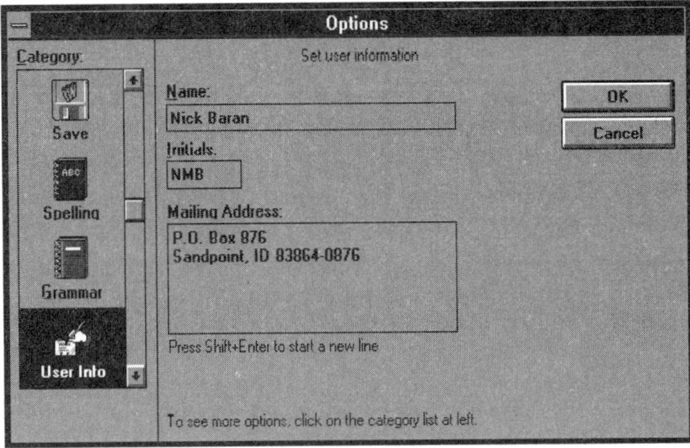

Figure 4.6 The User Info category.

Menus

The Menus option allows you to change menu options or add new ones to existing menus. Although it is possible to change the default menu options, the most common type of customization is to add macros. Figure 4.7 shows the Menus Option window. Note that the menu name is shown along with the various options belonging to that menu and the command associated with the option. For example, the Toolbar option in the View menu is associated with the ViewToolbar command. The Description field describes the function of the command.

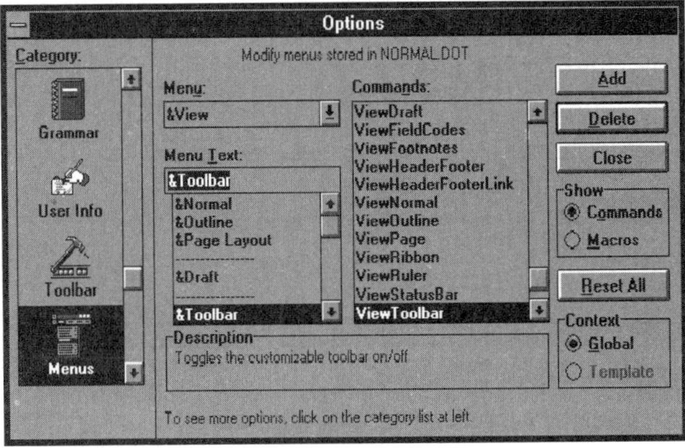

Figure 4.7 The Menus option.

The example shows the menu commands, but you can also display available macros using the Show option. The Reset All button resets the Word menus back to their default status. The Context field allows you to make the changes apply *globally* (to all Word documents) or to specific document templates. (The Template option is not available unless the currently active document is assigned to a template other than the default Normal template).

Keyboard

The Keyboard Option window shown in Figures 4.8(a) and 4.8(b) is similar to the Menus option, allowing you to modify or add commands or macros. The Show option allows you to display either keyboard commands or macros. As with the Menus option, keyboard changes can apply either globally or to specific document templates.

Notice in Figure 4.8(a) that the keyboard assignments apply to the PRESS.DOT template (a template supplied with Word for formatting press releases). In this case, the macros and keystrokes apply only to documents associated with the PRESS template. (For more on templates, see the section on the File menu later in this chapter.)

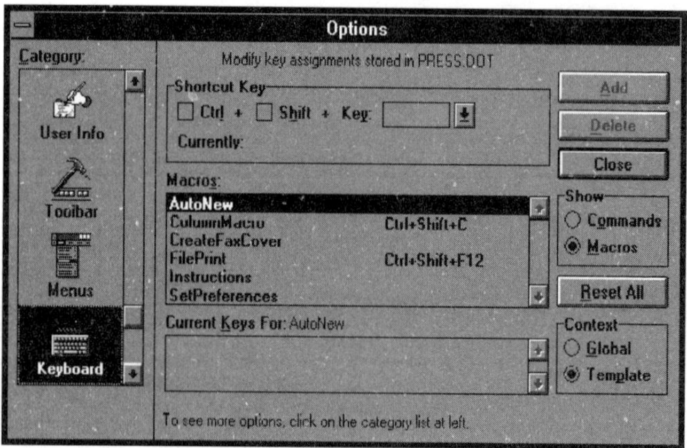

Figure 4.8(a) The keyboard layout and its associated macros belongs to the PRESS template.

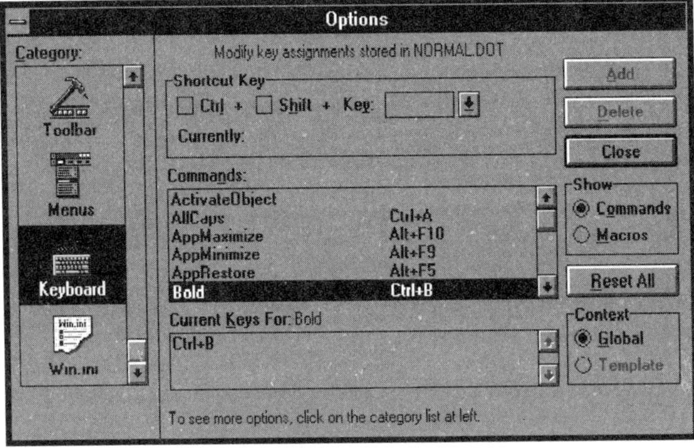

Figure 4.8(b) The keyboard and associated commands belong to the NORMAL template, which is the standard template for general-purpose documents.

In Figure 4.8(b), the key assignments apply to the NORMAL template and apply globally to all Word documents. Note that the commands and their corresponding keystroke sequences are listed in this example. In the example, the Bold command is activated with Ctrl+B. Unless you are an advanced user, we recommend that you do not tamper with key assignments for commands.

Navigating Microsoft Word

Word behaves much like other Windows applications, and much of the product will look familiar to you if you have mastered the basic Windows navigational and menu keystrokes discussed in Chapter 1.

A typical Word document window is shown in Figure 4.9. You access the Word menu bar like you would any other Windows menu bar. Pressing Alt activates the menu bar. Alt+Spacebar brings up the Word Control menu, which we discussed in Chapter 1. Alt+Hyphen brings up the document Control menu shown in Figure 4.9.

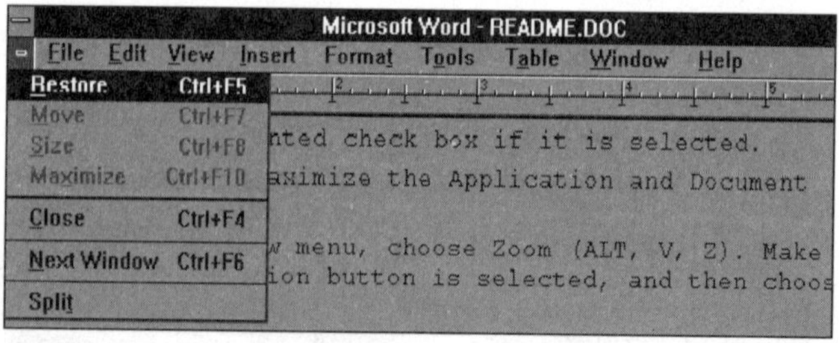

Figure 4.9 The Word document window and document Control menu.

Note the additional options in the document Control menu called Next Window and Split. The Next Window option (Alt+Hyphen,N or Ctrl+F6 from the document window) switches to the next document window if you are working with multiple documents. (See the next section on working with files.)

The Split option splits the window horizontally, allowing you to view different parts of the document simultaneously or to view formatting codes in one window and the resulting text in the other. See the section on split windows later in this chapter for an example.

Alt+F opens the File menu, Alt+E opens the Edit menu, and so forth. As in other Windows applications, the menu bar must be deactivated for keystrokes to take effect in the main document window. (If one of the menu bar options is highlighted, the menu bar is still active.) Press the Esc key to deactivate the menu bar.

It should be noted that unlike WordPerfect, which relies heavily on submenus for accessing commands belonging to a specific menu option, Microsoft Word uses dialog boxes for accessing most subcommands. As you may recall from Chapter 1, the easiest way to move to various fields in the dialog box is by pressing Alt+ the underlined letter in the heading of the field.

Working with Files

Unless you specify a file, Word opens with a blank document, and is ready for you to begin entering text. As we learned in the first two chapters, you can open files associated with an application directly by selecting the file's icon in Program Manager or the filename in File Manager and pressing Enter. The associated application opens automatically to display the file. If you open Word without specifying a file (by selecting the Word icon or the file \WINWORD\WINWORD.EXE and pressing Enter), you start with a blank document.

To open a file in Word, you can press Ctrl+F12 to open the Open File dialog box, or you can press Alt+F to open the File menu in the menu bar, as shown in Figure 4.10(a). One useful feature is the list of most recently opened files at the bottom of the menu. You simply type the number of the desired file to open it. In Figure 4.10(a), pressing "3" on the keyboard opens the file, GRAPHICS.DOC.

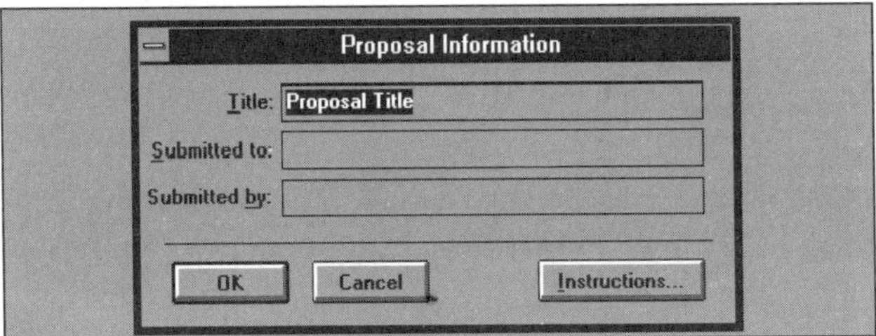

(a)

(b)

(c)

Figure 4.10(a) The Word File menu. (b) The Template dialog box. (c) The PROPOSAL template.

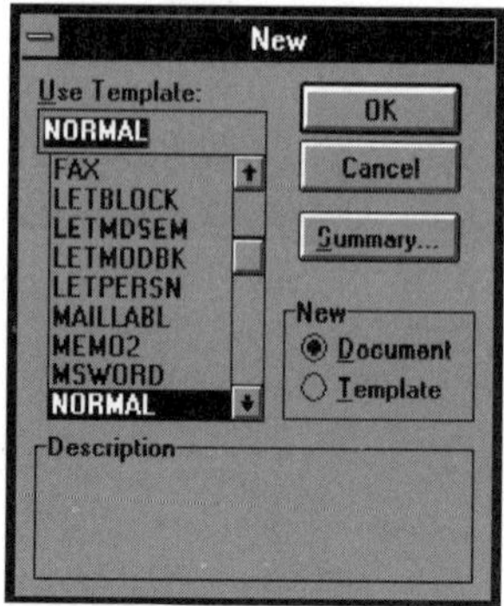

Figure 4.10(d) The New option.

Note that the Open command opens an existing file in a new window. If you want the file to appear in the current window, select the File option from the Insert menu, as discussed later in this chapter.

WORKING WITH MULTIPLE FILES

You can work with multiple documents simultaneously in Word. However, only one document can be active at a time. The easiest method to switch from one document to another is to press Ctrl+F6 until you reach the desired window. You can also press Alt+Hyphen to open the document Control menu and then select the Next Window option. Finally, you can open the Window menu (Alt+W), and select from the list of open documents displayed in the menu list.

Document Templates

Word uses document templates to provide specific patterns or styles for creating documents. Word provides a series of document templates for various standard types of documents, including business proposals, press releases, and academic term papers, to name a few. Document templates can include special macros and keystroke sequences as well as *boilerplate text* that always appears in the main document. You can add macros and other customized features to templates using the Options command in the Tools menu (Alt+O).

The supplied Word templates will probably meet the requirements for most types of documents. For example, Figure 4.10(c) shows a document being created using the Proposal template. The template automatically prompts you for information such as the proposal title, which it then inserts into the document. Of course, you can modify the supplied templates to meet your particular requirements.

In addition to using Word's supplied templates, you can also create your own. To create your own template, open a new document using the New option in the File menu, and then select Template as the document type, as shown in Figure 4.10(d). It is beyond the scope of this book to fully explain how to create your own templates, but Word's user's guide devotes an entire chapter to the subject.

You can attach a document to a template by selecting the Template option from the File menu. The Template dialog box is shown in Figure 4.10(b).

Moving the Insertion Point (Cursor)

The blinking vertical bar which tells you where you are in the document is called the *insertion point* or *cursor*. As we saw in Chapter 1, Windows provides a standard set of keystrokes for cursor movement and text selection. Cursor movement in Word is the same as it is in Windows Notepad or Write. For that matter, it's virtually the same as in other word processing packages such as WordPerfect and Lotus AmiPro, both of which are also covered in this book. There are a few minor differences between these packages, but if you're familiar with one of these word processors, you can easily adapt to any of the others.

The Arrow keys move one character at a time horizontally (Left and Right Arrows) and one line at a time vertically (Up and Down Arrows). To move one word at a time, press Ctrl+Right Arrow or Ctrl+Left Arrow. To move one paragraph at a time, press Ctrl+Up Arrow or Ctrl+Down Arrow.

The Home and End keys move the cursor to the beginning and end of the current line, respectively. PgUp and PgDn move the cursor to the top and bottom of the screen, respectively. If pressed repeatedly, these keys move the cursor up or down one screen of text at a time. To move the cursor up or down one page (the equivalent of one printed page of the document), press Alt+PgUp or Alt+PgDn. To move to the beginning or end of the document, press Ctrl+Home or Ctrl+End, respectively.

Selecting Text

Next to entering text, selecting text is probably the operation performed most frequently. Text is selected for Cut, Copy, and Paste operations and for changing fonts or other text attributes such as italic or boldface. To select text, you use the cursor movement keystrokes described above but add the Shift key. For example, to select one line of text at a time, press Shift+Up Arrow or Shift+Down Arrow. To select the word to the right of the cursor, press Shift+Ctrl and the Right Arrow. To select the next paragraph of text, press Shift+Ctrl and the Down Arrow. (Press the Up Arrow to select the previous paragraph.) To select the text in the entire document, position the cursor at the top of the document (Ctrl+Home) and then press Shift+Ctrl+End. To deselect text, simply press an Arrow key.

Another selection method is to press the F8 key to turn on Extend Selection mode and then simply move the navigation keys as you would normally (without holding down the Shift key). The text that you traverse with the navigation keys is automatically selected. (Pressing F8 again cancels the selection.) Pressing Shift+F8 reverses or "shrinks" the selection. (Pressing Shift+F8 repeatedly will bring you back to where you started selecting text.) Press the Esc key to cancel Extend Selection mode.

One handy feature with Extend Selection mode is that you can use it in conjunction with the Find or Go To commands in the Edit menu (Fig. 4.11) to select large chunks of text. You can also use the Select All command to select the entire document.

The figure shows a Microsoft Word window with the Edit menu open:

Microsoft Word - README.DOC

File Edit View Insert Format Tools Table Window Help

Undo Cut	Ctrl+Z
Repeat Cut	F4
Cut	Ctrl+X
Copy	Ctrl+C
Paste	Ctrl+V
Paste Special...	
Select All	Ctrl+NumPad 5
Find...	
Replace...	
Go To...	F5
Glossary...	
Links...	
Object...	

Figure 4.11 The Edit menu.

Working with Selected Text

Once you have selected text, you are obviously going to do something with it. You may want to move it, cut or copy it, delete it, save it as a file, change the font, change its margins or tabs, print it, and so on. There are two ways you can work with selected text: by using keystroke combinations or by executing commands from the menu bar. In some cases, you may have to use the menu bar if no keystroke combination is available. In most cases, however, it is much faster and more efficient to use keystroke combinations. The following paragraphs discuss the various ways you can work with selected text.

Cut, Copy, and Paste

There are several methods to cut, copy, or paste selected text. The easiest way is to select the text, and then press Ctrl+X or Ctrl+C to cut or copy the text, respectively. Cutting the text removes it from the document and places it in the Windows clipboard. (See Chapter 1 for more on the Windows clipboard.) Copying the text copies the text to the clipboard while at the same time leaving it in the original document. To paste the text into a different location or into another document, move the cursor to where you wish to paste the text, in either the current document or another one, and press Ctrl+V to paste. Press Ctrl+Z to undo the most recent Cut, Copy, or Paste operation.

Shift+Del, Ctrl+Ins, Shift+Ins, and Alt+Backspace, are alternative keystrokes for Cut, Copy, Paste, and Undo, respectively. However, as mentioned in Chapter 1, we strongly recommend getting in the habit of using the Ctrl combinations, which have become the standard keystroke combinations for Cut, Copy, and Paste, in most computer operating systems.

The alternative method for performing Cut, Copy, or Paste is using the Edit menu, as shown in Figure 4.11.

Deleting Text

The Backspace key deletes the character immediately before (to the left of) the current location of the cursor. The Del key deletes the character immediately after (to the right of) the cursor. Pressing Ctrl+Del deletes the word to the right of the cursor. Pressing Ctrl+Backspace deletes the word to the left of the insertion point. And, most importantly, pressing Ctrl+Z or Alt+Backspace will undo your deletion. The Undo function is also available using the Edit menu.

Working with Split Windows

The Split Windows option is accessible from the document Control menu (Alt+Hyphen). The split window allows you to work with the same document in two different ways. For example, you could have hidden codes and formatting characters shown in one pane (by turning these features on using the Options command in the Tools menu, discussed earlier in this chapter) and have the codes hidden in the other pane. Or, you could use the split window to view different parts of the document and cut and paste from one pane to the other.

To create a split window, select the Split option from the document Control menu. A horizontal bar then appears somewhere close to the middle of the document. You can move the bar up or down with the Arrow keys to the desired location of the split. Then press the Enter key to activate the split window. Pressing F6 moves you from one pane of the window to the other. You can navigate in each window separately and you can also use the display options in the Tools menu separately for each pane.

Figure 4.12 shows a split window showing the same parts of a document, with hidden characters and the field code for the date shown in the lower pane, and the finished result shown in the upper pane.

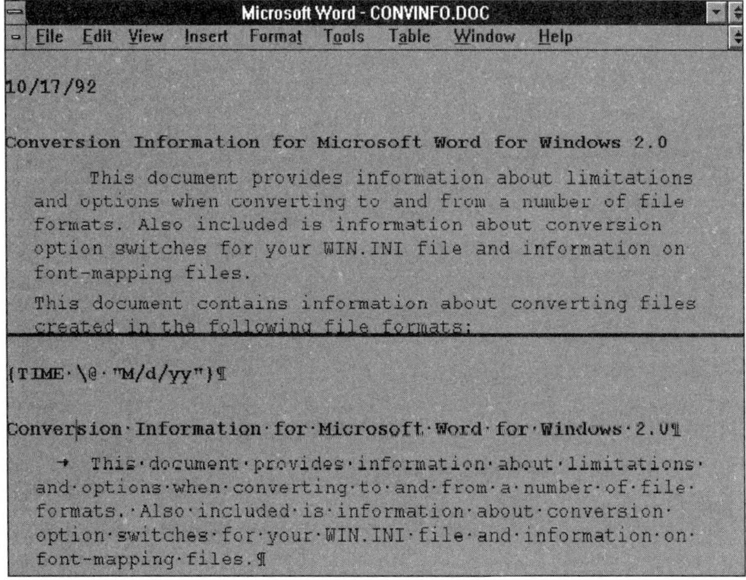

Figure 4.12 The split window.

Modifying Attributes of Selected Text

One of the main reasons to select text is to modify the text's attributes. For example, you may want to change some text to boldface or italics, or change from a right justified margin to a ragged margin. Here again, you can use keystroke combinations for many of the text modification commands, or you can access the commands in the menu bar. For example, pressing Ctrl+B changes the selected text to boldface. Pressing Ctrl+I changes it to italics. Or, you can select the Format menu (Alt+T) and select these same attributes from the Character dialog box. Note that the Undo command (Ctrl+Z) will undo the most recent text modification.

Changing Fonts and Other Character Attributes

You can change fonts and other character attributes by selecting the Character command from the Format menu, shown in Figure 4.13. The Character dialog box is shown in Figure 4.14. You can also bring up the Character dialog box directly from the document window by pressing Ctrl+F.

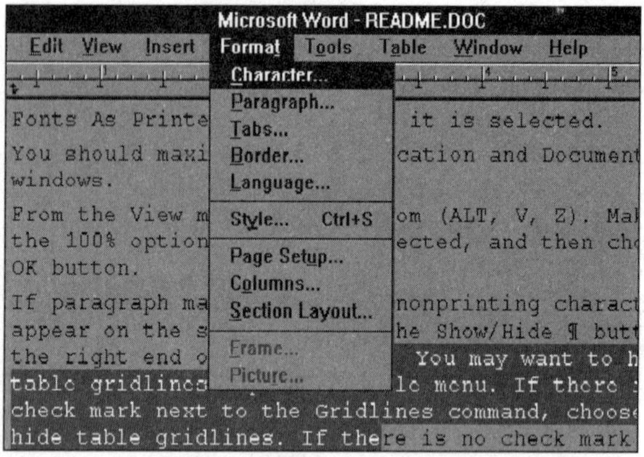

Figure 4.13 The Format menu provides commands for formatting documents, such as the Character command for modifying text attributes such as fonts.

Of course, many of the operations available in the Character dialog box can be executed directly from the document window. As mentioned above, Ctrl+B and Ctrl+I change characters to bold and italics, respectively. (Pressing those keys again returns the characters to the standard font.) Pressing Ctrl+= or Ctrl++ (Ctrl+ the plus sign) changes the selected text to Subscript or Superscript, respectively. You can also change the size of fonts incrementally from the keyboard using Ctrl+F2 to increase ("grow") the size, and Shift+Ctrl+F2 to decrease ("shrink") it.

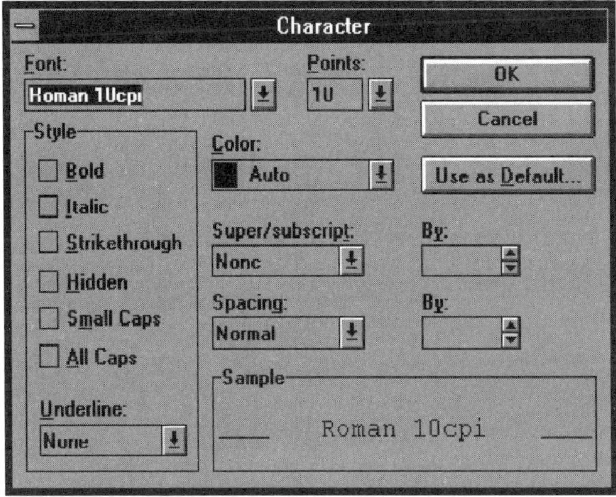

Figure 4.14 The Character dialog box.

Formatting Paragraphs

The Paragraph dialog box is shown in Figure 4.15. Here again, many of these operations can be performed directly from the document window. For example, the Alignment functions (left, right, and full justification) are represented by Ctrl+L (left), Ctrl+R (right), Ctrl+E (center), and Ctrl+J (full).

Indented or nested paragraphs can be started by pressing Ctrl+N, which will indent the paragraph starting with the first tab stop and maintain the indentation until you press Ctrl+M.

You can change the line spacing of selected text (or for the whole document if no text is selected) by pressing Ctrl+1 for single, Ctrl+5 for one and a half, and Ctrl+2 for double line spacing.

Tabs, Margins, and Columns

The Format menu provides separate dialog boxes for setting tabs, margins (Page Setup), and columns. These are shown in Figures 4.16, 4.17, and 4.18. As we noted earlier, it is possible to set tab stops using the ruler, but not margins or paragraph indentation. Note that the Tab, Margin, and Column commands can be applied to either selected text or to the entire document.

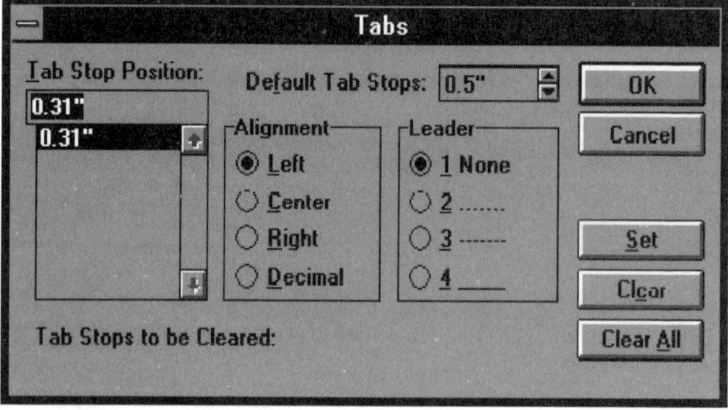

Figure 4.15 The Paragraph dialog box.

Figure 4.16 The Tabs dialog box.

The Insert Menu

The Insert menu provides the commands for inserting items into your document, from page breaks and special symbols to graphics images and other text files. The Insert menu is shown in Fig. 4.19.

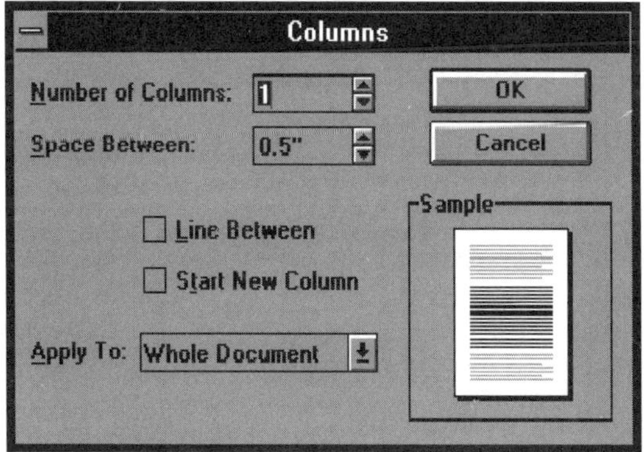

Figure 4.17 The Margins dialog box.

Figure 4.18 The Columns dialog box.

Inserting Graphics

To insert a graphic image in your document, position the cursor
at the desired location and then select the Picture command from

the Insert menu. Word provides a library of graphic images in the clipart directory to choose from, or you can import other graphic images in a variety of formats. Native Word images have the extension .WMF. To import other images such as TIFF, EPS, or PIC, simply type the filename in the Picture dialog box shown in Figure 4.20. Note the Preview option which allows you to first inspect the graphic before inserting it in your document. The inserted figure is shown in Figure 4.21(a).

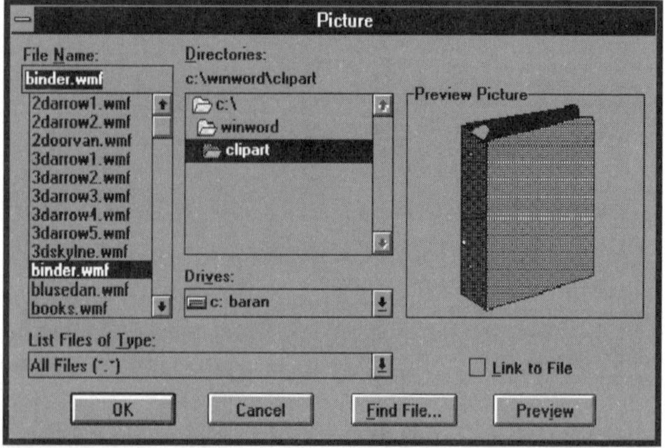

Figure 4.19 The Insert menu.

Figure 4.20 The Picture dialog box.

To remove a graphic image from your document, place the cursor on the left edge of the graphic and then press Shift+Right Arrow to select the image. Notice that when the image is selected, it will display rectangular "handles" as shown in Figure 4.21(b). Press the Del key to delete the image.

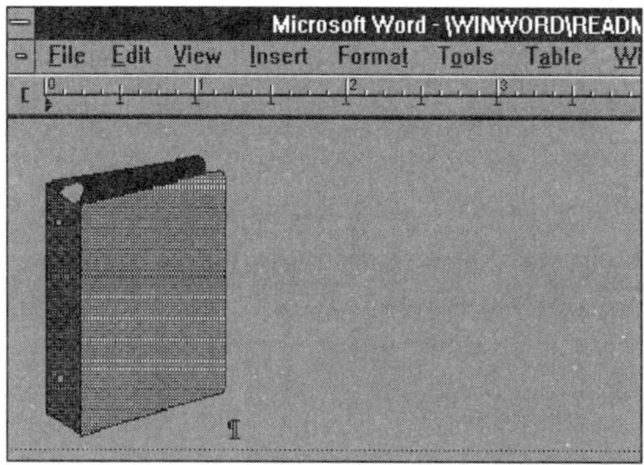

(a)

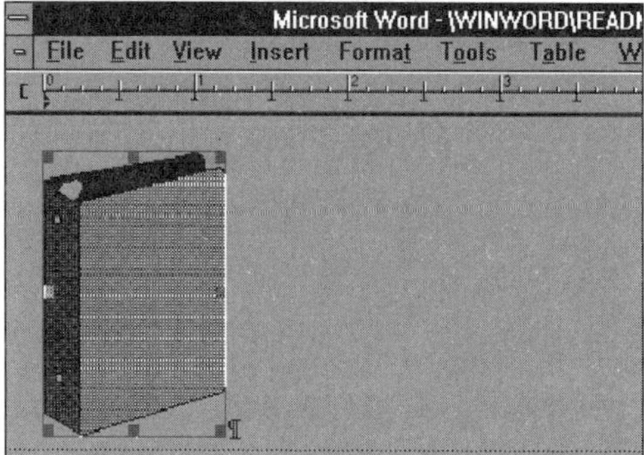

(b)

Figure 4.21(a) The figure inserted into the document. (b) Select the graphic image by placing cursor to the left of the image, and press Shift+Right Arrow.

Inserting Frames

Frame is another term for a text box. To insert a frame around a portion of text in your document, you must be in Page Layout mode, which can be activated from the View menu. The Page Layout mode displays the document in the same way that it will be printed, and enables you to move frames and graphic images and to view their relationship to the other elements on the page.

After selecting the text to be framed, select the Frame command from the Insert menu to insert the text box. A box will appear around the text as shown in Figure 4.22. Then select the Frame command from the Format menu to adjust the size of the frame. The Frame dialog box from the Format menu is shown in Figure 4.23. To remove the frame, select the Remove Frame option from the dialog box shown in Figure 4.23.

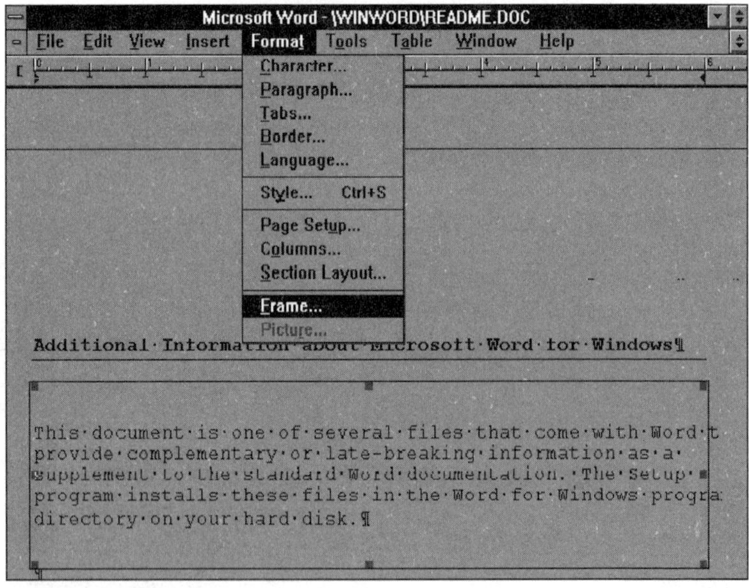

Figure 4.22 The Frame command places a box around selected text.

Inserting Objects

You can insert a variety of other elements called *objects* into your document. Objects are elements such as equations, drawings, graphs, and even sound files, developed in other Windows applications such as Microsoft Draw or Graph, or the Microsoft

Equation Editor. To insert an object, select the Object command from the Insert menu, which opens the Object dialog box, shown in Figure 4.24.

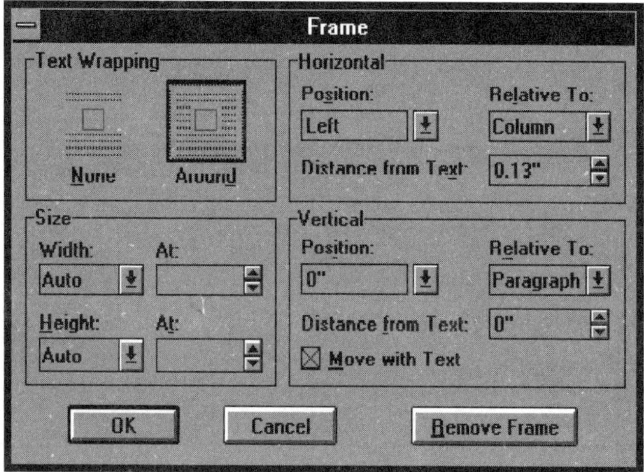

Figure 4.23 The Frame dialog box opened from the Format menu.

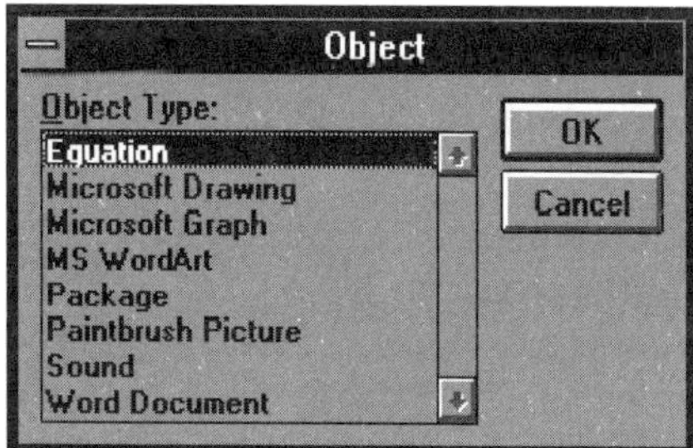

Figure 4.24 The Object dialog box.

As an example, you could insert a graph and chart from Microsoft Graph as shown in Figure 4.25. To insert the graph, open the File menu in the Microsoft Graph window and select the Update command. Then return to your original document. Notice that a field representing the object is placed in the original document as shown in Figure 4.26. To delete the object, simply select the field (place the cursor at the beginning of the field and press Shift+Right Arrow), and then the Del key. (For more information on embedding and linking objects, see the chapter "Using Word with Other Applications" in Word's user's guide.)

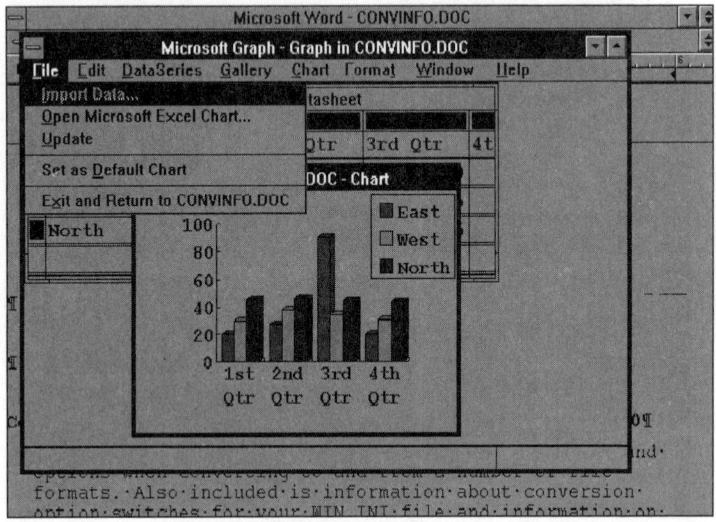

Figure 4.25 A graph generated in Microsoft Graph to be inserted in a Word document.

Inserting Page Breaks

To insert a *hard page break* (in other words, a user.defined page break), select the Break command from the Insert menu, bringing up the dialog box in Figure 4.27, or press Ctrl+Enter from the document. The page break is inserted immediately before the insertion point. To delete the page break, move the cursor to the page break and press the Del key. You can also search for hard page breaks using the Find command in the Edit menu, by entering ^d in the search field.

We have just covered some of the functions of the Insert menu. You can also insert footnotes, annotations, date and time fields, special symbols, bookmarks, index or table of contents markers, and the contents of other Word documents using the commands in the Insert menu.

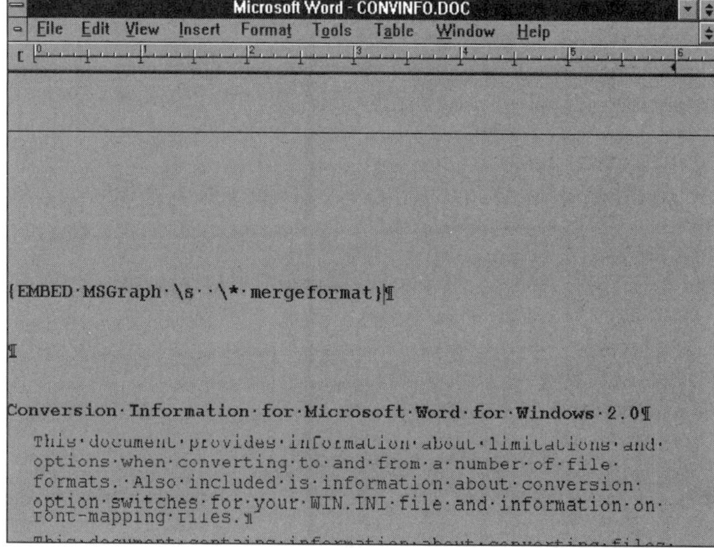

Figure 4.26 The object is represented in the document by an "embedded field" or pointer to the object.

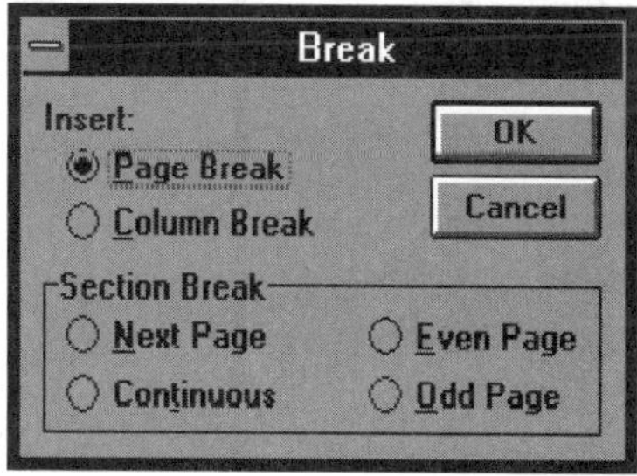

Figure 4.27 Insert a page break using the Break command in the Insert menu.

Tables and Calculated Fields

The Table menu provides commands for creating tables in your document. Figure 4.28 shows a simple table and the Table menu. You can create calculated fields by inserting formulas into the table as shown in the figure. To insert a formula, move the insertion point to the cell in which the result will be calculated, and press Ctrl+F9 to insert the formula brackets in the cell. Then type in the formula. Press Shift+F9 to see the result. (For more information, see the chapters on math calculations and fields in Word's user's guide.)

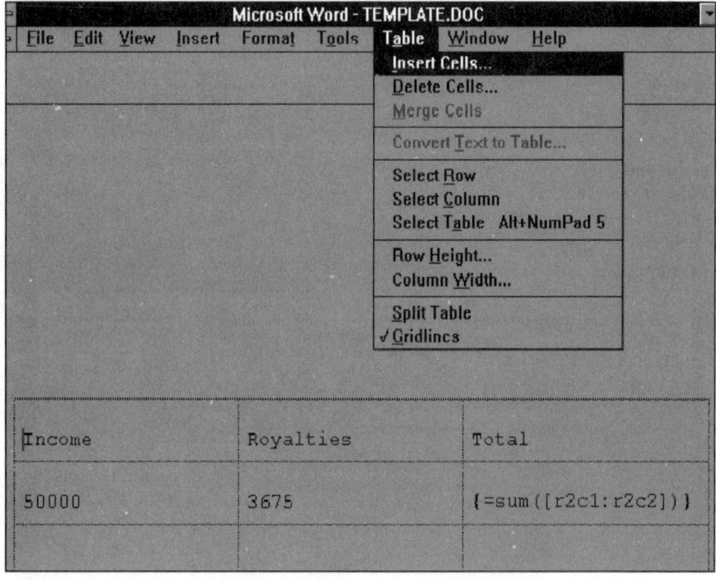

Figure 4.28 The Table menu.

Other Tools

Earlier in this chapter we looked at the customization features of the Options command in the Tools menu, shown in Figure 4.4. There are many other powerful tools in the Tools menu, such as the spelling checker, thesaurus, a special envelope printing utility, options for numbering paragraphs, bulleting items, recording and playing macros, and sorting text. We will cover this sorting option next.

Sorting

The sorting function is handy for sorting lists of names and addresses, for example. In fact, the sort function in modern word processors has made it possible to maintain mailing lists within your word processing application, rather than switching to a database program. In any case, Figure 4.29 shows a selected list of names and the Sorting dialog box.

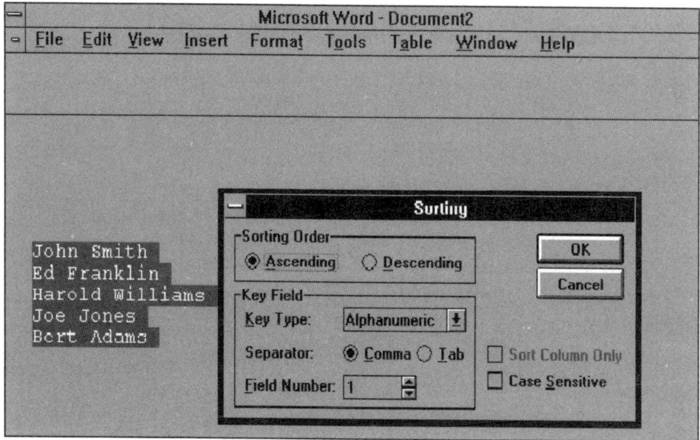

Figure 4.29 The Sort command from the Tools menu.

Macros

The Record Macro command allows you to record frequently used keystrokes and to store them as a macro. The Record Macro dialog box is shown in Figure 4.30. You assign a name to the macro and, if desired, assign a keyboard sequence starting with Ctrl+Shift, which will automatically play the macro. When you have finished recording the macro, open the Tools menu again, and select the Stop Recorder command, which has taken the place of the Record Macro option during the record operation. To edit macros, select the Macro command in the Tools menu.

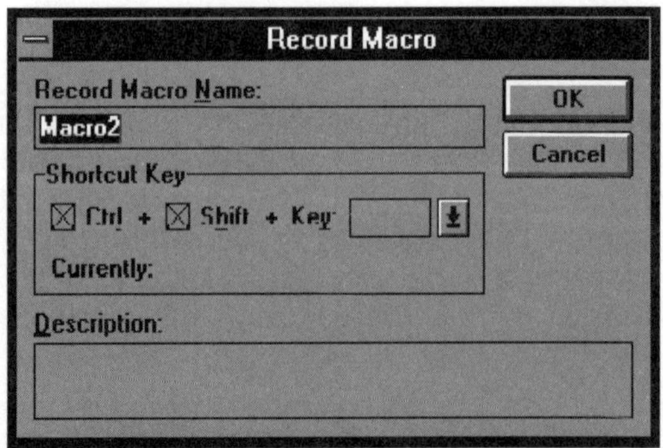

Figure 4.30 The Record Macro dialog box.

Headers and Footers

The primary method for creating headers or footers is to use the Header/Footer command in the View menu. If you just want to insert page numbers, use the Page Number command in the Insert menu.

The Header/Footer command opens the Header/Footer dialog box shown in Figure 4.31. Note that you should be in Normal view (Page Layout mode disabled from the View menu) when you are creating headers and footers, so that a separate window pane can be opened in which to create the header/footer, as shown in Figure 4.32. In the Header/Footer pane, you can insert page numbers using the key sequence, Alt+Shift+P. Alt+Shift+D and Alt+Shift+T insert the date and time, respectively. Press Alt+Shift+C to close the pane.

To delete a header or footer, open the header or footer by selecting the Header/Footer command from the View menu and then selecting a header or footer from the Header/Footer dialog box. Delete all the text in the pane and then press Alt+Shift+C to close the pane, thus deleting it. One convenient way to delete all the text is to use the Select All command from the Edit menu and then to press the Del key.

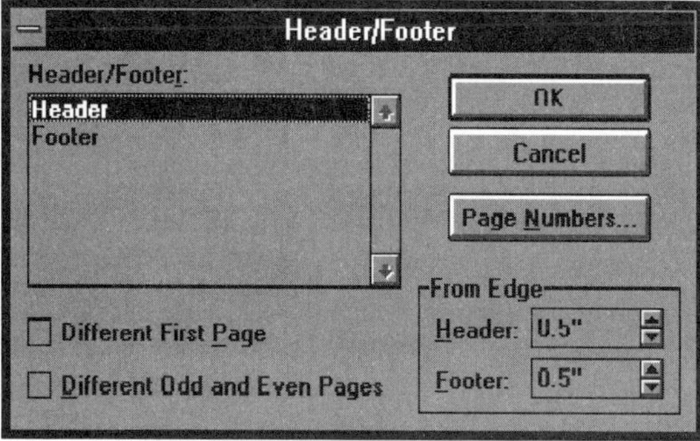

Figure 4.31 The Header/Footer dialog box.

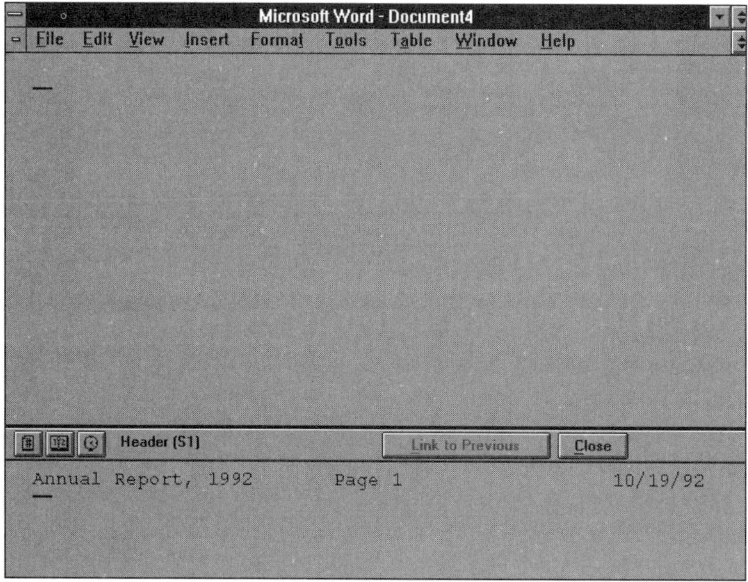

Figure 4.32 The Header/Footer pane is closed by pressing Alt+Shift+C.

Lotus Ami Pro

5

A concise list of Lotus Ami Pro keystrokes begins on page 260.

Lotus Ami Pro is a native Windows application. Unlike Word and WordPerfect (covered in the previous two chapters), the original Ami word processing application was designed to run under Windows. Since acquired by Lotus, subsequent versions of the product have been called Ami Pro.

Ami Pro is a full-featured word processor with capabilities comparable to those of Word and WordPerfect. The product places strong emphasis on a "WYSIWIG" (What You See Is What You Get) format, displaying graphics and text attributes such as special fonts and boldface directly on the screen, although a Draft Mode option allows you to switch to a character-based format for faster editing and display speed.

Like its competitors covered in this book, Ami Pro is a fully Windows-compliant application, using the standard Windows interface and supporting the clipboard and windowing system. Naturally, the program is optimized for operation with a mouse. Indeed, Ami Pro is the least "keyboard-friendly" of the word processors covered in this book. The product makes heavy use of icons for implementing many of its features and does not always provide a keyboard equivalent. (The Equation feature is a case in point.)

Ami Pro sports several mouse-driven features such as a *SmartIcons* bar, similar to Word's toolbar or WordPerfect's button bar, a *status bar* which provides mouse-accessible commands, and a *ruler* for visually formatting your document with the mouse. The ruler is the primary method for setting tabs and margins and is also accessible from the keyboard. The SmartIcons and mouse features of the status bar are not available to keyboard users.

Consistent with the other application chapters in this book, we'll start this chapter by reviewing what can't be done from the keyboard when using Ami Pro.

What You Can't Do from the Keyboard

The vertical and horizontal scroll bars do *not* work with the keyboard and can be removed by changing the display settings using the View Preferences command in the View menu, shown in Figure 5.1. (We will discuss the View Preferences command in greater detail later in this chapter.) From the keyboard, you can duplicate the function of the scroll bars with the Arrow and PgUp and PgDn keys, as we will discuss in greater detail later in this chapter.

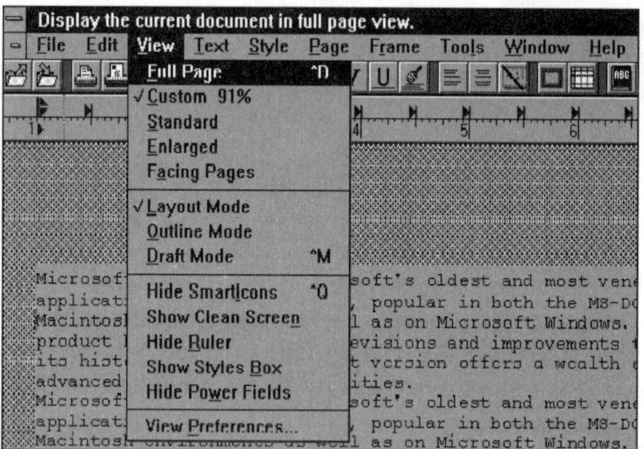

Figure 5.1 The View menu. The Show Clean Screen option produces a virtually blank screen for text editing.

The row of icons below the menu bar shown in Figure 5.2 is called *SmartIcons*. SmartIcons allows mouse users to point and click on icons representing frequently used commands such as opening, printing, and closing files, or activating other Ami Pro features such as the spelling checker. SmartIcons includes customizable buttons so that users can add other commands or macros represented by icons.

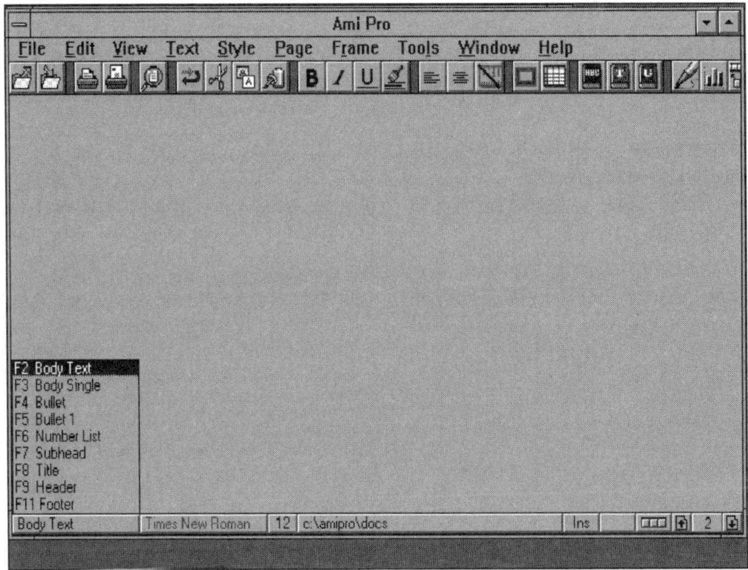

Figure 5.2 The icons below the menu bar are called SmartIcons. At the bottom of the screen is the status bar.

All of the functionality of SmartIcons can be duplicated from the keyboard using keystroke sequences or the Ami Pro menu options. If you are strictly using the keyboard, you can reclaim some space on the screen by removing SmartIcons. This is accomplished by selecting the Hide SmartIcons option in the View menu (Alt+V) and pressing Enter. (Note that the option then changes to "Show SmartIcons," indicating that SmartIcons is currently hidden.) Alternatively, you simply press the "I" key to toggle the Show/Hide Smarticons option.

You can also select the Show Clean Screen option to hide everything including the menu bar, if you want to leave the whole screen available for text. This option is discussed in greater detail in the next section on customizing Ami Pro.

As shown in Figure 5.2, another mouse-only feature in Ami Pro is the set of buttons in the status bar at the bottom of the screen. While the status bar presents useful information such as the filename, page number, type of font currently in use, and the paragraph type, mouse users can change these characteristics directly from the status bar by clicking on the item that they want to change. You can remove the status bar from the View menu, but even though keyboard users can't take advantage of its mouse capabilities, it's still useful for displaying the status of your document.

Ami Pro's *ruler* is fully accessible from the keyboard. You can adjust tabs directly from the ruler or from the Styles menu discussed later in this chapter.

The Drag and Drop feature requires a mouse. This feature allows you to select text and drag it to another location in the document or to another window. However, the same functionality can be achieved with Ami Pro's standard Cut, Copy, and Paste functions.

It should be noted that the Equation tool in Ami Pro has only limited functionality without a mouse. If you intend to work with math documents extensively in Ami Pro, you will need a mouse. Similarly, the Drawing tool virtually requires a mouse.

The Ami Pro Keyboard

The Ami Pro keyboard conforms to the Windows keyboard interface standard, which is consistent with the Common User Access (CUA) standard as we discussed in the Foreword. As we shall see, navigation keys and menu selection keys are virtually the same as in other Windows text and word processing applications.

Ami Pro offers limited keyboard customization capabilities within the program. (About all you can do is change the function key functions and assign macro keystrokes.) You can, however, open the Windows Control Panel directly from the Ami Pro Control menu, shown in Figure 5.3. You can select various keyboard layouts from the International option in the Control Panel as shown in Figure 5.4.

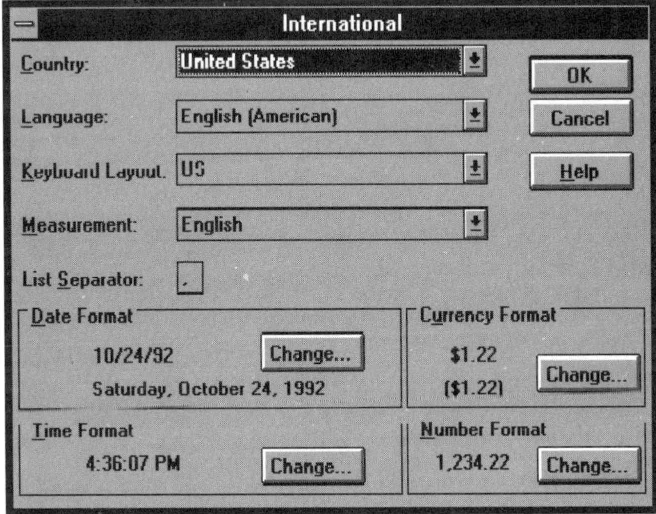

Figure 5.3 The Ami Pro Control menu.

Figure 5.4 The International dialog box.

The main method of document customization in Ami Pro is by means of style sheets, discussed later in this chapter.

Customizing Ami Pro

Ami Pro offers two primary menu options for customizing the features of the program. These are the View Preference command in the View menu and the User Setup command in the

Tools menu. To open the View Preference dialog box, select the View menu (Alt+V) and then the View Preference command. (Press P or move the Down Arrow to View Preference and press Enter.) To open the User Setup dialog box, select the Tools menu (Alt+L) and then the User Setup command (U).

View Preferences

The View Preference dialog box, shown in Figure 5.5, allows you to modify the visual and display characteristics of Ami Pro. Of particular interest is the Clean Screen Options button, which opens an additional dialog box, shown in Figure 5.6, for specifying what Ami Pro features should remain displayed when you select the Show Clean Screen option from the View menu. For example, if you un-check the Menu option, you can have a completely blank screen for text entry. Pressing Alt+ the underlined letter of the menu will display the menu when the screen is blanked (e.g., press Alt+V to open the View menu).

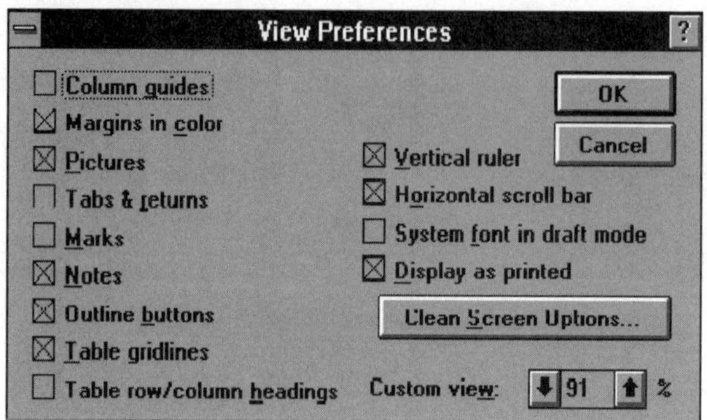

Figure 5.5 The View Preferences dialog box.

Other useful options in the View Preferences dialog box include the Pictures option. If you un-check Pictures, then graphic images are not displayed. Only the region in which the graphic would appear is marked off, which enables faster editing since Ami Pro doesn't have to constantly redraw the graphic image as you work with the document.

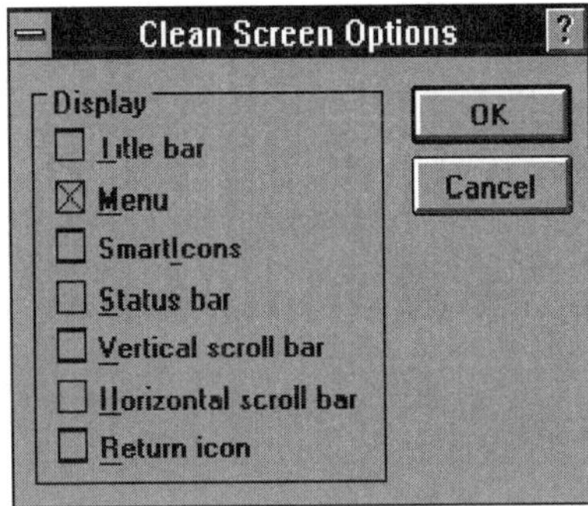

Figure 5.6 The Clean Screen Options dialog box is opened from the View Preferences dialog box.

Keyboard users may want to remove the horizontal scroll bar by un-checking the Horizontal Scroll Bar option in the View Preferences dialog box. The Vertical Ruler option places a ruler down the left-hand edge of the screen, which can be useful for identifying the location of the insertion point in relation to the page. Other options include specifying symbols for tabs and returns, and marks for various page elements such as column and page breaks.

The Custom View option allows you to adjust the percentage of the printed page to be displayed on the screen at one time. The default is 91% and can be specified from ten to 400%.

User Setup

The User Setup dialog box is shown in Figure 5.7. User Setup enables you to modify general Ami Pro functions such as where to save document files, what style sheets to load by default, automatic file backup, and so forth. The Undo Levels button allows you to specify how far back Ami Pro can go to undo your actions. The default is one action (e.g., the last deletion or editing change), but you can specify up to four levels (actions). There is, however, a decline in overall performance for each additional level.

User Setup allows you to disable Drag and Drop, which is probably a good idea for keyboard users since you can't use this feature. Disabling Drag and Drop may give Ami Pro a slight boost in performance.

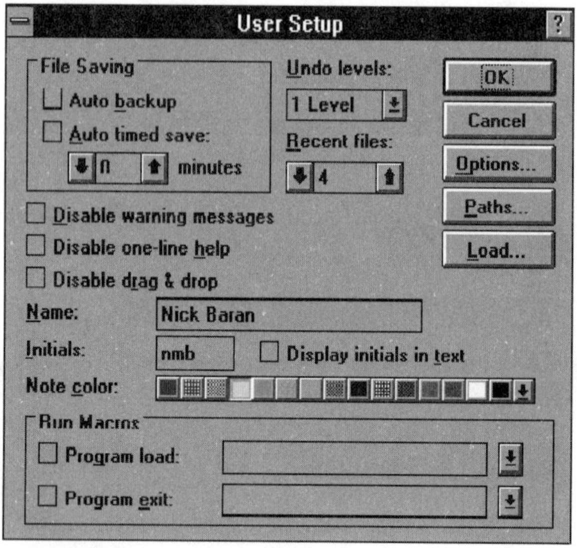

Figure 5.7 The User Setup dialog box.

The Run Macros option allows you to specify a macro to be executed when Ami Pro starts up (Program load), or when Ami Pro quits (Program exit), or both.

The Options, Paths, and Load buttons in User Setup all produce dialog boxes, shown in Figures 5.8, 5.9, and 5.10. The Options dialog box allows you to specify typographic options such as hyphenation and widow/orphan control. Speed options allow you to adjust performance by eliminating background printing or background text formatting (text flow). Most users will probably find the default settings for these options to be acceptable.

The Paths button opens the Default Paths dialog box, which allows you to specify directories for storing various types of Ami Pro files. Some users may want to change the directories for storing documents and backup files.

The Load Defaults dialog box provides options for specifying Ami Pro's configuration when you first start the program. For example, you could specify a different style sheet to load at startup, or a different type of screen view or page layout. The best course is to start out with the default configuration and then make changes as needed.

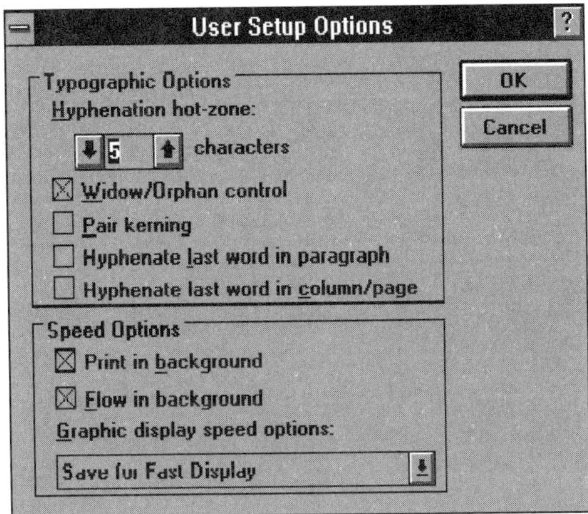

Figure 5.8 The User Setup Options dialog box.

Figure 5.9 The Default Paths dialog box.

Navigating Ami Pro

Ami Pro behaves very much like other Windows applications, and much of the product will look familiar to you if you have mastered the basic Windows navigational and menu keystrokes discussed in Chapter 1.

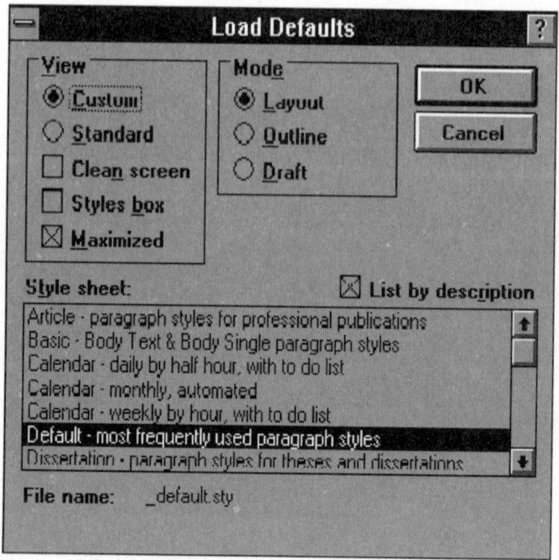

Figure 5.10 The Load Defaults dialog box.

A typical Ami Pro document window is shown in Figure 5.11. You access the Ami Pro menu bar like you would any other Windows menu bar. Pressing Alt activates the menu bar. Alt+Spacebar brings up the application Control menu, which we discussed in Chapter 1. Alt+Hyphen brings up the document Control menu shown in Figure 5.11.

Note the additional option in the document Control menu called Next, which is short for "next window." The Next option (Alt+Hyphen,T or Ctrl+F6 from the document window) switches to the next document window if you are working with multiple documents. (See the next section on working with files.)

Alt+F opens the File menu, Alt+E opens the Edit menu, and so forth. As in other Windows applications, the menu bar must be deactivated for keystrokes to take effect in the main document window. (If one of the menu bar options is highlighted, the menu bar is still active.) Press the Esc key to deactivate the menu bar.

It should be noted that unlike WordPerfect, which relies heavily on submenus for accessing commands belonging to a specific menu option, Ami Pro uses dialog boxes for accessing most subcommands. As you may recall from Chapter 1, the easiest way to move to various fields in the dialog box is by pressing Alt+ the underlined letter in the heading of the field.

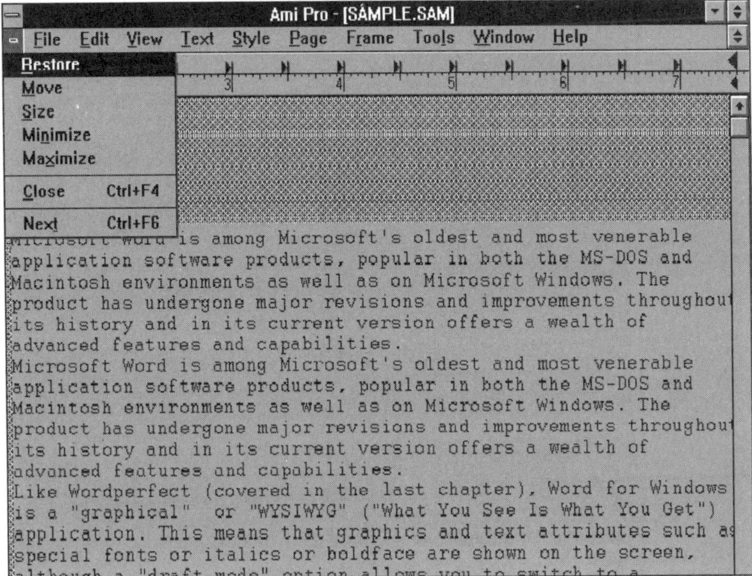

Figure 5.11 A typical Ami Pro document window.

Working with Files

Unless you specify a file, Ami Pro opens with a blank document and is ready for you to begin entering text. As we learned in the first two chapters, you can open files associated with an application directly by selecting the file's icon in Program Manager or the filename in File Manager and pressing Enter. The associated application opens automatically to display the file. If you open Word without specifying a file (by selecting the Ami Pro icon or the file \AMIPRO\AMIPRO.EXE and pressing Enter), you start with a blank document.

To open a file in Ami Pro, you can press Ctrl+O from the document window to open the Open File dialog box, or you can press Alt+F to open the File menu in the menu bar, as shown in Figure 5.12. One useful feature is the list of most recently opened files at the bottom of the menu. You simply type the number of the desired file to open it. In Figure 5.12, pressing the "1" key opens the file, SAMPLE.SAM.

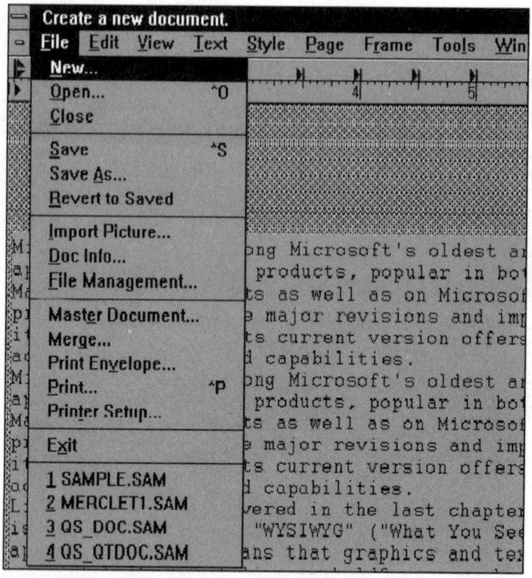

Figure 5.12 The Ami Pro File menu.

Note that the Open command normally opens an existing file in a new window. If you want the file to appear in the current window, select the Insert option from the Open File dialog box as shown in Figure 5.13.

WORKING WITH MULTIPLE FILES

You can work with multiple documents simultaneously in Ami Pro. However, only one document can be active at one time. To switch from one document to another, the easiest method is to press Ctrl+F6 until you reach the desired window. You can also press Alt+Hyphen to open the document Control menu and then select the Next Window option. Finally, you can open the Window menu (Alt+W), and select from the list of open documents displayed in the menu list.

Style Sheets

Ami Pro uses style sheets to provide specific patterns or styles for creating documents. Ami Pro provides a series of style sheets for various standard types of documents, including business proposals, press releases, academic term papers, and so forth. Style sheets can include special macros and keystroke sequences as well as *boilerplate text* that always appears in the main document. You can add macros and other customized features to style sheets using the Modify Style Sheet command in the Style menu (Alt+S), shown in Figure 5.14.

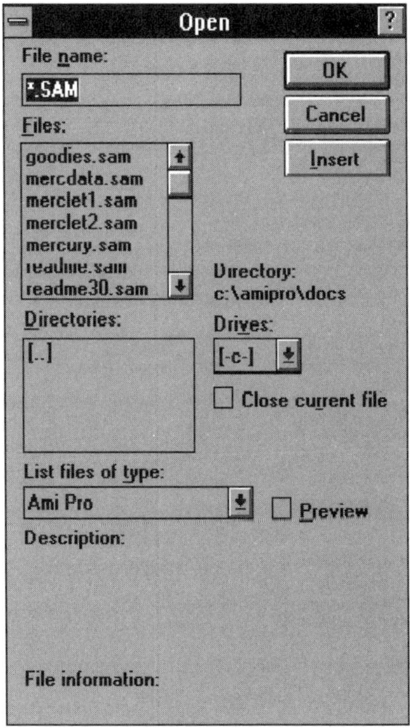

Figure 5.13 The Open dialog box.

When you start a new document (by selecting New from the File menu), Ami Pro starts by prompting you for the style sheet that you want to use with the document, which is initially set to the default style sheet as shown in Figure 5.15.

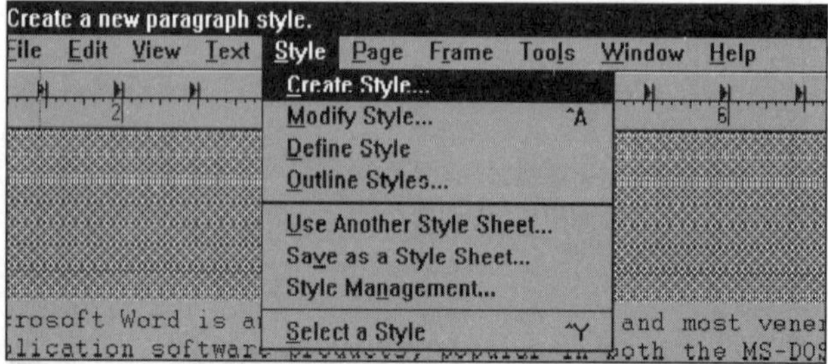

Figure 5.14 The Style menu.

Figure 5.15 The New dialog box for opening new files asks you to specify a style sheet to go with the document. If you just press Enter, the Ami Pro default style sheet is used.

The supplied style sheets will probably meet the requirements for most types of documents. For example, Figure 5.16 shows a document being created using the Expense Report style sheet. This style sheet automatically supplies the fields and columns for filling out an expense report. Of course, you can make modifications to the style sheet, which should then be saved as a new style sheet. In fact, the best way to create your own style sheets is to start with one of the supplied sheets and then make the desired modifications.

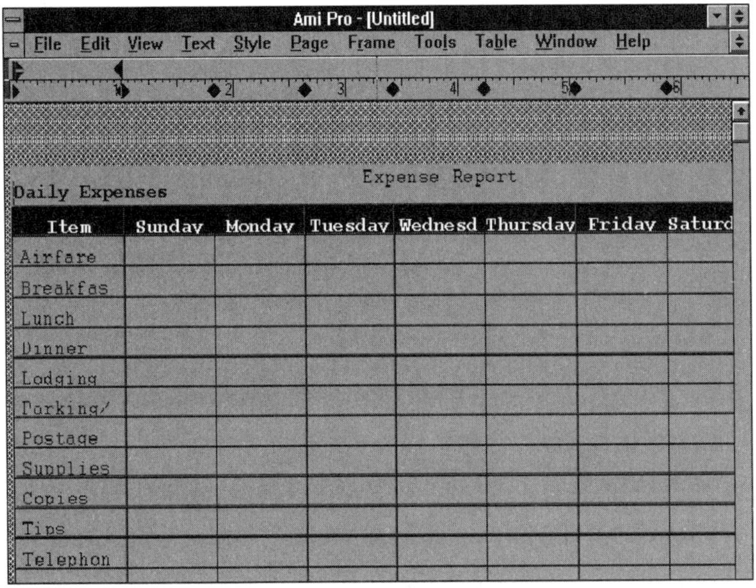

Figure 5.16 The Expense Report style sheet.

Moving the Insertion Point (Cursor)

The blinking vertical bar which tells you where you are in the document is called the *insertion point* or *cursor*. As discussed in Chapter 1, Windows provides a standard set of keystrokes for cursor movement and text selection. Cursor movement in Ami Pro is the same as it is in Windows Notepad or Write. For that matter, it's virtually the same as in other word processing packages such as WordPerfect and Microsoft Word, both of which are also covered in this book. There are a few minor differences between these packages, but if you're familiar with one of these word processors, you can easily adapt to one of the others.

The Arrow keys move one character at a time horizontally (Left and Right Arrows) and one line at a time vertically (Up and Down Arrows). To move one word at a time, press Ctrl+Right Arrow or Ctrl+Left Arrow. To move forward one sentence at a time, press Ctrl+ the period (.) key. To move backward one sentence at a time, press Ctrl+ the comma (,) key. To move one paragraph at a time, press Ctrl+Up Arrow or Ctrl+Down Arrow.

The Home and End keys move the cursor to the beginning and end of the current line, respectively. PgUp and PgDn move the cursor to the top and bottom of the screen, respectively. If pressed repeatedly, these keys move the cursor up or down one screen of text at a time. To move the cursor up or down one page (the equivalent of one printed page of the document), press Ctrl+PgUp or Ctrl+PgDn. To move to the beginning or end of the document, press Ctrl+Home or Ctrl+End, respectively.

Selecting Text

Next to entering text, selecting text is probably the operation performed most frequently. Text is selected for Cut, Copy, and Paste operations and for changing fonts or other text attributes such as italic or boldface, for example. To select text, you use the cursor movement keystrokes described above but add the Shift key.

For example, to select one line of text at a time, press Shift+Up Arrow or Shift+Down Arrow. To select the word to the right of the cursor, press Shift+Ctrl and the Right Arrow. To select the next paragraph of text, press Shift+Ctrl and the Down Arrow. (Press the Up Arrow to select the previous paragraph.) To select the text in the entire document, position the cursor at the top of the document (Ctrl+Home) and then press Shift+Ctrl+End. To deselect text, simply press an Arrow key or the Esc key.

Working with Selected Text

Once you have selected text, you are obviously going to do something with it. You may want to move it, cut or copy it, delete it, save it as a file, change the font, change its margins or tabs, print it, and so on. There are two ways you can work with selected text: by using keystroke combinations or by executing commands from the menu bar. In some cases, you may have to use the menu bar if no keystroke combination is available. In most cases, however, it is much faster and more efficient to use keystroke combinations. The following paragraphs discuss the various ways you can work with selected text.

Cut, Copy, and Paste

There are several methods to cut, copy, or paste selected text. The easiest way is to select the text, and then press Ctrl+X or Ctrl+C to cut or copy the text, respectively. Cutting the text removes it from the document and places it in the Windows clipboard. (See Chapter 1 for more on the Windows clipboard.) Copying the text copies the text to the clipboard while at the same time leaving it in the original document. To paste the text into a different location or into another document, move the cursor to where you wish to paste the text, in either the current document or another one, and press Ctrl+V to paste. Press Ctrl+Z to undo the most recent Cut, Copy, or Paste operation.

Shift+Del, Ctrl+Ins, Shift+Ins, and Alt+Backspace, are alternative keystrokes for Cut, Copy, Paste, and Undo, respectively. However, as mentioned in Chapter 1, it is strongly recommended to get in the habit of using the Ctrl combinations, which have become the standard keystroke combinations for Cut, Copy, and Paste, in most computer operating systems.

The alternative method for performing Cut, Copy, or Paste is using the Edit menu, as shown in Figure 5.17.

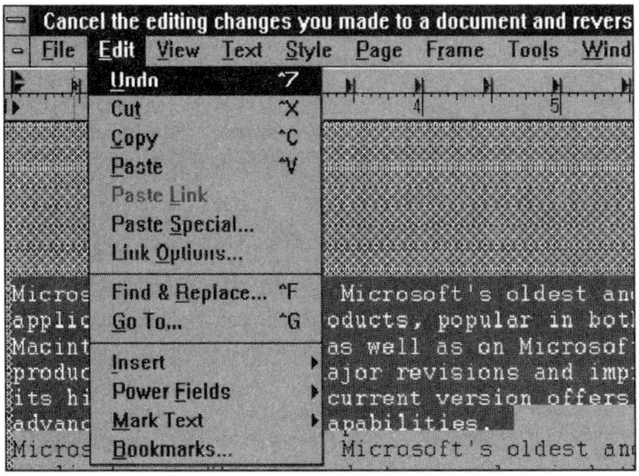

Figure 5.17 The Edit menu provides Cut, Copy, and Paste commands.

Deleting Text

You can delete selected text by pressing the Del key. When working with unselected text, the Backspace key deletes the character immediately before (to the left of) the current location of the cursor. The Del key deletes the character immediately ahead (to the right of) the cursor. Pressing Ctrl+Del deletes the word to the right of the cursor. Pressing Ctrl+Backspace deletes the word to the left of the insertion point. Note that the Del key deletes. And, most importantly, pressing Ctrl+Z or Alt+Backspace will undo your deletion. The Undo function is also available from the Edit menu.

Modifying Attributes of Selected Text

One of the main reasons to select text is to modify the text's attributes. For example, you may want to change some text to boldface or italics, or change from a right justified margin to a ragged margin. Here again, you can use keystroke combinations for many of the text modification commands, or you can access the commands in the menu bar. For example, pressing Ctrl+B changes the selected text to boldface. Pressing Ctrl+I changes it to italics. Or you can select these same attributes from the Text menu (Alt+T) shown in Figure 5.18. Note that the Undo command (Ctrl+Z) will undo the most recent text modification. Pressing Ctrl+N (Normal Text) removes any applied text formats.

Changing Fonts and Other Character Attributes

You can change fonts and other character attributes by selecting the Font command from the Text menu, shown in Figure 5.18. Note the keyboard equivalents given for a number of commands in the Text menu. The Font dialog box is shown in Figure 5.19. The Special Effects command provides options for specifying Subscript, Superscript, and several other special character options.

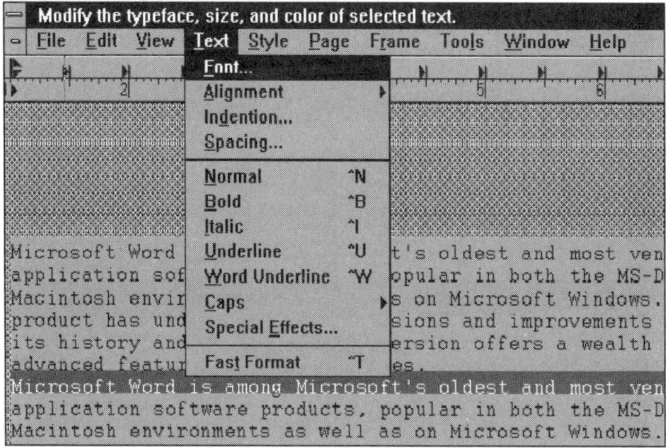

Figure 5.18 The Text menu provides commands for modifying attributes of selected text.

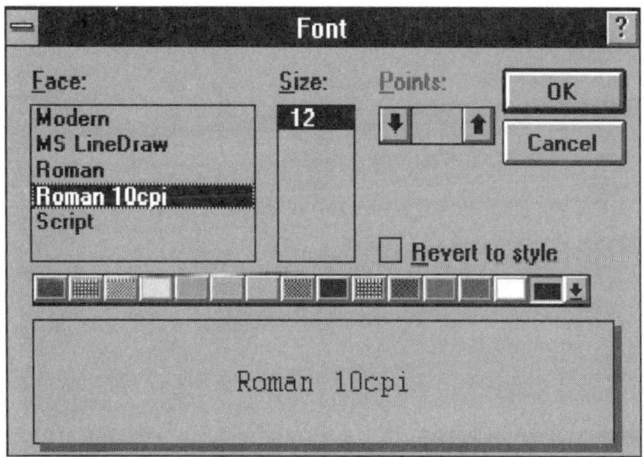

Figure 5.19 The Font dialog box.

Formatting Paragraphs

You can change text alignment, indentation, and line spacing, from the Text menu as shown in Figure 5.18. To change text justification directly from the document window, you can press Ctrl+L for left justification, Ctrl+R for right justification, and Ctrl+J for full justification. Pressing Ctrl+E centers the selected text.

The Indention and Spacing commands bring up dialog boxes for changing paragraph indentation and text line spacing.

The Fast Format command lets you copy format information from one paragraph to another. For example, if you have a paragraph with special indentation and fonts and you want to apply that same format to another paragraph later in the document, you can use the Fast Format command as shown in Figure 5.20.

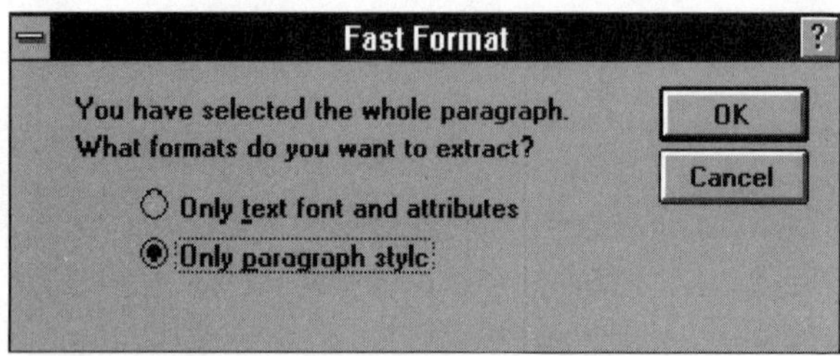

Figure 5.20 The Fast Format dialog box.

Page Layout

The primary tools in Ami Pro for laying out the page are contained in the Page menu (Alt+P), shown in Figure 5.21. From this menu, you can insert headers and footers, page breaks, and set margins and tabs as well as columns and other special page attributes.

Figure 5.21 The Page menu provides tools for page layout and creating headers and footers.

Tabs, Margins, and Columns

The Modify Page Layout command in the Page menu is probably the one you will use most frequently for setting tabs, margins, and columns, as well as other page elements. The Modify Page Layout dialog box is shown in Figure 5.22. Use the Tab key to move to the box that you want to change. You can use the Arrow keys to move tabs on the ruler shown in the dialog box. Note the number of columns is underlined. To select the desired number of columns, press Alt+ the desired number (e.g., Alt+3 will set the number of columns to three).

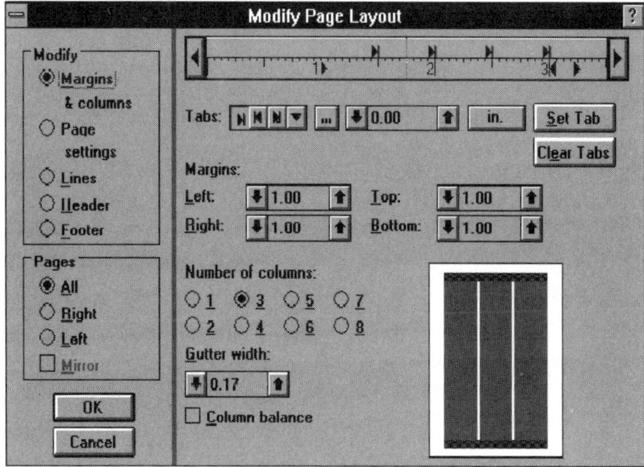

Figure 5.22 The Modify Page Layout dialog box.

Note the box entitled "Modify" in the upper left of the dialog box. Each of the options in the Modify box have their own dialog box. For example, the Page Settings dialog box is shown in Figure 5.23.

USING THE RULER FROM THE KEYBOARD

If you prefer, you can use the ruler to set tabs and margins, although I find it easier to use the Modify Page Layout dialog box. In any case, if you want to use the ruler, open the Edit menu (Fig. 5.17) and select the Go To command. This opens the

Go To dialog box shown in Figure 5.24. Select Ruler from the Next Item option and press Enter to open the ruler as shown in Figure 5.25. You can then use the Tab and Arrow keys to adjust the settings on the ruler.

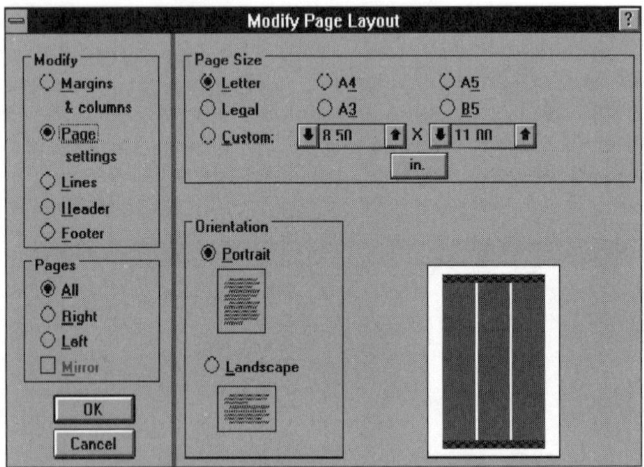

Figure 5.23 The Page settings option from the Modify Page Layout dialog box.

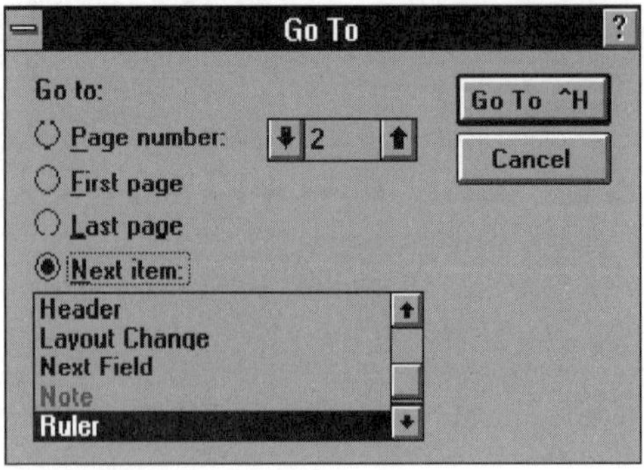

Figure 5.24 The Go To dialog box is opened from the Edit menu.

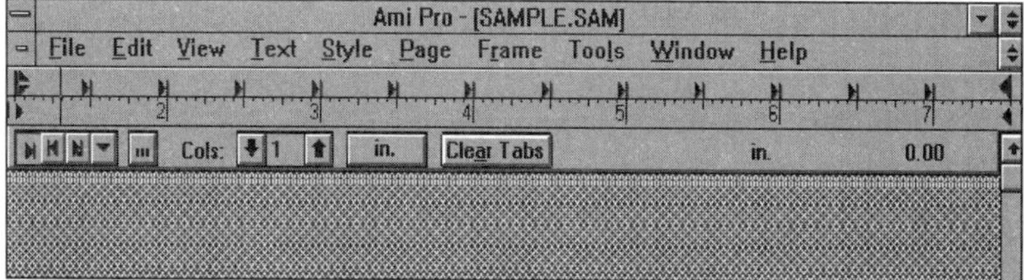

Figure 5.25 The Ami Pro ruler can be accessed from the keyboard, though it may be easier to use the Modify Page Layout dialog box.

Headers and Footers

You create headers or footers by using the Headers/Footers command in the Page menu (Fig. 5.21). This command opens a dialog box shown in Figure 5.26. The shaded portion at the top of the figure is the header area, where we have inserted some sample text and the page number. Use the Page Numbering command in the Page menu to insert the page number at the insertion point. To remove headers or footers, simply delete the text or graphics using the Del key.

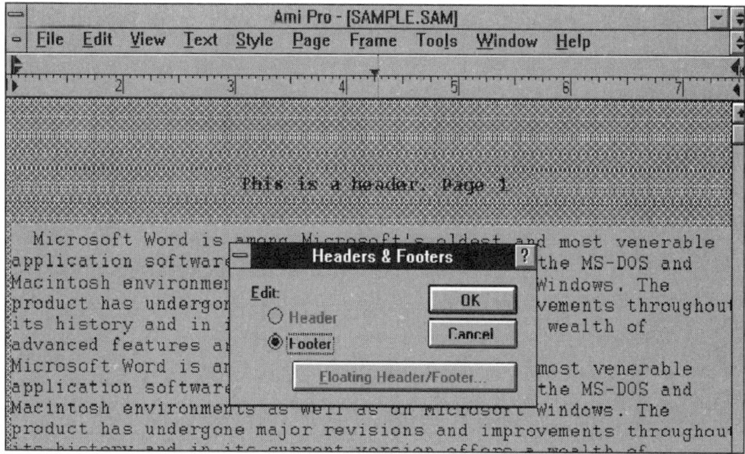

Figure 5.26 The Headers/Footers dialog box opened from the Page menu.

Graphics and Frames

Ami Pro uses the concept of frames for inserting graphics, charts, or equations into your document. You can first create the frame using the Create Frame command in the Frame menu (Alt+R), shown in Figures 5.27(a) and 5.27(b), and then insert a graphic image or other item into the frame.

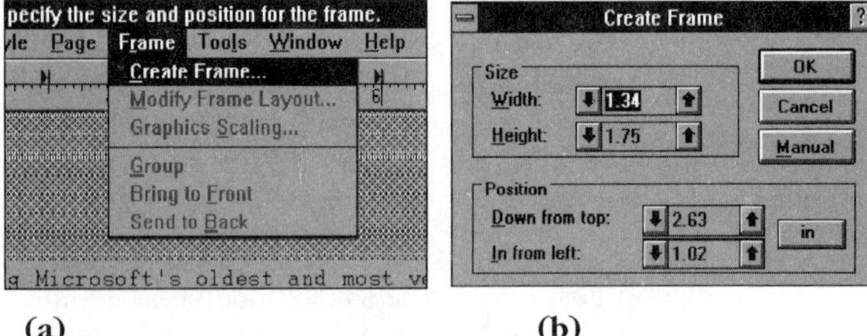

(a)   **(b)**

Figure 5.27(a–b) The Create Frame command in the Frame menu.

If you are simply inserting an existing graphic image, it's easier to execute the Import Picture command from the File menu, the dialog box of which is shown in Figure 5.28. Note that Ami Pro supports a wide variety of graphics file formats.

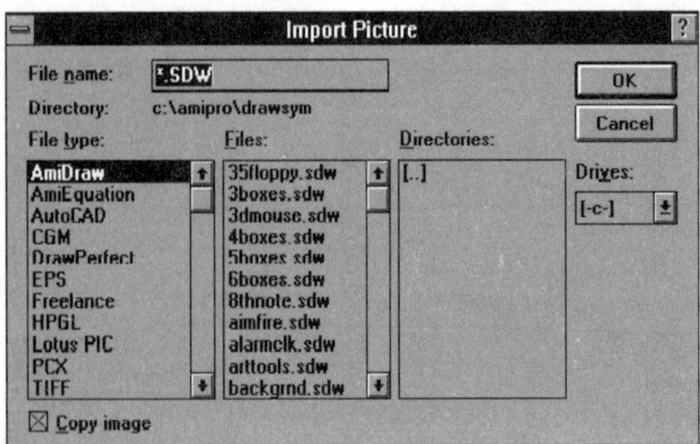

Figure 5.28 The Import Pictures command opened from the File menu.

A sample graphic is shown in Figure 5.29. You can modify the layout or scale of the image using the tools available in the Frame menu as shown in the figure. Figure 5.30 shows the Modify Frame Layout dialog box, which provides a variety of tools for working with frames. Note that you can create text and equation boxes, as well as charts, using the Modify Frame Layout tools as well as the charting and drawing tools in the Tools menu.

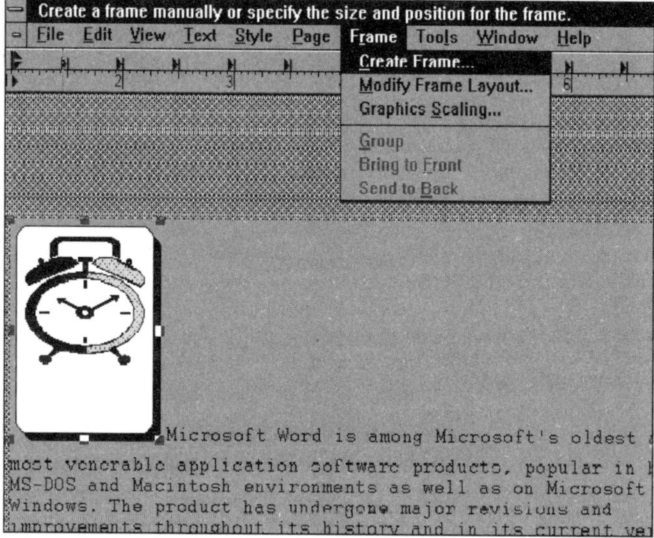

Figure 5.29 A graphic image imported using the Import Pictures command.

Selecting and Deleting Frames

You must use the Go To command from the Edit menu as described in the section on using the ruler earlier in this chapter to select frames from the keyboard. You can also press Ctrl+G from the document window to open the Go To dialog box. In this case, choose the Next Item option and then Frame to select the frame. You can then modify the frame or delete the frame by pressing the Del key.

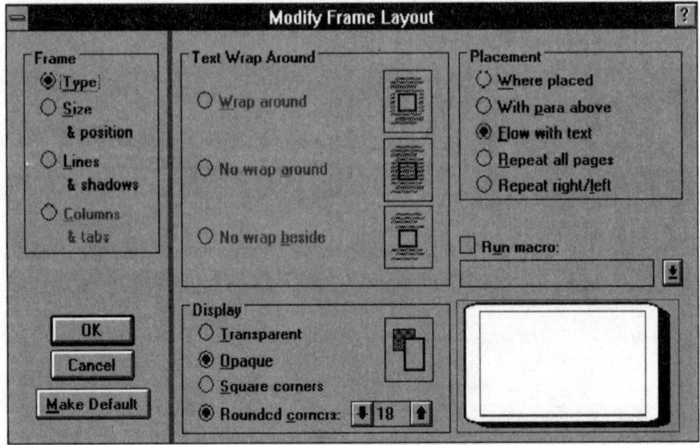

Figure 5.30 The Modify Frame Layout dialog box.

Macros

Ami Pro offers a variety of built-in macros as well as the capability to record and create your own macros. Figure 5.31 shows the Macro menu, which is a submenu of the Tools menu (Alt+L). Figure 5.32 shows the Play Macro dialog box. Note that you can assign keystrokes to playback macros. Lotus also offers a macro developer's kit for a nominal fee, which provides detailed instructions on writing macros using the Ami Pro macro language. This can be ordered directly from Lotus.

Tables

Like its competitors covered in this book, Ami Pro offers powerful capabilities for creating tables within your document, including calculated fields. In fact, Ami Pro's Table function supports Lotus 1-2-3 formulas. When you execute the Tables command from the Tools menu, you specify the number of columns and rows in the Table dialog box (Fig. 5.33), and then Ami Pro inserts the table at the insertion point in your document. When a table is present in your document, a new menu called Table appears in the menu bar as shown in Figure 5.34. The Quick Add command automatically adds totals in either rows or columns and inserts the result in the current cell. In the example in Figure 5.34, executing the Quick Add command with the insertion point in the third cell in the second row would total up the values in the first two columns.

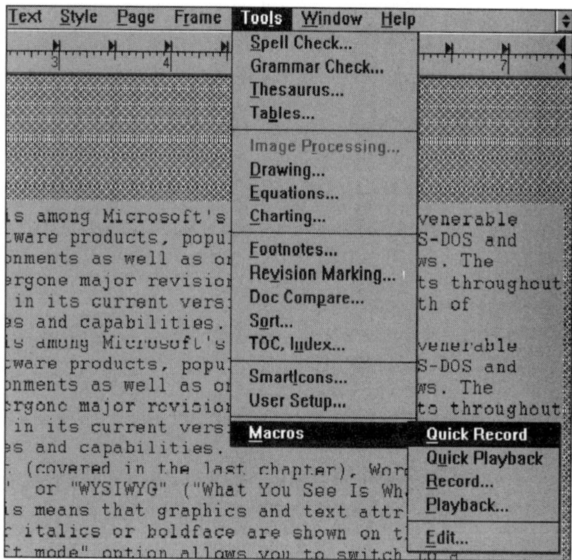

Figure 5.31 The Macro menu.

Other Tools

We have only skimmed the surface of the capabilities of Ami Pro. Like the other word processors covered in this book, there are simply too many features and capabilities to cover in this limited space. Nevertheless, some additional features are worth noting.

The Tools menu offers the usual array of document editing and preparation tools such as a spelling checker and thesaurus, outlining and document revision utilities, a tables of contents and index feature, and drawing and charting utilities, to name a few examples.

The Edit menu's Insert command shown in Figure 5.35 provides tools for procedures such as inserting the date and time, annotations, and merge fields. The Power Fields command (Fig.

5.36) allows you to set up fields in your document which prompt the user for input. In conjunction with macros, you can set up complex form entry capabilities with the Power Fields command.

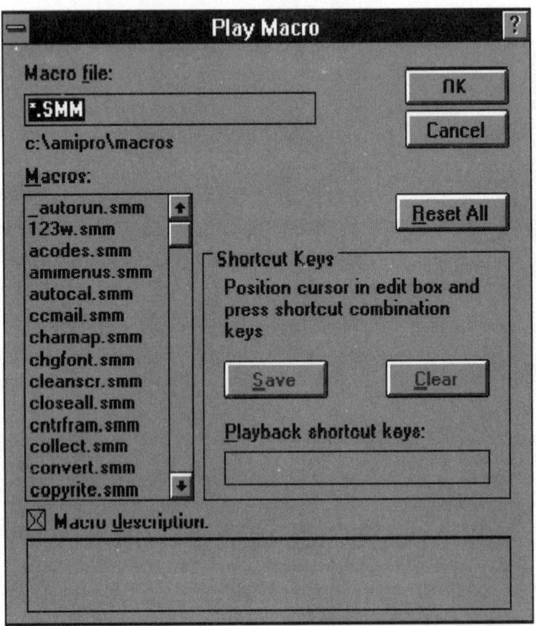

Figure 5.32 The Play Macro dialog box.

Figure 5.33 The Create Table dialog box.

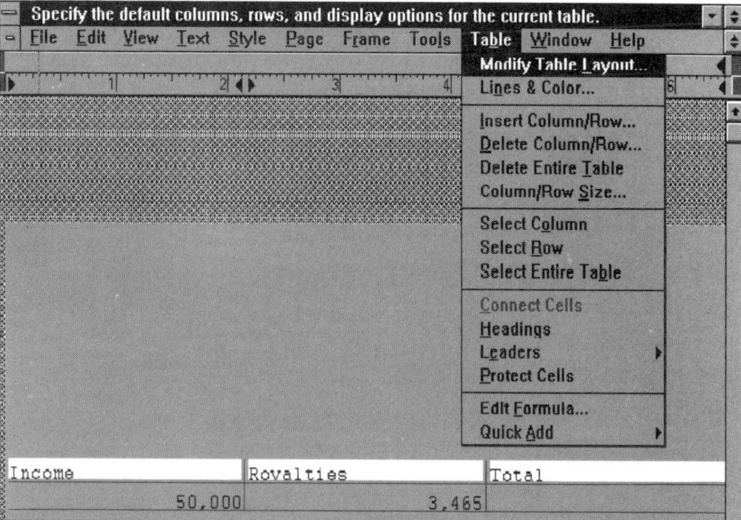

Figure 5.34 When a table is present, a new Tables menu appears in the menu bar with extensive formatting and computational capabilities.

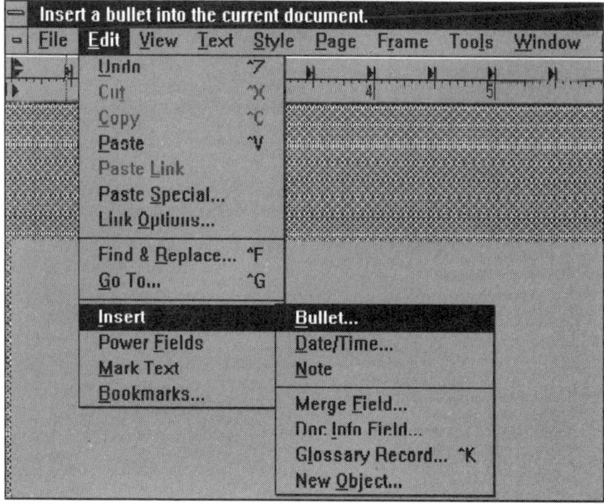

Figure 5.35 The Insert command in the Edit menu.

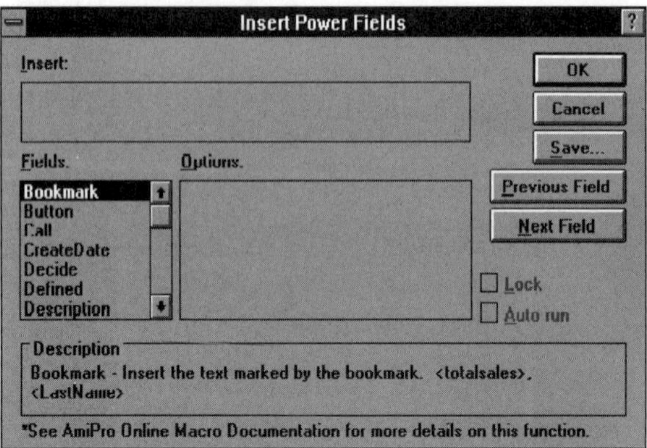

Figure 5.36 The Insert Power Fields dialog box.

Microsoft Excel

6

A concise list of Microsoft Excel keystrokes begins on page 268.

This chapter covers the basic keystrokes for the Microsoft Excel spreadsheet application.

Like Microsoft Word, Microsoft Excel is one of the company's most venerable and successful application software products. First introduced on the Macintosh in 1985, it's been available for the DOS and Windows environments since 1987. The product has undergone major revisions and improvements throughout its history, and in its current version offers a wealth of advanced features and capabilities.

Not surprisingly, Excel is a fully Windows-compliant application. In other words, it is consistent with the Windows interface, using the Windows menu bar and supporting the Windows clipboard and windowing system. Naturally, Excel for Windows is also designed to take advantage of the mouse.

In the most recent wars among spreadsheet applications, the emphasis has been on mouse-driven features such as toolbars and button bars, similar to those we encountered in the chapters on the word processors. And indeed, Excel has some features that only work with the mouse. Fortunately, Excel provides equivalent keystroke functionality for virtually every mouse feature. As in the earlier chapters, however, we'll start off by examining what *can't* be done from the keyboard.

What You Can't Do from the Keyboard

The vertical and horizontal scroll bars do not work with the keyboard and can be removed by changing the settings using the Workspace command in the Options menu. (See the section on customizing Excel later in this chapter.) From the keyboard, you can duplicate the function of the scroll bars with the Arrow and PgUp and PgDn keys, as described later in this chapter.

Like Microsoft Word, Excel features an optional graphical *toolbar*, which allows mouse users to point and click on icons representing frequently used commands such as opening, printing, and closing files, or activating other Excel features such as changing fonts or copying cells. The toolbar includes customizable buttons so that users can add other commands or macros represented by icons. Excel includes a variety of "specialty" toolbars such as a *drawing toolbar* and a *formatting toolbar*. The *standard toolbar*, which is the default toolbar when you open a spreadsheet, is shown in Figure 6.1.

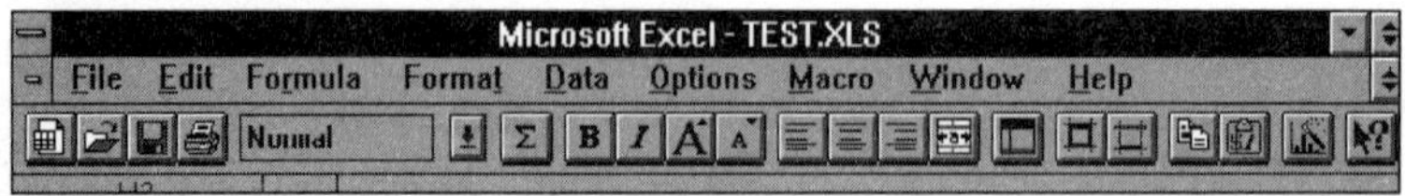

Figure 6.1 The standard toolbar.

Most, if not all, of the functionality of the toolbars can be duplicated from the keyboard using either keystroke sequences or the Excel menu options. If you are strictly using the keyboard, you can reclaim some space on the screen by removing the toolbar. This is accomplished by "hiding" the toolbar using the Toolbars command in the Options menu, which is covered in more detail in the next section on customizing Excel.

The Cell Drag and Drop feature does not work without a mouse. This feature allows you to select cells or cell ranges with the mouse and drag them to another location in the spreadsheet or to another window. The same functionality can be achieved with Excel's standard Cut, Copy, and Paste functions, however. The Drag and Drop feature can be disabled using the Workspace command in the Options menu.

Other features such as the *ChartWizard* and *Autofill* also only work with the mouse. ChartWizard allows you to embed charts directly into your worksheet, whereas you have to create charts in a separate window using the keyboard. The Autofill feature automatically copies a cell formula to neighboring cells by dragging with the mouse. Again, the standard Copy and Paste functions can duplicate the Autofill feature.

The Excel Keyboard

The Excel keyboard conforms to the Windows keyboard interface standard which is consistent with the Common User Access (CUA) standard, as discussed in the Foreword. Navigational keystrokes in Excel are somewhat similar to those used for navigating text in word processing applications, and there are many similarities between keystroke functions in Excel and Microsoft Word. For example, both programs use the F12 key and combinations of Shift, Alt, and Ctrl, for file operations, and both use the F8 key for extending selections.

Customizing Excel with the Options Menu

The primary means of customizing the Excel is the Options menu (Alt+O), shown in Figure 6.2. In particular, the Display, Toolbars, and Workspace commands allow you to control what you see on the screen.

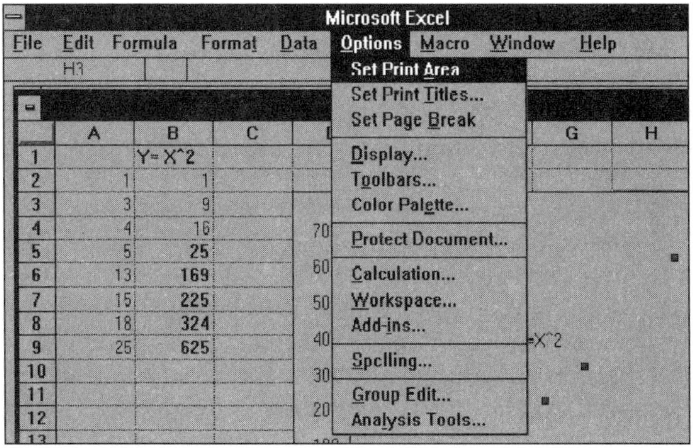

Figure 6.2 The Options menu.

The Display Options dialog box, shown in Figure 6.3, allows you to control the appearance of the spreadsheet itself and what is displayed in the cells. For example, the Zero Values option determines whether zero or a blank space appears in a cell in which the value is zero. If you un-check the Zero Values box (press Alt+Z to toggle the X on and off in the box), then zero value cells will appear as blanks. Among other options in the Display Options dialog box, you can remove gridlines, or display or hide cell formulas.

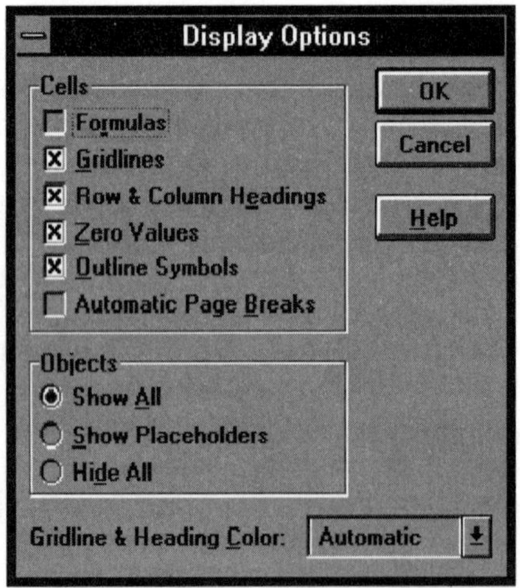

Figure 6.3 The Display Options dialog box.

The Toolbars command, which we briefly mentioned earlier in this chapter, gives you the option to display or hide the various Excel toolbars. As mentioned earlier, the toolbars require a mouse, so you may want to remove toolbars if you're not using a mouse. The Toolbars dialog box is shown in Figure 6.4. To hide the currently selected toolbar, select the Hide button by pressing Alt+I or the Tab key and then Enter.

The Workspace Options dialog box, shown in Figure 6.5, allows you to modify the appearance of the entire workspace, in contrast to the Display command, which deals with the appearance of the spreadsheet. Using the Workspace command, you can remove scroll bars and even the formula bar or status bar, if so desired. You can select alternate navigation keys, which conform to the Lotus 1-2-3 set of navigational keystrokes, and you can disable Cell Drag and Drop, which requires a mouse.

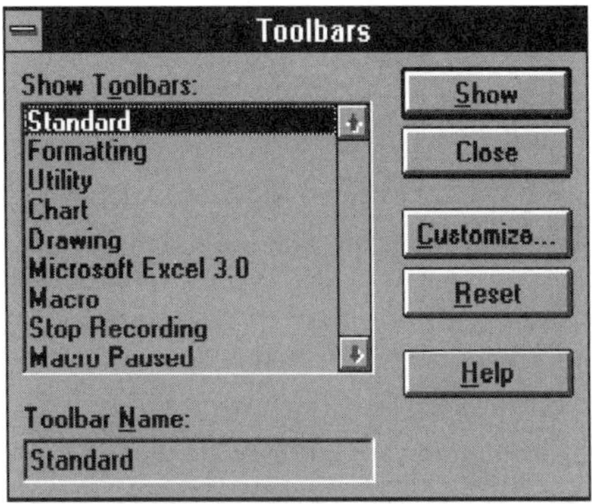

Figure 6.4 The Toolbars dialog box.

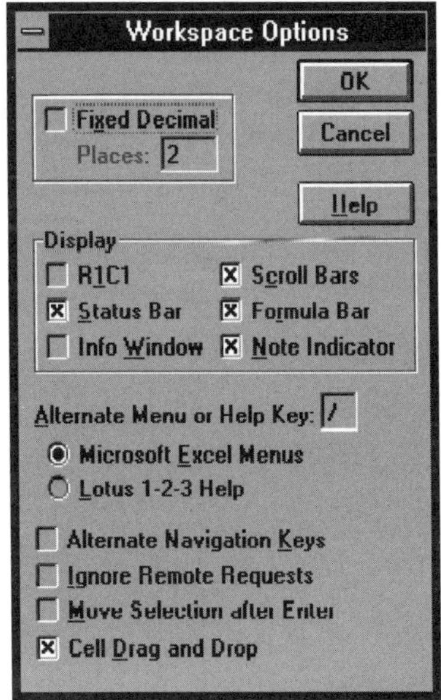

Figure 6.5 The Workspace Options dialog box.

Getting Started in Excel

Excel behaves very much like other Windows applications, and much of the product will look familiar to you if you have mastered the basic Windows navigational and menu keystrokes discussed in Chapter 1.

A typical Excel document window is shown in Figure 6.6. You access the Excel menu bar like you would any other Windows menu bar. Pressing Alt activates the menu bar. Alt+Spacebar brings up the application Control menu, which we discussed in Chapter 1. Alt+Hyphen brings up the document Control menu shown in Figure 6.6.

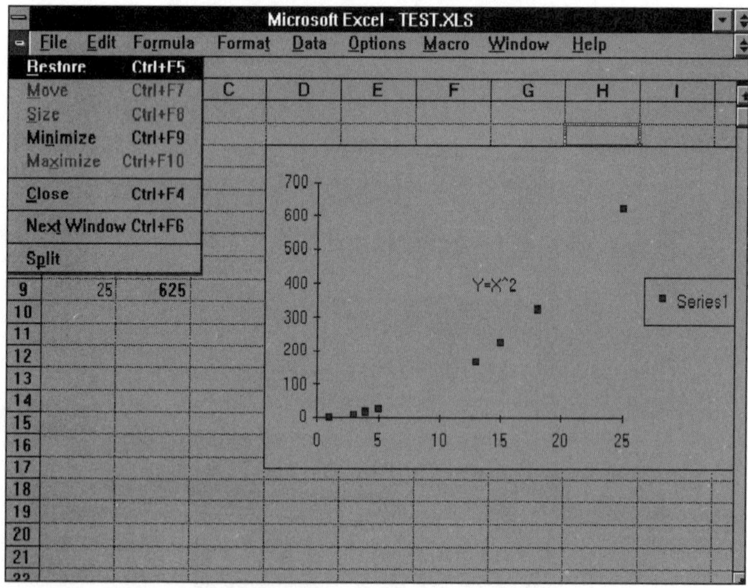

Figure 6.6 A typical Excel document and the document Control menu.

Note the additional options in the document Control menu called Next Window and Split. The Next Window option (Alt+Hyphen,N or Ctrl+F6 from the document window) switches to the next document window if you are working with multiple documents. (See the next section on working with files.)

The Split option splits the window horizontally or vertically, allowing you to view different parts of the spreadsheet simultaneously. Note that this command is also available from the Windows menu, and that split windows may be removed using the Windows menu, but not using the document Control menu. Therefore, it is better to use the Windows menu when executing the Split command.

Alt+F opens the File menu, Alt+E opens the Edit menu, and so forth. As in other Windows applications, the menu bar must be deactivated for keystrokes to take effect in the main document window. (If one of the menu bar options is highlighted, the menu bar is still active.) Press the Esc key to deactivate the menu bar.

It should be noted that Microsoft Excel relies heavily on dialog boxes for implementing most menu commands. As you may recall from Chapter 1, the easiest way to move to various fields in a dialog box is by pressing Alt+ the underlined letter in the heading of the field.

Working with Files

There are four types of files (or documents, as Microsoft calls them) in Excel. The basic file type is the *worksheet* or *spreadsheet*. (We will use the terms worksheet and spreadsheet interchangeably.) These files have an extension .XLS. There are also *macro sheets* (file extension .XLM), *charts* (file extension .XLC), and *workbooks* (file extension .XLW).

Workbooks are like folders or directories, in that you can keep a number of associated spreadsheets, charts, and macro sheets together in a workbook file, so that they are all opened and accessible when you open the workbook. Excel also supports templates, with the file extension .XLT, which are documents that store a specific pattern to use in creating other documents.

Unless you specify a file, Excel opens with a blank worksheet, and is ready for you to begin entering data. As we learned in the first two chapters, you can open files associated with an application directly by selecting the file's icon in Program Manager or the filename in File Manager and pressing Enter. The associated application opens automatically to display the file. If you open Excel without specifying a file (by selecting the Excel icon or the file \EXCEL\EXCEL.EXE and pressing Enter), you start with a blank worksheet.

To open a file in Excel, you can press Ctrl+F12 to open the Open File dialog box, or you can press Alt+F to open the File menu in the menu bar, as shown in Figure 6.7. One useful feature is the list of most recently opened files at the bottom of the menu. You simply type the number of the desired file to open it. In Figure 6.7, pressing the 1 key opens the file, TEST.XLS.

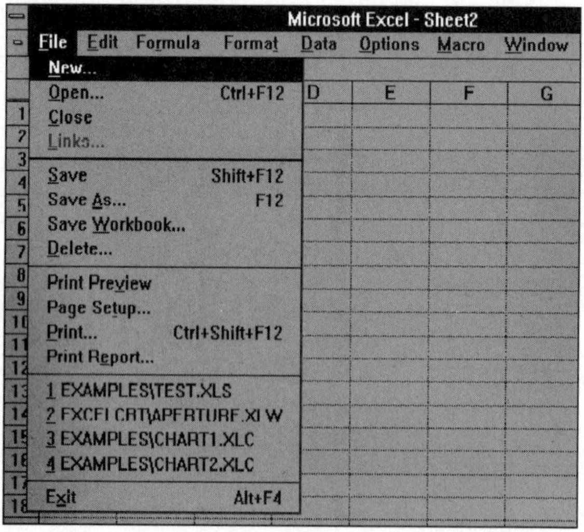

Figure 6.7 The Excel File menu.

Note that the Open command opens an existing file in a new window. If you want the file to appear in the current window, you must either use the Cut, Copy, and Paste functions to copy the data from a different window into the current window, or use the Consolidate function in the Data menu.

WORKING WITH MULTIPLE FILES

You can work with multiple documents simultaneously in Excel. However, only one document can be active at a time. To switch from one document to another, the easiest method is to press Ctrl+F6 until you reach the desired window. You can also press Alt+Hyphen to open the document Control menu and then select the Next Window option. Finally, you can open the Window menu (Alt+W), and select from the list of open documents displayed in the menu list.

Navigating the Worksheet

There are two distinct regions comprising a worksheet: the *main worksheet area,* where the cells of the worksheet are located, and the *formula bar,* located directly above the main worksaheet area. A typical worksheet is shown in Figure 6.8(a). The currently active cell is indicated by the shaded border around the cell. In the example in Figure 6.8(a), the currently active cell is B3. The formula bar is the area immediately above the spreadsheet's title bar and indicates the currently active cell and the contents of the cell. In the example, the contents of cell B3 is the formula, "A3^2." If we move to cell A3, note the corresponding change in the formula bar as shown in Figure 6.8(b).

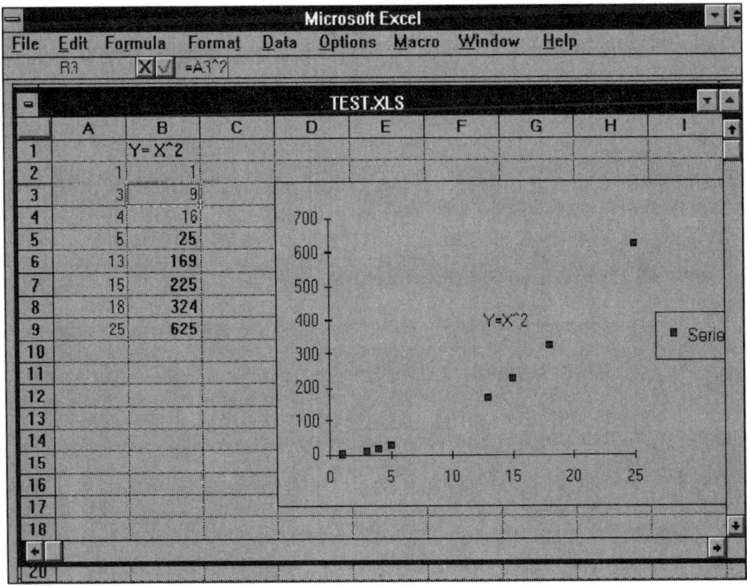

Figure 6.8(a) A typical worksheet. The active cell has the shaded border around it (in this case, cell B3).

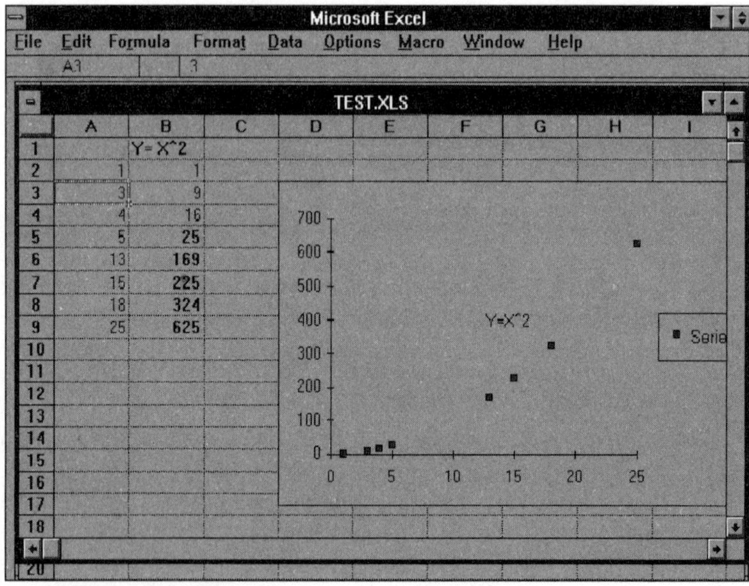

Figure 6.8(b) Now the active cell is A3. Note the change in the formula bar (the bar below the main menu bar).

The bottom of the spreadsheet shows the *status bar,* which provides information on what commands are currently active in the spreadsheet. For example, when the status bar displays "Edit," that means you are in the formula bar and not in the main worksheet. The status bar displays "Ready" when you are in the spreadsheet and can enter data.

Moving around the Worksheet

Most work can be done directly in the main worksheet area. You move from cell to cell with the Arrow keys and other navigation keys as described in the next paragraph. You enter new data by simply typing directly in the cell and then pressing the Enter key or moving the navigation keys to the next cell. You can replace the contents of a cell simply by moving to the cell and typing over the contents of the cell. Pressing the Esc key will cancel whatever you entered into the cell, leaving the cell's original contents unchanged.

Moving from cell to cell in a spreadsheet is analogous to moving from character to character in a word processing document. The Arrow keys move one cell at a time. Pressing Ctrl+ an Arrow key moves to the end of a data block or range in the direction of the Arrow key. Pressing Ctrl+Home brings you to the beginning of the worksheet. Ctrl+End takes you to the end. The PgUp and PgDn keys move one screen up or down. Pressing Ctrl+PgUp or Ctrl+PgDn moves one screen to the left or right, respectively.

Selecting Cells in the Worksheet

As with navigation, selecting cells is similar to selecting text. Shift+ an Arrow key or other navigation key combinations will select the cells as they are traversed. For example, pressing Shift+Ctrl+End will select all cells from the current cell to the end of the worksheet. To select an entire column, press Ctrl+Spacebar. Pressing Shift+Spacebar selects an entire row.

Another selection method is to press the F8 key to turn on Extend Selection mode and then simply move the navigation keys as you would normally (without holding down the Shift key). The cells that you traverse with the navigation keys are automatically selected. (Pressing F8 again or pressing Esc cancels select mode.)

Pressing Shift+F8 allows you to add non-adjacent cells to your selection. To do this, make your first selection and then press Shift+F8. You'll see the word "ADD" in the status bar, indicating that you are in Add mode. The move to the additional cells that you want to add and press Enter. Press Esc to cancel Add mode.

You can also select cells by reference or range name using the Goto command in the Formula menu or by pressing the F5 key from the main document window, which opens the Goto dialog box shown in Figure 6.9. The Goto dialog box displays the available cell range names. For more information on creating cell ranges, consult Excel's user's guide.

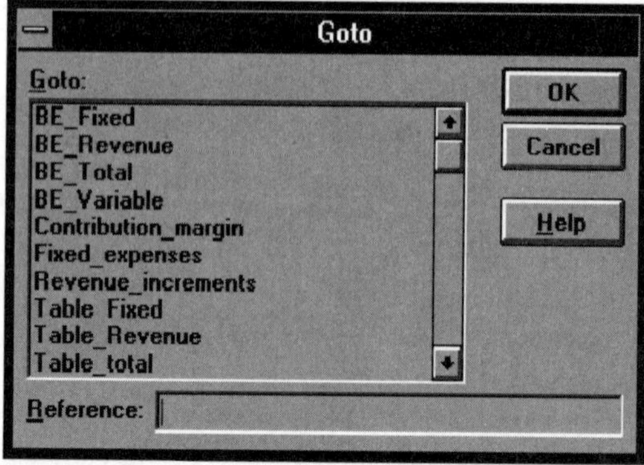

Figure 6.9 The Goto dialog box.

Moving within Selected Cells

After you have selected a group of cells, you may need to move
the active cell within the selection. If you use the normal navigation keys (e.g., the Arrow keys), you will cancel the entire selection. Therefore, you must use alternative keys, primarily Tab and
Enter, to move around within a block of selected cells. Press the
Enter key to move down while in a column of cells, or
Shift+Enter to move up. To move horizontally, press the Tab key
to move to the right, or Shift+Tab to move to the left.

Editing with the Formula Bar

You use the *formula bar* to edit the contents of a cell, rather than
completely replacing the contents. To activate the formula bar,
move to the desired cell and press the F2 key. When the formula
bar is active, two boxes, called the Enter box and the Cancel
box, appear in the formula bar. The Enter box is denoted by a
check and the Cancel box by an X. These boxes can be used by
mouse users to complete or cancel an editing operation, simply
by clicking on either box. From the keyboard, pressing Esc cancels the operation and returns you to the main cell area. Pressing
the Enter key returns you to the cell with your editing changes
reflected in the cell. An active formula bar is shown in Figure

6.10. Note that the status bar at the bottom of the screen displays the word, "Edit," when the formula bar is active.

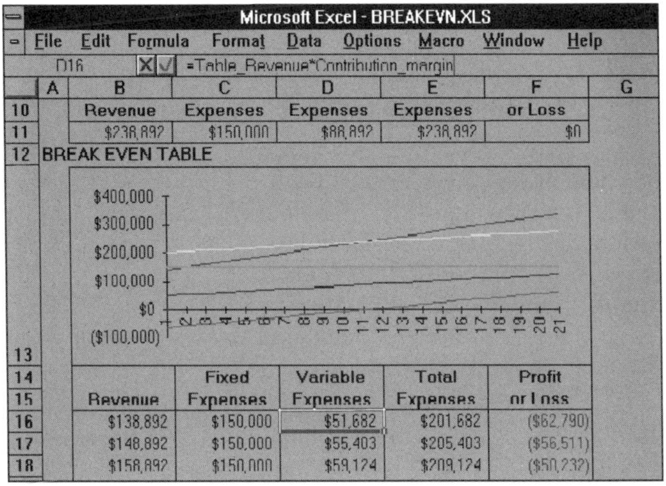

Microsoft Excel - BREAKEVN.XLS

<u>F</u>ile <u>E</u>dit Fo<u>r</u>mula Forma<u>t</u> <u>D</u>ata <u>O</u>ptions <u>M</u>acro <u>W</u>indow <u>H</u>elp

D16   X √   =Table_Revenue*Contribution_margin

	A	B	C	D	E	F	G
10		Revenue	Expenses	Expenses	Expenses	or Loss	
11		$238,892	$150,000	$88,892	$238,892	$0	
12	BREAK EVEN TABLE						

	Revenue	Fixed Expenses	Variable Expenses	Total Expenses	Profit or Loss
14		Fixed	Variable	Total	Profit
15	Revenue	Expenses	Expenses	Expenses	or Loss
16	$138,892	$150,000	$51,682	$201,682	($62,790)
17	$148,892	$150,000	$55,403	$205,403	($56,511)
18	$158,892	$150,000	$59,124	$209,124	($50,232)

Figure 6.10 An activated formula bar. The "X" and check boxes indicate that the bar is active.

Editing in the formula bar is just like editing in a Windows-compliant word processor. The insertion point is a vertical bar and can be moved with the Arrow keys. Pressing Ctrl+ the Arrow keys moves the insertion point one word at a time. The Home key brings you to the beginning of the cell text. The End key brings you to the end of the text.

Pressing Alt+Enter inserts a carriage return if you are entering multiple lines of text. Use the Shift key with the above navigational keystrokes to select text (e.g., Shift+Ctrl+Right Arrow selects the word to the right). The Cut, Copy, Paste, and Undo commands (Ctrl+X, Ctrl+Y, Ctrl+V, and Ctrl+Z) all work in the formula bar.

DELETING TEXT IN THE FORMULA BAR

The Backspace key deletes the character immediately before (to the left of) the current location of the cursor. The Del key deletes the character immediately ahead (to the right of) the cursor.

Pressing Ctrl+Del deletes the word to the right of the cursor, and pressing Ctrl+Backspace deletes the word to the left of the insertion point. Most importantly, pressing Ctrl+Z or Alt+Backspace will undo your deletion.

Working with Selected Cells

Once you have selected cells, you are obviously going to do something with them. You may want to cut, copy, and paste, perform calculations, copy formulas, create graphs, and so forth. Microsoft has thoughtfully included what's called a Shortcut menu that contains the commands most often used with selected cells. If you can't find the command in the Shortcut menu, it's most likely available from the main menu.

The Excel Shortcut Menu

Whenever you are working in a spreadsheet, you can press Shift+F10 to open the Shortcut menu. If you try this and the menu doesn't open, make sure that the formula and main menu bars are both inactive. (If you're not sure, press the Esc key a couple of times.) The Shortcut menu is shown in Figure 6.11.

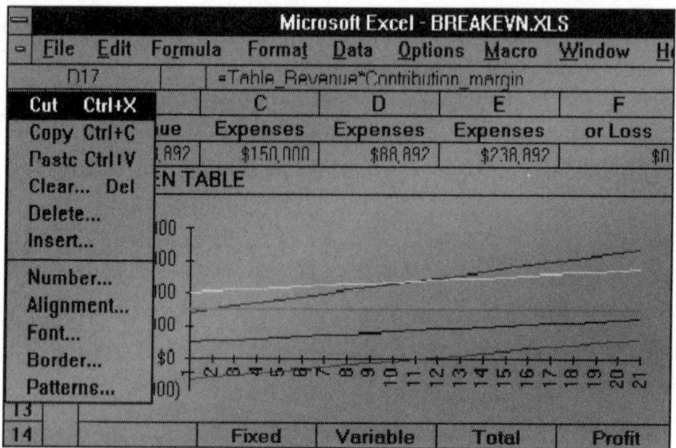

Figure 6.11 The Excel Shortcut menu.

Note that the Cut, Copy, Paste, Clear, and Font commands have keystroke equivalents which allow you to execute those commands directly from the spreadsheet, without opening the Shortcut menu. Typing the first letter of the command in the Shortcut menu will open that command. As you get used to using the Shortcut menu, you can simply type Shift+F10, followed by the first letter of the menu you want to open (e.g., Shift+F10,F to open the Font dialog box).

Commands in the Shortcut menu can be executed with either individual or groups of cells selected. For example, if you want to change the numerical format of an entire column of numbers, first select the column (Ctrl+Spacebar), and then press Shift+F10,N to open the Shortcut menu and the Number dialog box described below.

CUT, COPY, AND PASTE

There are several methods to cut, copy, or paste the contents of selected cells. The easiest way is to select the cell, and then press Ctrl+X or Ctrl+C to cut or copy the contents of the cell, respectively. Cutting the contents removes it from the cell or cells and places it in the Windows clipboard. (See Chapter 1 for more on the Windows clipboard.) Note that the cell contents is not actually removed until you paste it into another location. If you wish to delete the contents, you must use the Clear command rather than the Cut command, as described in the next section.

Copying the contents copies it to the clipboard while at the same time leaving it in the original cell location. The Copy command is particularly useful for copying formulas into additional cells, as discussed in a separate section later in this chapter.

To paste the contents into a different location or into another spreadsheet, move the active cell to where you wish to paste the contents, in either the current document or another one, and press Ctrl+V to paste. Press Ctrl+Z to undo the most recent Cut, Copy, or Paste operation. As mentioned earlier, the Cut operation is not completed until you execute the Paste command.

Shift+Del, Ctrl+Ins, Shift+Ins, and Alt+Backspace, are alternative keystrokes for Cut, Copy, Paste, and Undo, respectively. However, as mentioned in Chapter 1, we strongly recommend getting in the habit of using the Ctrl combinations, which have become the standard keystroke combinations for Cut, Copy, and Paste, in most computer operating systems.

CLEAR AND DELETE

The Clear command deletes the contents of the selected cells, while the Delete command deletes the cells themselves; usually rows or columns. The Clear and Delete dialog boxes are shown in Figure 6.12(a) and Figure 6.12(b), respectively. Note the important difference between these two commands. You can use the Undo command to restore the most recent deletions made with either the Clear or Delete commands. Note that the Del key is a shortcut key for the Clear command.

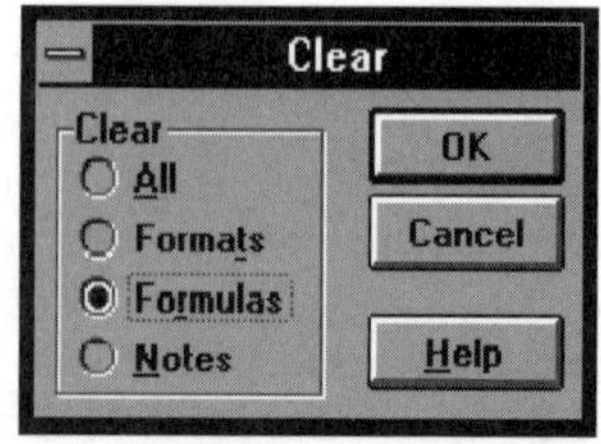

(a)

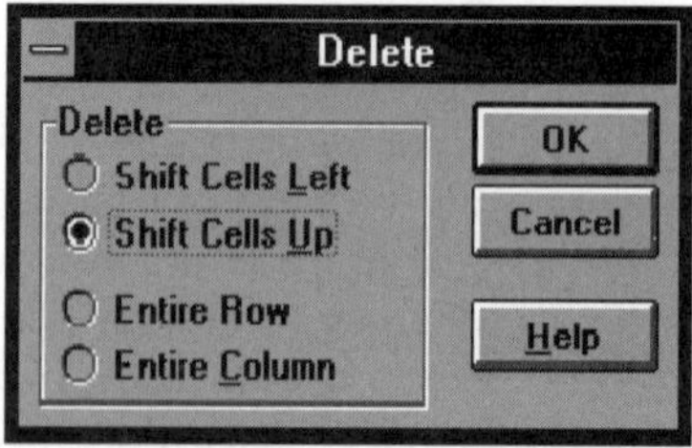

(b)

**Figure 6.12(a) The Clear dialog box.
(b) The Delete dialog box.**

THE INSERT COMMAND

The Insert command allows you to shift individual cells down or to the right, or you can insert new rows and columns. The Insert dialog box is shown in Figure 6.13. Note that the Shift option (which is also provided in the Delete dialog box) does not insert or remove rows or columns, but instead simply moves the cells.

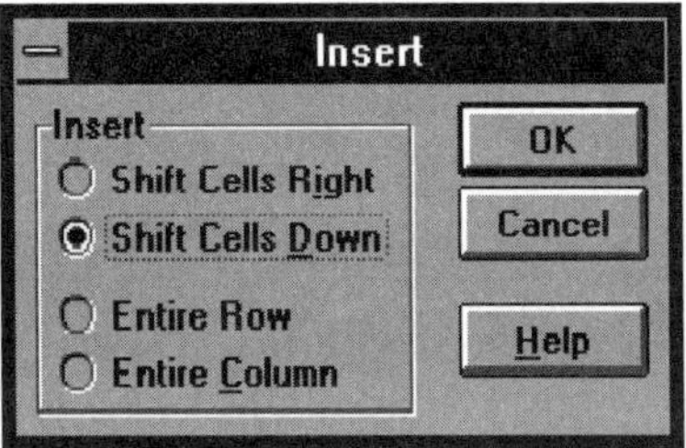

Figure 6.13 The Insert dialog box.

THE NUMBER COMMAND

The Number command allows you to change the numerical format of numbers in your spreadsheet. For example, you may want numbers to appear in currency format, rounded to the nearest integer, or in date and time format. The Numbers dialog box is shown in Figure 6.14. Note that many number formats can be entered directly from the keyboard. For example, Ctrl+Shift+$ changes the selected cells to currency format. On the other hand, trying to memorize the various keystrokes for applying number formats is probably more trouble than opening the Shortcut menu.

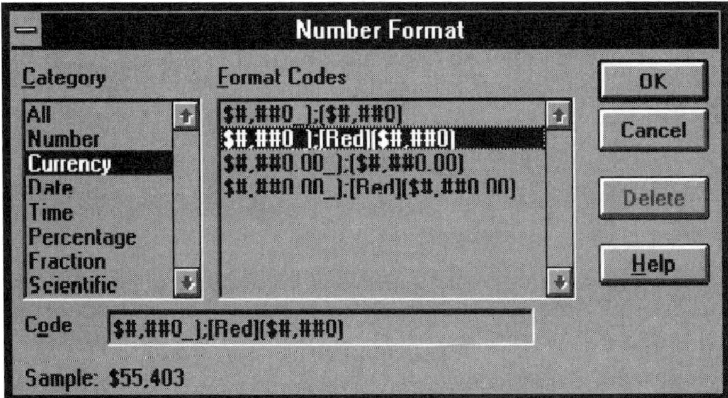

Figure 6.14 The Numbers dialog box.

THE ALIGNMENT COMMAND

The Alignment command allows you to align the contents of the selected cells. You can center, left and right justify text, change the orientation of the text, wrap text, and so forth. The Alignment dialog box is shown in Figure 6.15.

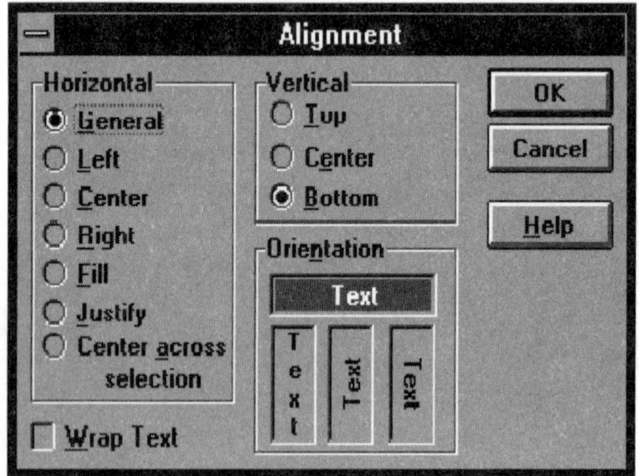

Figure 6.15 The Alignment dialog box.

FONT COMMAND

You can use many of the same keystroke commands as in word processors for setting boldface, italics, and so forth, directly from the document without opening the Shortcut menu. For example, Ctrl+B will change the contents of the current cell to boldface. Ctrl+I sets the font to italics. Ctrl+N returns the text to normal. If you want to change fonts, you must open the Font dialog box as shown in Figure 6.16.

BORDER AND PATTERNS

The Border and Patterns dialog boxes are shown in Figure 6.17(a) and Figure 6.17(b). These commands allow you to enhance the appearance of the spreadsheet. Using the Borders command, a border can be applied to a group of cells, or, using the Patterns command, you can apply shading to certain cells that should stand out, as shown in Figure 6.17(c).

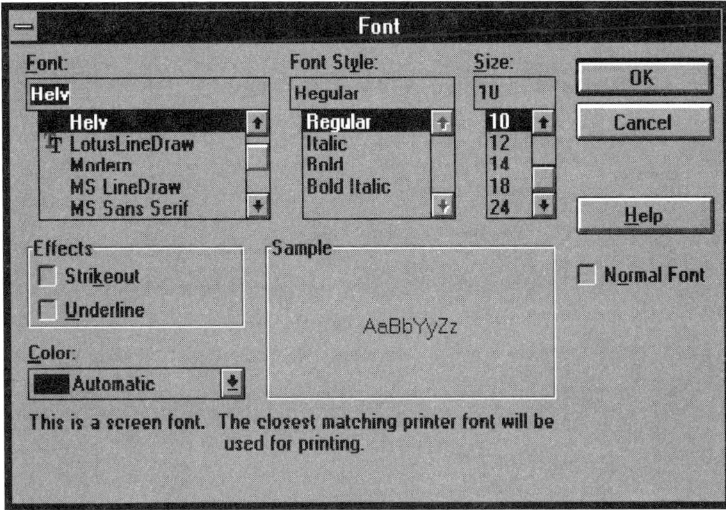

Figure 6.16 The Font dialog box.

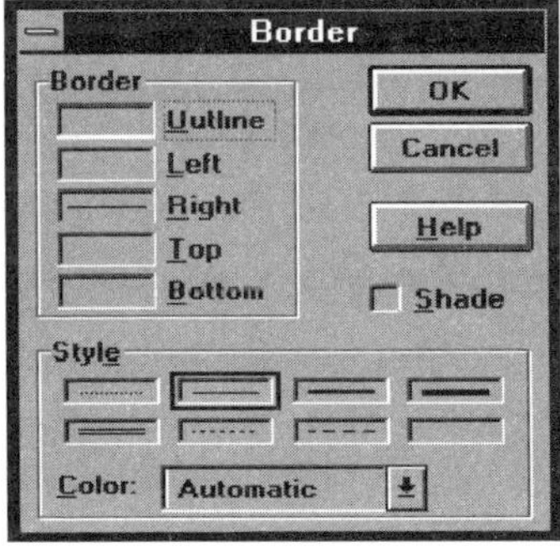

Figure 6.17(a) The Border dialog box.

Figure 6.17(b) The Pattern dialog box.

Figure 6.17(c) An outline border and shaded background.

Formulas and Calculations

Spreadsheets are most useful for performing calculations: adding up totals, multiplying cell values by other values, and so forth. And to perform calculations, you need to use formulas. The first character in a formula is the equal sign (=). For example, Figure 6.18(a) shows a simple spreadsheet that calculates the square of the value in the first column and puts that value in the second column. The third column adds the first two columns together (y + x^2). In cell B2, the formula is "=A2^2." As shown in Figure 6.18(b) the formula in cell C2 is "=A2+B2."

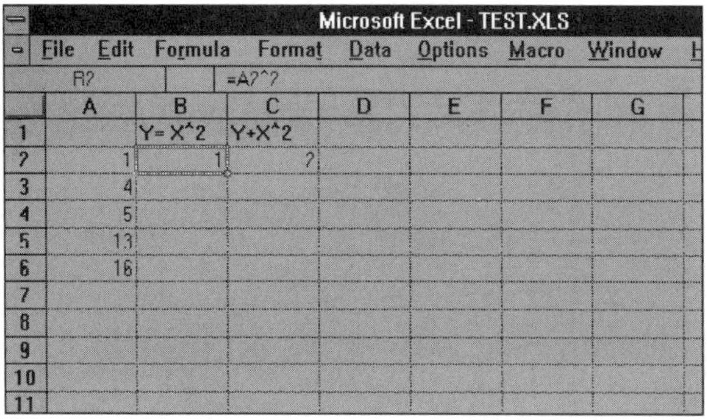

Figure 6.18(a) Cell B2 squares the value in cell A2. (b) Cell C2 calculates the sum of A2 and B2. (c) We copy the formulas in cells B2 and C2 into the selected cells below.

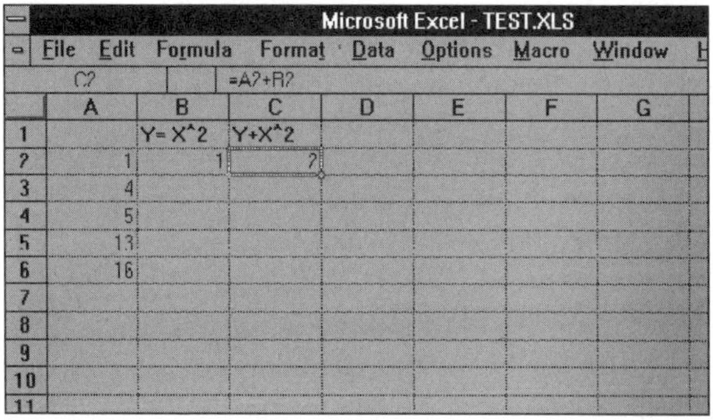

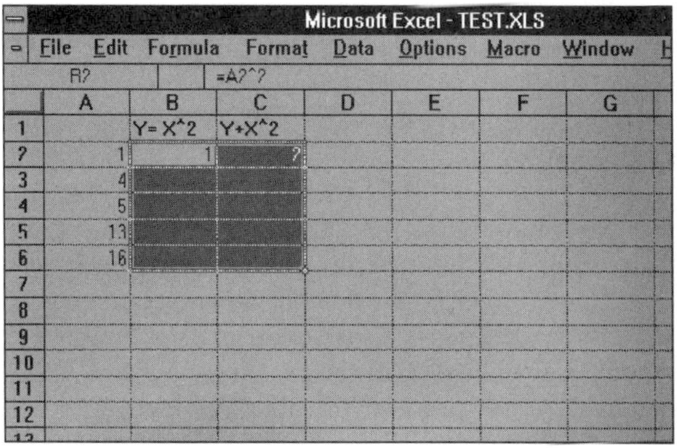

Microsoft Excel - TEST.XLS

File   Edit   Formula   Format   Data   Options   Macro   Window

R1   Y=X^?

	A	B	C	D	E	F	G
1		Y=X^2	Y+X^2				
2	1	1	2				
3	4	16	20				
4	5	25	30				
5	13	169	182				
6	16	256	272				
7							
8							
9							
10							
11							
12							
13							
14							

Figure 6.18(d) Results of copying formulas in B2 and C2 into cells selected in Figure 6.18(c).

Copying Formulas

Now, we want to replicate these formulas in the remaining cells of the spreadsheet. There are two ways to copy formulas. One is to simply select the cell in which the formula exists and then press Ctrl+C. Then select the cells in which you want this same formula to appear, and press Ctrl+V to paste the formula.

Another and often more efficient method is to use the Fill command. Using the Fill command, you can copy multiple cell formulas simultaneously. In our example, we need to copy both the formulas in B2 and C2 to the cells below them. To do this using the Fill command, first select cells B2 and C2. Still holding down the Shift key, press the Down Arrow to select the remaining cells so that you have a block of selected cells as shown in Figure 6.18(c). Now execute the Fill Down command. The most efficient way to do this is to type Ctrl+D for Fill Down. (Ctrl+R executes Fill Right.) The result is shown in Figure 6.18 (d).

Alternatively, you can use the Edit menu to execute the Fill commands as shown in Figure 6.19.

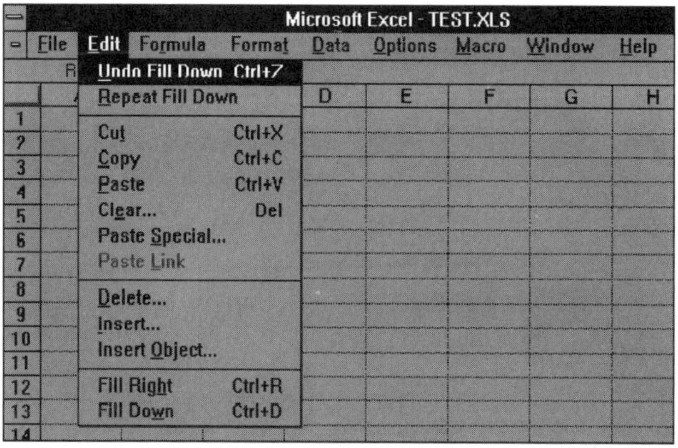

Figure 6.19 The Edit menu provides the Fill Right and Fill Down commands.

Using Autosum for Totals

One of the handiest features in Excel is the Autosum command. This command automatically creates a total of the numbers in adjacent cells. The command is designed to make an educated guess as to which adjacent cells should be totaled. If the cell which will display the total is below a column of numbers, the Autosum command assumes that the column of cells is to be totaled. If the cell for displaying the total is at the end of a row, Autosum assumes that the row of cells is to be totaled.

To execute the Autosum command, move to the cell in which you want the total to appear and press Alt+=. The command will show the cell range which it assumes is to be totaled. You can press the Enter key to use the range supplied by the command, or you can press F2 to enter the formula bar and change the range. Note that you do not have to select any cells to use the Autosum command. Simply move to the cell in which you want the sum to appear.

Adjusting Column Width

Surprisingly, one command missing from the Shortcut menu is the Column Width command, which is located in the Format menu (Alt+T), shown in Figure 6.20(a). You will often want to adjust column widths to accommodate text strings that require more space than is available with the default column width. The Column Width Command dialog box is shown in Figure 6.20(b). Note that the Best Fit option will usually set the column width to the appropriate size for existing data. Obviously, you can set the column width to your own specifications when necessary.

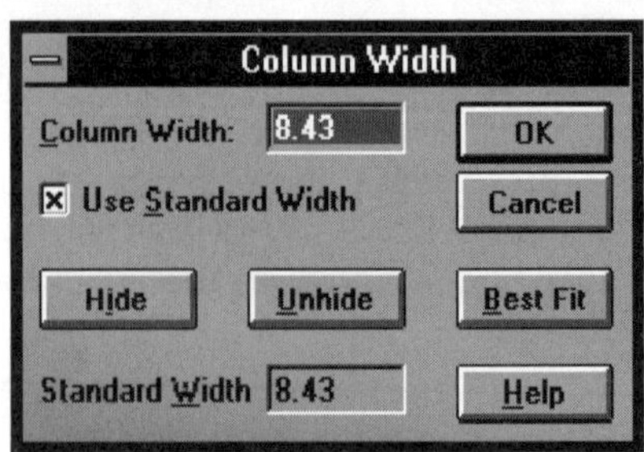

(a)

(b)

Figure 6.20(a) The Format menu. (b) The Column Width dialog box.

Creating Graphs

Here is one area where mouse users have a distinct advantage. A mouse-driven feature called the ChartWizard is included which allows mouse users to create charts directly in the spreadsheet with simple drag and drop functions. Nevertheless, keyboard users can also create graphs. And you can embed them in your spreadsheet. It's just a slightly more tedious process using the keyboard.

The first step is to select the data that you want to graph. Then press the F11 key to activate the Chart command. An example is shown in Figure 6.21(a). The resulting graph and the Chart menu is shown in Figure 6.21(b). You can choose from a variety of chart styles, including linear XY, bar graphs, pie charts, and so on.

Note that you work with charts in a separate Excel document window with a separate menu bar. When you have finished creating the chart, you can save it as a file. To close the charting application, press Alt+Hyphen and select Close from the Control menu or press Ctrl+F4 from the document window.

Inserting the Chart in Your Spreadsheet

The easiest way to insert the chart in your spreadsheet is to open the chart file (which you presumably saved after creating it), and press Ctrl+C to copy the chart into the clipboard. Then return to your spreadsheet, move to the area on the spreadsheet where you want to insert the graph, and press Ctrl+V to paste the chart as shown in Figure 6.22.

To remove the chart from the spreadsheet, open the Select Special dialog box from the Formula menu and select objects as shown in Figure 6.23. The chart will then display little square handles around its border, indicating that it is selected. Press the Del key to delete the chart or Ctrl+X to cut it and copy it into the clipboard.

Note that you can use the Insert Object command in the Edit menu to insert other types of files into your spreadsheet. You can also use the object linking features of Excel to update charts automatically as the spreadsheet is updated. *OLE* (Object Linking and Embedding) is beyond the scope of this book but is covered in detail in Book Two of Excel's user's guide.

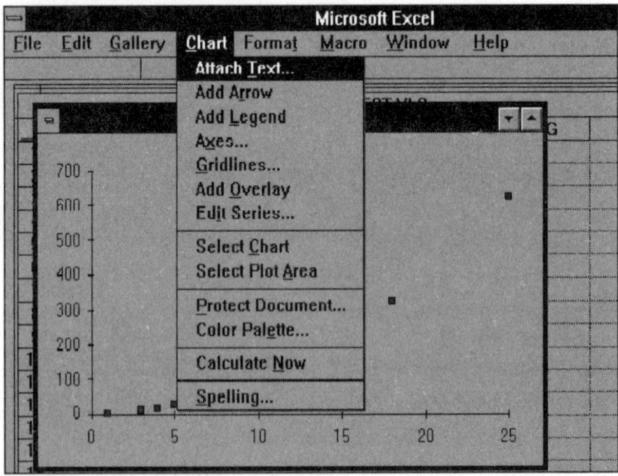

(a)

(b)

Figure 6.21(a) The New Chart dialog box is opened by pressing the F11 key after selecting the cells that you want to graph. (b) The Chart menu is part of the separate Excel charting application. Save your chart as a file (it will automatically receive the extension .XLC), which you can then paste back into your spreadsheet, if so desired.

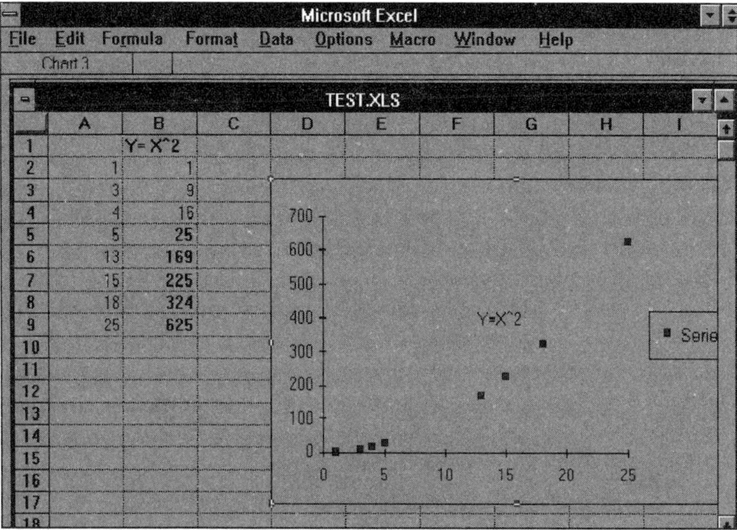

Figure 6.22 The chart pasted into the spreadsheet. Note the little square handles which indicate that the chart is selected.

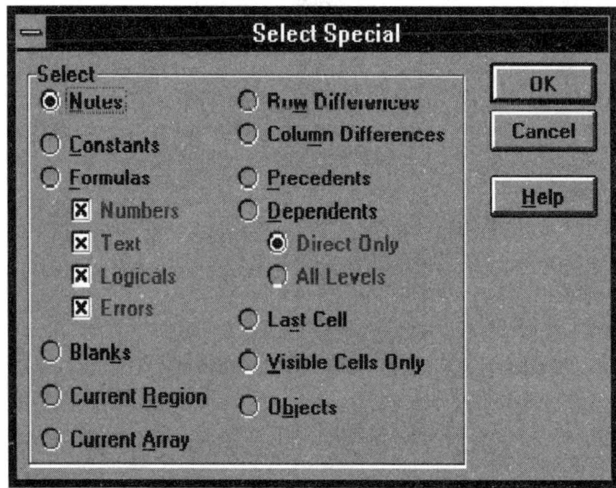

Figure 6.23 Use the Select Special dialog box and select Objects to select a chart or other item embedded in your spreadsheet.

Working with Databases in Excel

While spreadsheets are known mainly for their ability to work with rows and columns of numbers, they can also be used effectively as databases if the spreadsheet application supports this function. Most full-featured spreadsheet programs, including Excel, allow you to work with the spreadsheet as you would with a flat file database, treating each cell as a database field and each row as a database record. Among other data manipulation functions provided in the Data menu, shown in Figure 6.24, Excel provides functions for entering data into a simple data entry form, performing queries, and sorting records.

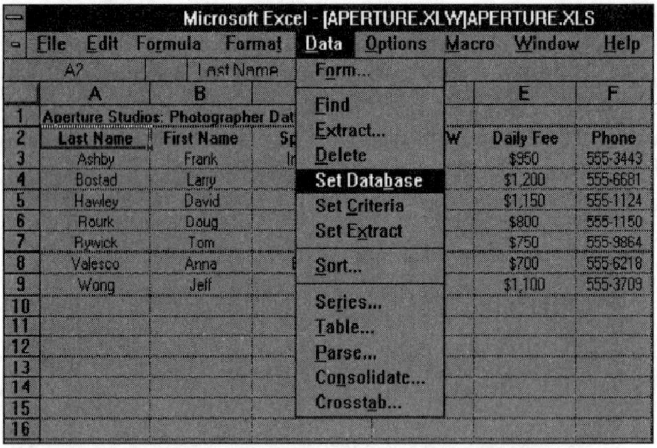

Figure 6.24 The Data menu.

To create a database in Excel, type in the fieldnames in the first row of the spreadsheet area that you will use for the database. (This can be the entire spreadsheet or a particular range of cells within the spreadsheet.) Enter data into the fields below each fieldname to create a database record. Select all the cells plus a blank row below the last record you entered, and then execute the Set Database command from the Data menu. This command establishes the selected region as a database. To enter additional records, you can use the Form command in the Data menu.

An example of creating a database is shown in Figure 6.25. Here we have entered the fieldnames and adjusted the column widths using the Column Width command to accommodate the data. We then select the row with the fieldnames in addition to the two following rows and then execute the Set Database command from the Data menu.

Figure 6.25 In this example, we enter some fieldnames and then select two additional blank rows. We then execute the Set Database command to establish the database, which allows you to use data entry forms and perform database queries.

We can then enter records into the *database entry form*, which opens when you execute the Form command in the Data menu. Notice that the form, shown in Figure 6.26, provides buttons for searching for records and performing queries based on specific criteria. Press Alt+ the underlined letter in the fieldname to enter data into that field, or press the Tab key to move to that field. Do not press Enter or the Arrow keys until you have completed the form, since those keystrokes are interpreted as completion of the data entry process for that record.

Macros

Excel provides a comprehensive macro language with over 400 functions for developing sophisticated macros for everything from analysis and computation to document formatting. Coverage of this capability is beyond the scope of this book, and the reader is referred to Book Two of Excel's user's guide. We will, however, briefly look at recording command macros, which can be accomplished from the Macro menu in the main menu bar as shown in Figure 6.27.

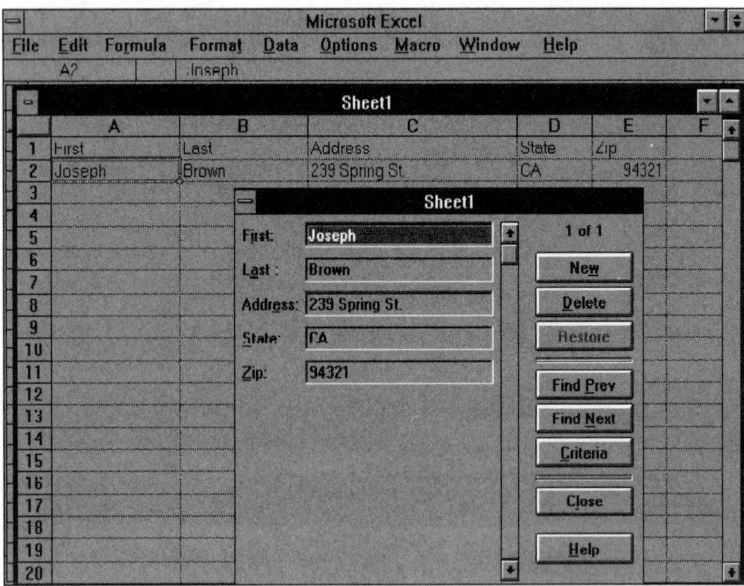

Figure 6.26 The Excel data entry form for databases.

Figure 6.27 The Macro menu allows you to record keystrokes and then replay them.

To record a macro, select the Record command in the Macro menu (Alt+M). You are then presented with the Record Macro dialog box shown in Figure 6.28. After assigning a name and key sequence to the macro (do not use Excel's built in key sequences such as Ctrl+I), select OK or press Enter and begin executing the operations and commands you want to record.

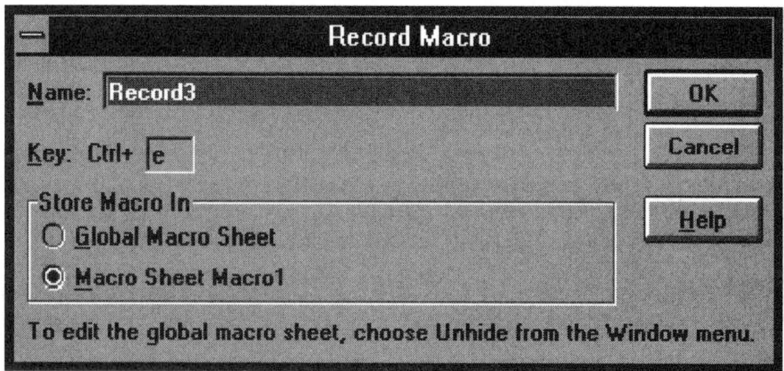

Figure 6.28 The Record Macro dialog box.

When you have finished, open the Macro menu again and execute the Stop Recorder command. Note that the command sequences in recorded macros are stored in a macro sheet file, which can be edited and further customized. To open the macro sheets associated with the active worksheet, open the Windows menu and select the Unhide command to open the macro sheet. For more on macro sheets, see Book Two of Excel's user's guide.

Borland Quattro Pro

7

A concise list of Quattro Pro
keystrokes begins on page 276.

This chapter covers keyboard usage of Borland's Quattro Pro spreadsheet application, which has become a major competitor of both Lotus 1-2-3 and Microsoft Excel.

Of the applications covered in this book, Quattro Pro is the least consistent with the standard Windows user interface. Some of the keystrokes that work universally in the other applications either do not work in Quattro Pro or do not work in the same way. For example, the standard Cut, Copy, Paste, and Undo keystrokes (Ctrl+X, Ctrl+C, Ctrl+V and Ctrl+Z) do not work in Quattro Pro. Quattro Pro also uses somewhat different keyboard conventions in some of its dialog boxes. (For example, the Object Inspector dialog boxes in the Property menu use a nonstandard Ctrl+PgUp or Ctrl+PgDn sequence to move through various subcategories in the dialog box.)

Nevertheless, Quattro Pro is a solid spreadsheet application and can be used successfully from the keyboard. The manual provides an appendix with a list of keyboard equivalents and includes a keystroke template that fits along the top of the keyboard. But it should be noted that if you have become particularly accustomed to some of the standard Windows selection and Cut/Copy/Paste keystrokes, you might find Quattro Pro a little more difficult to use than the other spreadsheet applications covered in this book. On the other hand, Quattro Pro is tightly integrated with Borland's Paradox database application, and would be the better choice if you are a Paradox user. These sorts of considerations, of course, apply to selecting any application software.

Like its competitors, Quattro Pro is particularly optimized for mouse usage. Quattro Pro offers a number of features that are only accessible using a mouse, such as the so-called *SpeedBar*, which is similar to the toolbar of Microsoft Word and Excel. Fortunately, Quattro Pro provides equivalent keystroke or menu functionality for virtually every mouse feature, although some operations may not be as fast or efficient from the keyboard as they are with a mouse. As in the other chapters on applications, we'll cover what you *can't* do from the keyboard and how to remove "mouse-only" features from the screen. But before we do, we must explain one unique concept in Quattro Pro, and that is the concept of *objects*.

Notebooks and Objects in Quattro Pro

The various components that comprise spreadsheets in Quattro Pro are called objects. Not to be confused with object-oriented programming, the term "object" in Quattro Pro refers to various components of the application and also to the Quattro Pro application itself. The primary types of Quattro objects are:

1) *Blocks:* Blocks consist of one or more cells (called ranges in 1-2-3 and Excel). The active cell or a group of selected cells is called a block.

2) *Pages:* Spreadsheet data in Quattro Pro can be organized into separate pages, which together comprise a notebook.

3) *Notebooks:* Notebooks are a set of pages representing one or more spreadsheets and other objects such as graphs and macros.

4) *Graphs* and *graphic images, custom dialog boxes,* and *SpeedButtons.*

5) The Quattro Pro application itself, called the *Application Object.*

You need to know about objects so that you can customize them to your requirements. In particular, if you're strictly a keyboard user, you may want to remove some of the mouse features found in these various objects.

What You Can't Do from the Keyboard

The vertical and horizontal scroll bars do not work with the keyboard and can be removed by changing the settings using the Active Notebook command in the Property menu. (See the section on customizing Quattro Pro later in this chapter.) From the keyboard, you can duplicate the function of the scroll bars with the Arrow and PgUp and PgDn keys, as described later in this chapter.

The SpeedBar allows mouse users to point and click on icons representing frequently used commands for performing calculations, changing fonts, or copying cells, for example. The SpeedBar includes customizable buttons so that users can add other commands or macros represented by icons. Quattro Pro includes a seperate SpeedBar for preparing graphics.

In addition to the SpeedBar, Quattro Pro provides a graphical tab system for organizing multiple spreadsheets into notebooks as described earlier. The idea is to organize different types of data into separate pages of a notebook. You can then click on the various pages using the notebook tab buttons at the bottom of Spreadsheet window. The SpeedBar and notebook tabs are shown in Figure 7.1.

You can remove the SpeedBar and notebook tabs using the Application command in the Property menu as discussed in the next section on customizing Quattro Pro.

The Drag and Drop feature requires a mouse. This feature allows you to select cells or cell ranges with the mouse and drag them to another location in the spreadsheet or to another window. However, the same functionality can be achieved with Quattro Pro's standard Cut, Copy, and Paste functions.

The Quattro Pro Keyboard

As mentioned earlier, the Quattro Pro keyboard does not strictly conform to the Windows user interface standard. It's sort of a hybrid between Windows standards and keystrokes from the DOS version of Quattro Pro. You can make the keyboard a little more Windows-like by un-checking the Compatible Keys option in the Startup section of the Application dialog box opened from the Property menu, as described in the next section on customizing Quattro Pro. If compatibility is checked, then the keyboard works exactly like it does in the DOS version of Quattro Pro. If you un-check compatibility, then some, though not all, of the Windows navigation keys will work like they do in other Windows applications. For example, in the DOS version of Quattro Pro, Ctrl+Right Arrow or Ctrl+Left Arrow moves the cursor five spaces to the right or left, respectively, rather than moving the cursor one word to the right or left as in Windows. We'll discuss editing and navigating in Quattro Pro in more detail later in this chapter.

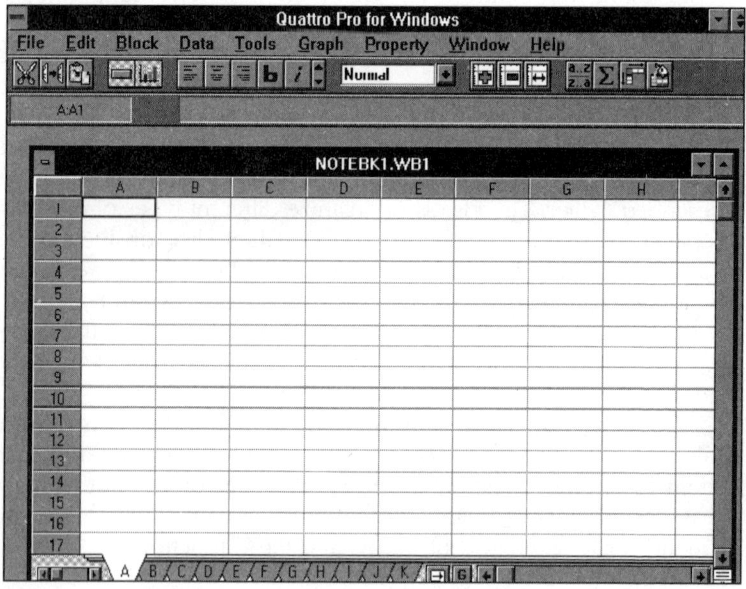

Figure 7.1 Quattro Pro's mouse-driven SpeedBar is directly below the main menu bar, while the notebook page tabs are at the bottom of the Spreadsheet window.

Customizing Quattro Pro with the Property Menu

The Property menu shown in Figure 7.2 is the main vehicle for customizing Quattro Pro. However, the concept of objects and assigning properties to those objects (i.e., customizing them) makes customization in Quattro Pro a far more comprehensive function than in Excel or 1-2-3, because it includes customizing selected cells. In other words, in Quattro Pro, you do everything from removing scroll bars to changing column width or fonts using the Property menu. Operations such as changing column widths or fonts are handled in separate menus in Excel or 1-2-3. In Quattro Pro, these operations are handled using the Current Object command in the Property menu.

Figure 7.2 The Property menu.

The other menu options deal with more general customization operations such as removing scroll bars or SpeedBars. Therefore, we'll cover the Application, Active Notebook, and Active Page commands in this section and then return to the Current Object command after we've discussed selecting cells.

The Application Command

The Application command in the Property menu allows you to modify settings that apply globally to the Quattro Pro application. Note that you can open the Application dialog box directly from the document window by pressing Alt+F12. The Application dialog box is shown in Figure 7.3(a).

Before going any further, it is important to note that the interface of this and the other Property menu dialog boxes do not follow Windows conventions for dialog boxes. The list on the left side of the dialog box represents the various categories that can be customized from this dialog box. Each category displays a different set of options. In Figure 7.3(a), the Display category is shown. Note that you can remove the SpeedBar, Input Line (the editing area immediately above the main spreadsheet area), and Status Line. Press Alt+ the underlined letter to check or un-check these options.

To move to the next category, press Ctrl+PgDn. To move up the category list, press Ctrl+PgUp. Again, these are non-standard keystrokes for navigating dialog boxes. Figure 7.3(b) shows the International dialog box. You can modify various defaults such as the currency and date/time formats as well as the language format used for sorting text.

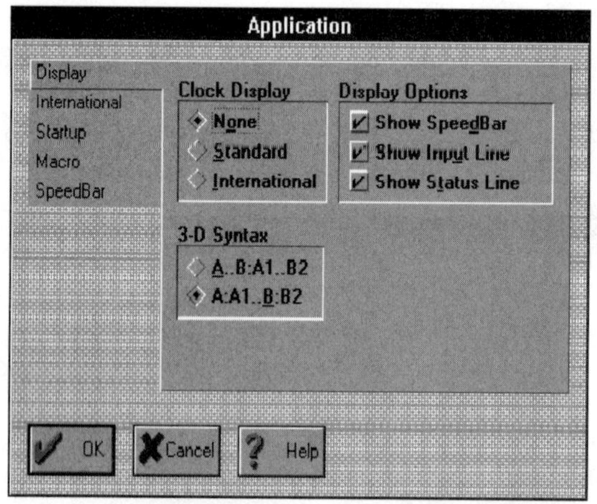

(a)

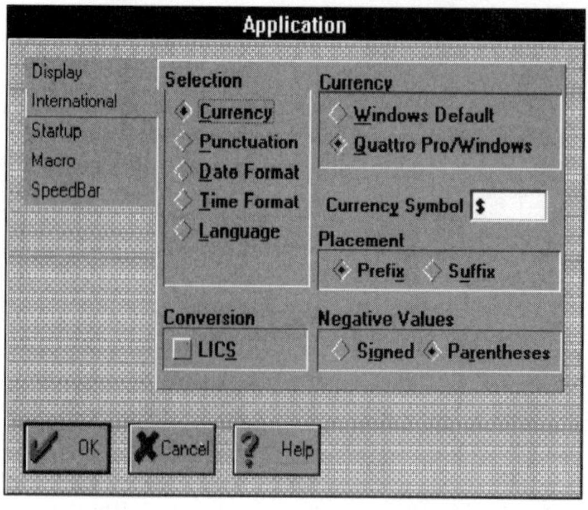

(b)

Figure 7.3(a–b) The Application dialog box is shown with three different categories displayed.

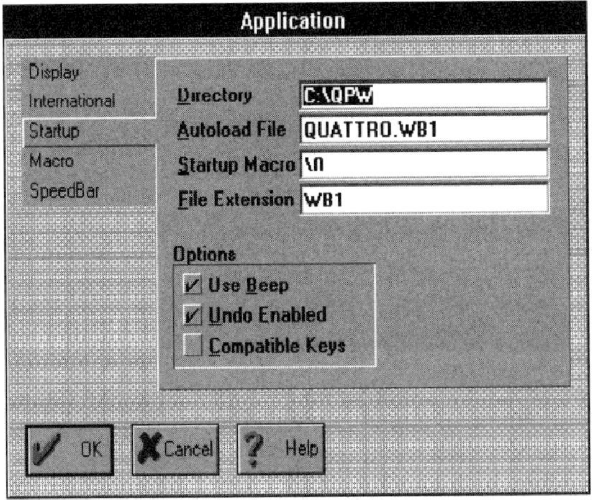

Figure 7.3(c) The Application dialog box *(continued)*.

The Startup category is shown in Figure 7.3(c). Note the compatible keys option, which we discussed in the section on the Quattro Pro keyboard. If Compatible keys is checked, then the keyboard conforms exactly to the DOS version of the product. If it is un-checked, then navigation and selection keys are more consistent with Windows keystroke conventions.

The Active Notebook Command

Properties specified with the Active Notebook command apply to the currently active notebook. Of particular interest is the Display category, shown in Figure 7.4. (Press Ctrl+PgDn to open this category.) You can hide both scroll bars as well as the notebook page tabs by un-checking the appropriate boxes. Press Alt+ the underlined letter to toggle these settings on or off. Note that you can open the Active Notebook dialog box directly from the main document window by pressing Shift+F12.

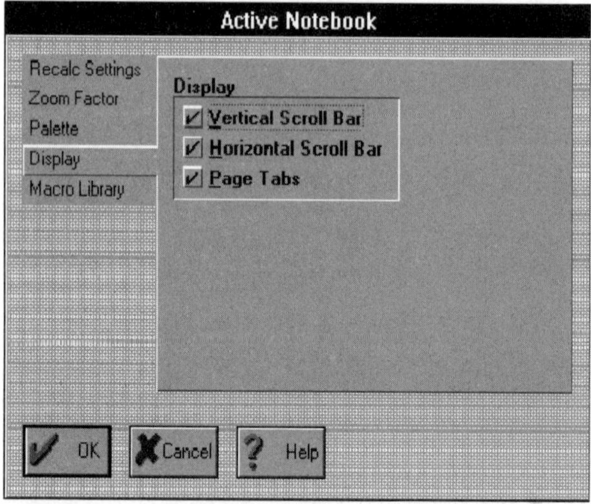

Figure 7.4 The Active Notebook command's Display category.

The Active Page Command

Properties specified with the Active Page command apply to the currently active page in the notebook. Shown in Figure 7.5, you can change the appearance of the spreadsheet with the various color, border, and grid options. You can assign names to pages in the notebook. These names will then appear as tabs in the notebook tab bar at the bottom of the screen if the bar is displayed, as shown in Figure 7.5.

You can also set the default column width, set cell protection (preventing cell contents from being modified), specify whether zero values should be displayed as zeros or as blanks, and set the text justification of cell labels (centered, right, or left).

Getting Started in Quattro Pro

Although we have pointed out that Quattro Pro is less consistent with the Windows interface than the other applications covered in this book, it is nevertheless a Windows application and is easy to learn if you have mastered the basic Windows navigational and menu keystrokes discussed in Chapter 1.

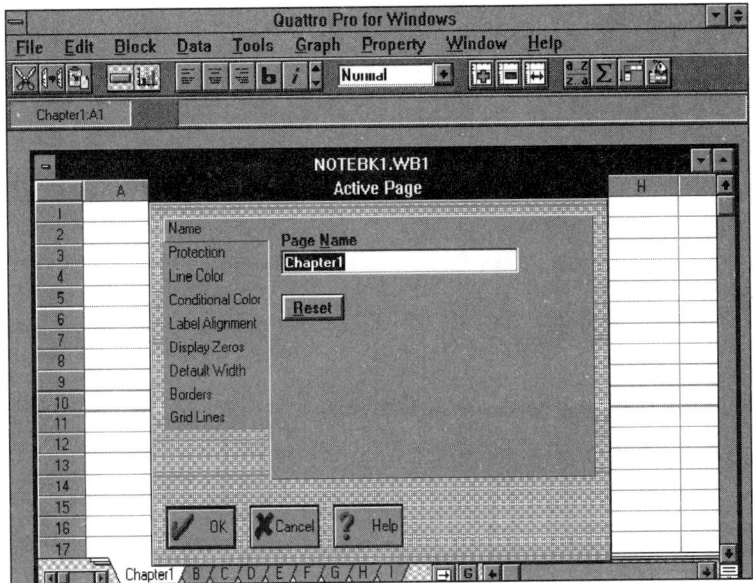

Figure 7.5 The Active Page command.

A typical Quattro Pro spreadsheet is shown in Figure 7.6. You access the Quattro Pro menu bar like you would any other Windows menu bar. Pressing Alt activates the menu bar. Alt+Spacebar brings up the application Control menu, which we discussed in Chapter 1. Alt+Hyphen brings up the document Control menu.

Alt+F opens the File menu, Alt+E opens the Edit menu, and so forth. As in other Windows applications, the menu bar must be deactivated for keystrokes to take effect in the main document window. (If one of the menu bar options is highlighted, the menu bar is still active.) Press the Esc key to deactivate the menu bar.

Working with Files

Quattro Pro saves spreadsheet files and associated graphs in a notebook. The default notebook extension is .WB1.

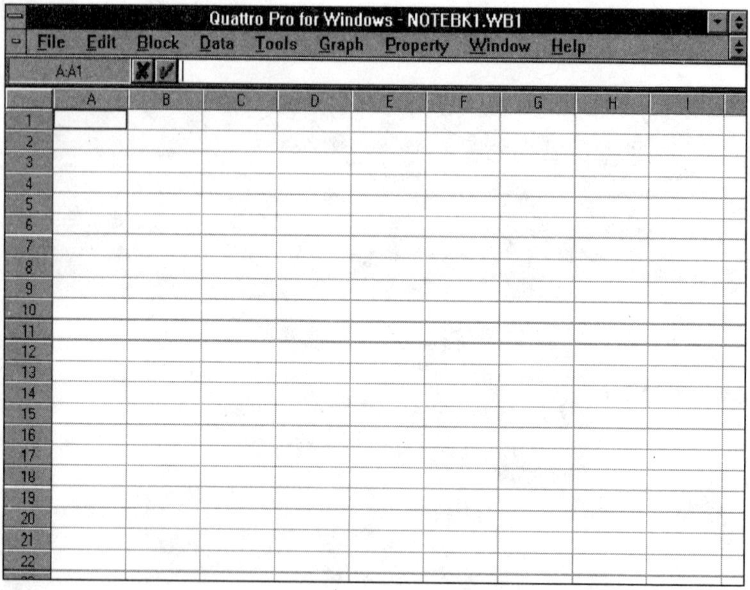

Figure 7.6 The Quattro spreadsheet with scroll bars, notebook tabs, and SpeedBar removed.

Unless you specify a file, Quattro Pro opens with a blank spreadsheet and is ready for you to begin entering data. As we learned in the first two chapters, you can open files associated with an application directly by selecting the file's icon in Program Manager or the filename in File Manager and pressing Enter. The associated application opens automatically to display the file. If you open Quattro Pro without specifying a file (by selecting the Quattro Pro icon or the file \QPW\QPW.EXE and pressing Enter), you start with a blank spreadsheet.

To open a file in Quattro Pro, you must open the File Menu (Alt+F) shown in Figure 7.7 and select the Open command. To open a new notebook, use the New command. Note that the Open command opens an existing file in a new window. If you want the file to appear in the current window, you must use the Insert File command in the Block menu or the Cut, Copy, and Paste functions to copy the data from a different window into the current window. To consolidate data, use the Combine command in the Tools menu.

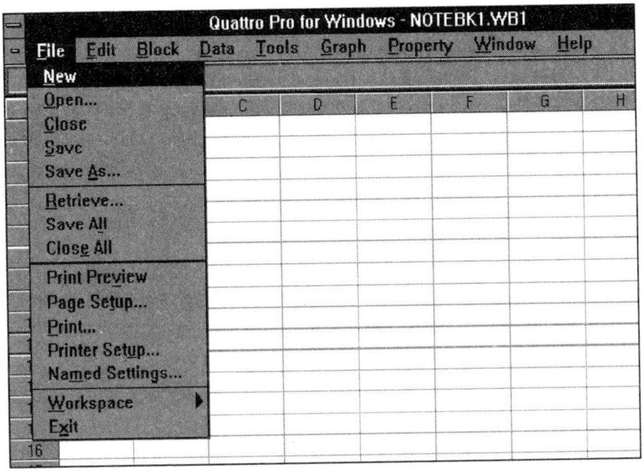

Figure 7.7 The Quattro Pro File menu.

WORKING WITH MULTIPLE FILES

You can work with multiple documents simultaneously in Quattro Pro. However, only one document can be active at a time. To switch from one document to another, the easiest method is to press Ctrl+F6 until you reach the desired window. You can also press Alt+Hyphen to open the document Control menu and then select the Next Window option. Finally, you can open the Window menu (Alt+W), and select from the list of open documents displayed in the menu list.

Navigating the Spreadsheet

There are two distinct regions comprising a Quattro Pro spreadsheet: the *input line,* which is the bar immediately above the main spreadsheet area, and the *main spreadsheet area,* where the cells of the spreadsheet are located. A typical spreadsheet is shown in Figure 7.8(a). The currently active cell is indicated by the shaded border around the cell. The input line is the area immediately above the top row of the spreadsheet, indicating the currently active cell and the contents of the cell. In the example in Figure 7.8(a), the currently active cell is A:B3. Note that B3 is the cell's coordinates, and A is the page. In the example, the contents of cell B3 is the formula, "A3^2." If we move to cell C3, note the corresponding change in the formula bar as shown in Figure 7.8(b).

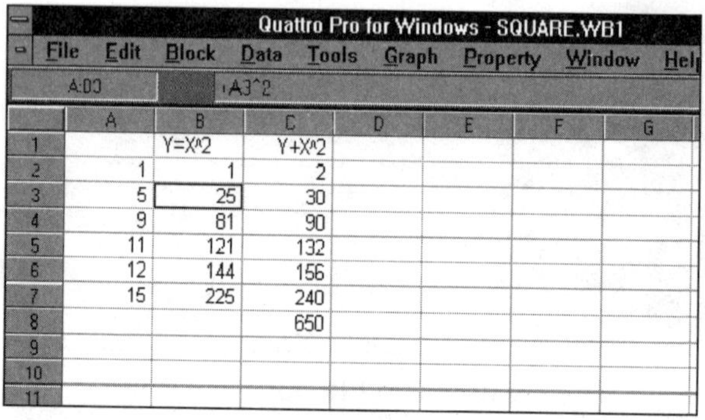

(a)

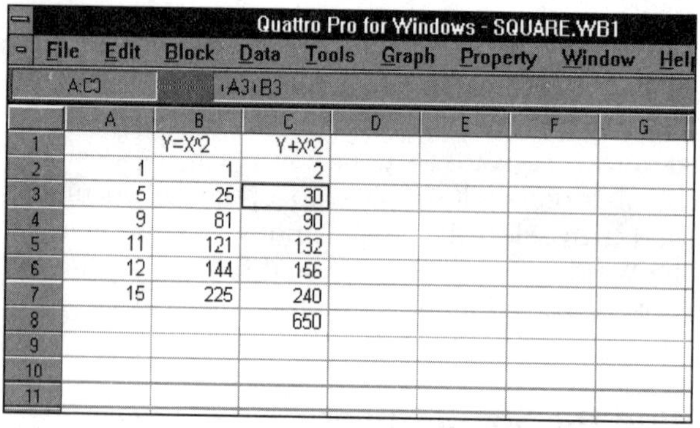

(b)

Figure 7.8(a–b) The currently active cell is displayed in the Input line directly above the main spreadsheet area. Note that the cell address A:B3 indicates page A, column B, row 3.

The bottom of the spreadsheet shows the *status bar,* which provides information on what commands are currently active in the spreadsheet. For example, when the status bar displays "Edit," that means you are in the input line and not in the main spreadsheet. The status bar displays "Ready" when you are in the spreadsheet and can enter data.

Moving around the Spreadsheet

Most work can be done directly in the main spreadsheet area. You move from cell to cell with the Arrow keys and other navigation keys as described in the next paragraph. You enter new data by simply typing directly in the cell and then pressing the Enter key or moving the navigation keys to the next cell. You can replace the contents of a cell simply by moving to the cell and typing over the contents of the cell. Note, however, that your typing first appears in the input line rather than in the cell itself until you either press Enter or move the active cell. Pressing the Esc key will cancel whatever you entered into the cell, leaving the cell's original contents unchanged.

Moving from cell to cell in a spreadsheet is analogous to moving from character to character in a word processing document. The Arrow keys move one cell at a time. Pressing Ctrl+Left Arrow or Ctrl+Right Arrow moves one screen to the left or right, respectively. Pressing Ctrl+Home brings you to the beginning of the spreadsheet. The PgUp and PgDn keys move one screen up or down. Pressing Ctrl+PgUp or Ctrl+PgDn moves one page up or down.

Selecting Cells in the Worksheet

As with navigation, selecting cells is similar to selecting text. Pressing the Shift key simultaneously with the arrow keys or other navigation key combinations will select the cells as they are traversed. Pressing an Arrow key without the Shift key cancels the selection.

Another selection method is to press Shift+F7 to turn on Extended Block Selection mode and then simply move the navigation keys as you would normally (without holding down the Shift key). The cells that you traverse with the navigation keys are automatically selected. (Pressing Esc cancels Select mode.)

You can also select cells by reference or range name using the Goto command in the Edit menu or by pressing the F5 key from the main document window, which opens the Goto dialog box shown in Figure 7.9. The Goto dialog box displays the available cell range names or block names as they are called in Quattro Pro. You can name blocks using the Name command in the Block menu. For more information on naming blocks, consult Quattro Pro's user's guide.

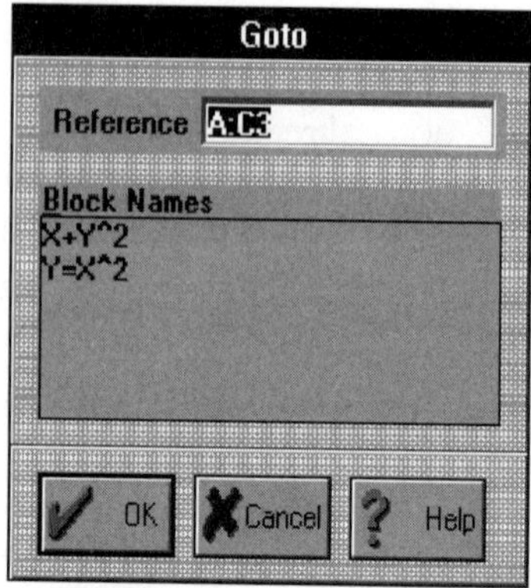

Figure 7.9 The Goto dialog box.

Editing from the Input Line

You use Edit mode to edit the contents of a cell rather than completely replacing the contents, which you can do by typing over the existing cell contents. All text editing takes place in the input line. To edit a cell's contents, move to the desired cell and press the F2 key to activate Edit mode. When the input line is active, two boxes denoted by a check and an X appear in the input line. These boxes can be used by mouse users to complete or cancel an editing operation, simply by clicking on either box. From the keyboard, pressing Esc cancels the operation and returns you to the main cell area. Pressing the Enter key returns you to the cell with your editing changes reflected in the cell. An active input line is shown in Figure 7.10. Note that the status bar at the bottom of the screen displays the word, "Edit," when Edit mode is active.

Editing in the input bar is similar to editing in a word processor. The insertion point is a vertical bar that can be moved with the Arrow keys. Pressing Ctrl+ an Arrow key moves the insertion point one word at a time if you have the Compatible Keys option disabled as discussed earlier in this chapter. (Otherwise the insertion point moves five spaces at a time.) The Home key brings you to the beginning of the cell text. The End key brings you to the end of the text. Use the Shift key with the above navigational keystrokes to select text (e.g., Shift+Ctrl+Right Arrow selects the word to the right). The Cut, Copy, Paste, and Undo commands all work in the input line.

Quattro Pro for Windows - SQUARE.WB1

	A	B	C	D	E	F	G
1		Y=X^2	Y+X^2				
2	1	1	2				
3	5	25	30				
4	9	81	90				
5	11	121	132				
6	12	144	156				
7	15	225	240				
8			650				
9							
10							
11							
12							
13							

Figure 7.10 The input line.

DELETING TEXT IN THE INPUT LINE

The Backspace key deletes the character immediately before (to the left of) the current location of the cursor. The Del key deletes the character immediately ahead (to the right of) the cursor. Pressing Ctrl+Del deletes the word to the right of the cursor, and pressing Ctrl+Backspace deletes the word to the left of the insertion point.

To Undo your editing if you haven't pressed Enter, simply press Esc. If you have pressed Enter, open the Edit menu and select the Undo Entry command.

Working with Selected Cells

Once you have selected cells, you are obviously going to do something with them. You may want to cut, copy, and paste, perform calculations, copy formulas, create graphs, and so forth. Selected cells in Quattro Pro are called blocks and most operations are performed from the Block menu or using the Current Block command in the Property menu.

Cut, Copy, and Paste

As mentioned earlier, Quattro Pro does not support the standard Ctrl+X, Ctrl+C, Ctrl+V, and Ctrl+Z keystrokes for Cut, Copy, Paste, and Undo. Instead, you use the old DOS keystrokes, Shift+Del for Cut, Ctrl+Ins for Copy, and Shift+Ins for Paste. There is no keystroke equivalent for Undo. You must use the Undo command in the Edit menu shown in Figure 7.11.

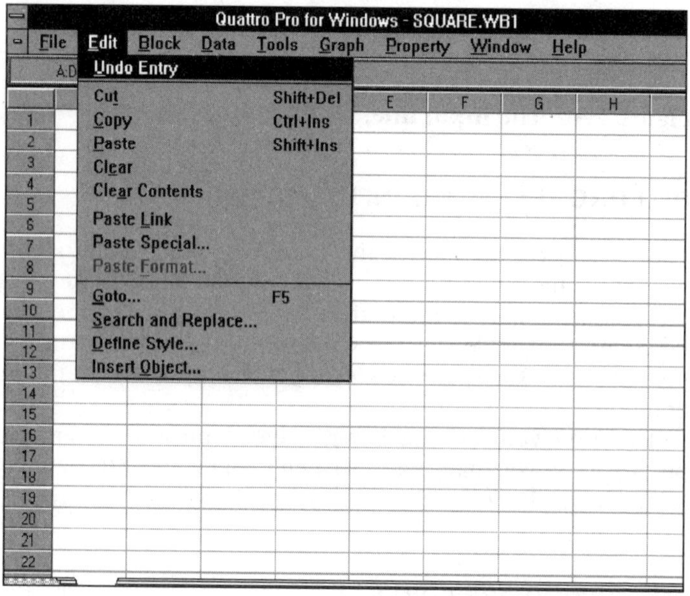

Quattro Pro for Windows - SQUARE.WB1

File   Edit   Block   Data   Tools   Graph   Property   Window   Help

Undo Entry

Cut   Shift+Del
Copy   Ctrl+Ins
Paste   Shift+Ins
Clear
Clear Contents
Paste Link
Paste Special...
Paste Format...

Goto...   F5
Search and Replace...
Define Style...
Insert Object...

Figure 7.11 The Quattro Pro Edit menu. Note that the Undo command is only accessible from the Edit menu. (There is no keyboard equivalent.)

Cutting the contents removes it from the cell or cells and places it in the Windows clipboard. (See Chapter 1 for more on the Windows clipboard.) If you wish to delete the contents without storing the deleted contents in the clipboard, you must use the Clear command in the Edit menu or press the Del key.

Copying the contents copies it to the clipboard while at the same time leaving it in the original cell location. The Copy command is particularly useful for copying formulas into additional cells, as discussed in a separate section later in this chapter.

To paste the contents into a different location or into another spreadsheet, move the active cell to where you wish to paste the contents, in either the current worksheet or another one, and press Shift+Ins to paste.

Modifying Selected Cells with the Current Object Command

The Current Object command in the Property menu opens the Active Block dialog box shown in Figures 7.12(a), (b), and (c). Note that you can open this dialog box directly from the document window by pressing the F12 key. The Active Block dialog box provides most of the commands for modifying the format and appearance of selected cells in your spreadsheet.

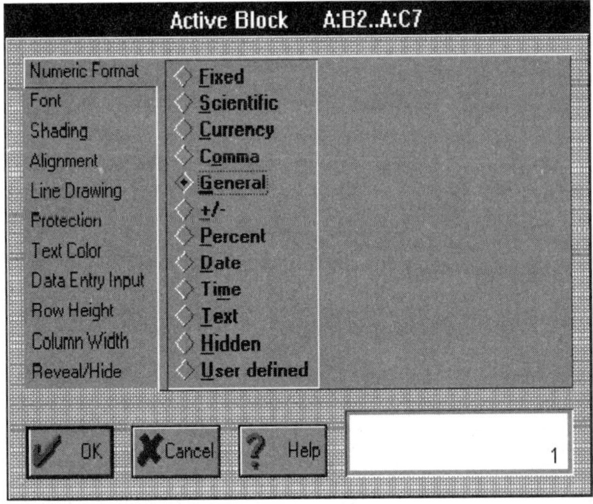

(a)

Figure 7.12(a–c) The Current Object command in the Property menu opens the Active Block dialog box, which allows you to modify the properties of selected cells. The screens show the numeric format, font, and column width categories.

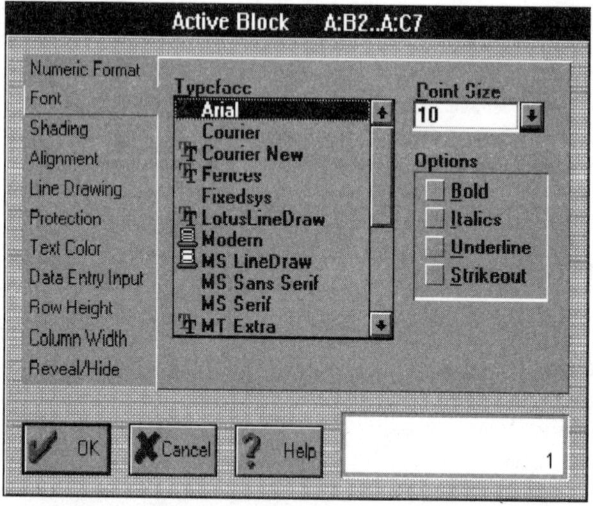

(b)

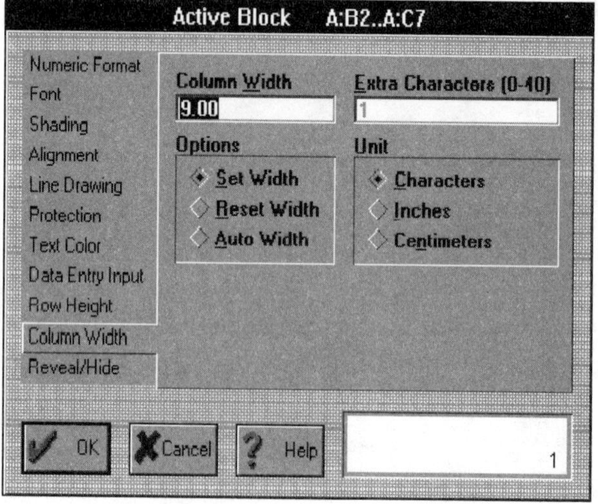

(c)

Figure 7.12(a–c) The Current Object command *(continued).*

As mentioned in the section on customizing Quattro Pro, the interface of this and the other Property menu dialog boxes does not follow Windows conventions for dialog boxes. The list on the left side of the dialog box represents the various categories that can be customized from this dialog box. You press Ctrl+PgDn to move down the category list and Ctrl+PgUp to move back up the list. Use the Arrow keys to select the available options within the category or press Alt+ the underlined letter of the desired option.

As shown in the figure, the Active Block title bar shows the currently selected cell range to which any changes will apply. The Numeric, Font, and Column Width categories are shown in the figures. The dialog box also provides an extensive array of options for customizing the appearance of selected cells.

Formulas and Calculations

Spreadsheets are most useful for performing calculations: adding up totals, multiplying cell values by other values, and so forth. And to perform calculations, you need to use formulas. Formulas must begin with one of the following characters: 0 1 2 3 4 5 6 7 8 9 + - $. (@ # $. If the formula begins with a letter (such as a cell address, for example), then start the formula with a plus sign (+). For example, Figure 7.13(a) shows a simple spreadsheet that calculates the square of the value in the first column and puts that value in the second column. The third column adds the first two columns together (y + x^2). In cell B2, the formula is "+A2^2." As shown in Figure 7.13(b), the formula in cell C2 is "+A2+B2."

```
Quattro Pro for Windows - NOTEBK3.WB1
File  Edit  Block  Data  Tools  Graph  Property  Window  Help
A:D2            'A2^2
```

	A	B	C	D	E	F	G	H
1		Y=X^2	Y+X^2					
2	1	1	2					
3	5	25	30					
4	9	81	90					
5	11	121	132					
6	12	144	156					
7	15	225	240					
8			650					
9								
10								
11								
12								
13								

Figure 7.13(a) An example of formulas used to make calculations in the spreadsheet.

	Quattro Pro for Windows - NOTEBK3.WB1						
File Edit Block Data Tools Graph Property Window Help							
A:C2		+A2+B2					

	A	B	C	D	E	F	G	H
1		Y=X^2	Y+X^2					
2	1	1	2					
3	5	25	30					
4	9	81	90					
5	11	121	132					
6	12	144	156					
7	15	225	240					
8			650					
9								
10								
11								
12								
13								
14								
15								
16								
17								
18								
19								

Figure 7.13(b) Note that formulas that begin with a letter (such as a cell address) must start with the plus sign (+).

Copying Formulas

Now, we want to replicate these formulas in the remaining cells of the spreadsheet. There are two ways to copy formulas. One is to simply select the cell or cells in which the formula or formulas exist and then press Ctrl+Ins to copy the formula. Then select the cells in which you want this same formula or block of formulas to appear, and press Shift+Ins to paste the formula. Note that you can copy multiple formulas this way. In the example, if you select both cells B2 and C2, copy them, and then select the two columns below them, and paste, each formula will be replicated with the correct cell addresses.

Another method is to use the Block Copy command. In this case, you select the formulas that you want to copy and then execute the Block Copy command. You then type in the cell range to which the formulas should be copied. For example, the dialog box in Figure 7.14 indicates that we have copied the formulas in cells B2 and C2 and want to copy them from B3 to C6. The result is shown in Figure 7.15.

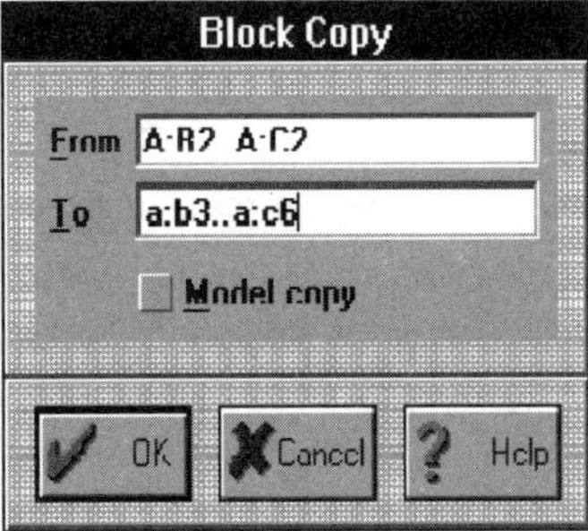

Figure 7.14 You can use the Copy command in the Block menu to copy blocks of cells or their formulas. In this case, we are copying the block for B2 to C2 to the block of B3 to C6, which is the block of cells four rows directly below B2 and C2.

Figure 7.15 The results of the Block copy.

Using @SUM for Totals

To calculate totals in Quattro Pro, use the @SUM function in the cell in which you wish to display the total. (Mouse users have the luxury of clicking on a *SpeedSum button* to do this automatically, but this feature is not available from the keyboard.) An example of using the @SUM function is shown in Figure 7.16(a). Note that if you insert additional rows in the range for which totals are calculated, these new values are automatically included and the @SUM formula is adjusted accordingly, as shown in Figure 7.16(b).

Quattro Pro for Windows - NOTEBK3.WB1

File   Edit   Block   Data   Tools   Graph   Property   Window   H

A:C7   @SUM(C2..C6)

	A	B	C	D	E	F	G
1		Y=X^2	Y+X^2				
2	1	1	2				
3	5	25	30				
4	9	81	90				
5	12	144	156				
6	15	225	240				
7			518				
8							
9							

(a)

Quattro Pro for Windows - NOTEBK3.WB1

File   Edit   Block   Data   Tools   Graph   Property   Window

A:C0   @SUM(C2..C7)

	A	B	C	D	E	F	G
1		Y=X^2	Y+X^2				
2	1	1	2				
3	5	25	30				
4	9	81	90				
5	11	121	132				
6	12	144	156				
7	15	225	240				
8			650				
9							
10							

(b)

Figure 7.16(a) Using the @SUM function to calculate totals. Note in (b) that we have inserted an additional row, which is automatically compensated for by the @SUM function.

The Block Menu

The Block menu shown in Figure 7.17 provides commands for manipulating selected cells. In fact, a single cell is also considered a block, so that you can use this menu without selecting cells. For example, to delete or insert a row, use the appropriate commands in the Block menu. The Move and Copy commands perform essentially the same functions as Copy and Paste, but allow you to enter specific cell addresses.

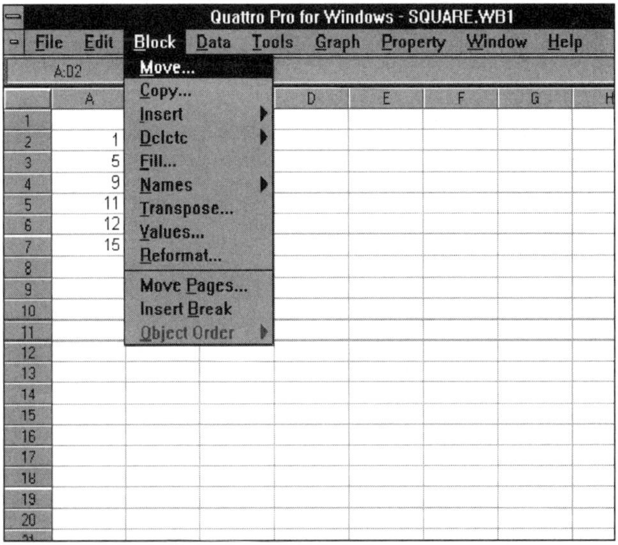

Figure 7.17 The Block menu.

Note that you can use the Insert command shown in Figure 7.18 to insert another file into your spreadsheet. The Fill command allows you to generate a sequence and fill up a row or column of cells with the sequence. You can use a variety of parameters to specify the sequence as shown in the Block Fill dialog box in Figure 7.19.

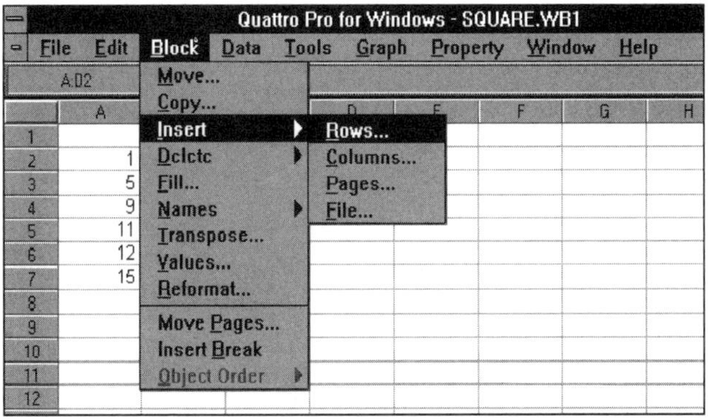

Figure 7.18 The Insert command in the Block menu.

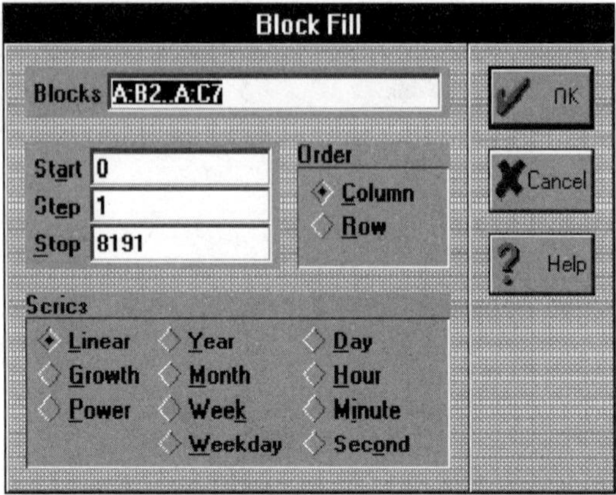

Figure 7.19 The Block Fill command allows you to create sequences in your spreadsheet. For example, you can quickly create a row with the 12 months of the year using the Month option in the dialog box. You can also use Quattro Pro formulas to create sequences.

Use the Names command to name blocks of cells. Use the Transpose command to switch columns to rows and rows to columns. Use the Values command to only store the values of cells but not the formulas. The Reformat command allows you to edit blocks of text like you would in a word processor.

Graphs

Keyboard users suffer a major disadvantage when it comes to graphing in Quattro Pro. The graph interface is really optimized for mouse users. Nevertheless, it is possible to create and insert graphs in your spreadsheet. Figure 7.20 shows a sample spreadsheet with an inserted bar graph.

To create a graph, select the cell ranges that you want to graph and then press Alt+G to open the Graphics menu. Select New to open the Graph New dialog box shown in Figure 7.21. Once you have created the graph you can open the Graph menu again to change the graph type, edit the graph, insert or delete it from a spreadsheet, and so forth.

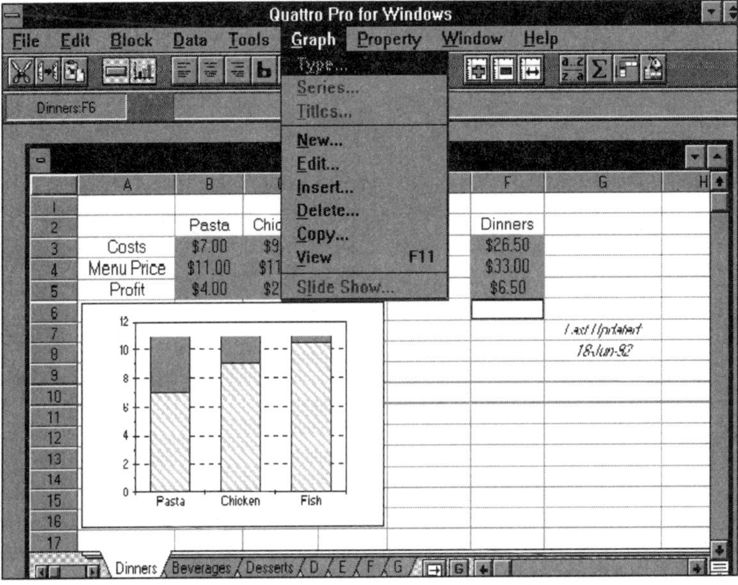

Figure 7.20 The Quattro Pro Graph menu.

Figure 7.21 The New Graph dialog box.

Working with Databases

While spreadsheets are mainly known for their ability to work with rows and columns of numbers, they can also be used effectively as databases if the spreadsheet application supports this function. Most full-featured spreadsheet programs, including Quattro Pro, allow you to work with the spreadsheet as you would with a flat file database, treating each cell as a database field and each row as a database record. Among other data manipulation functions provided in the Data menu, shown in Figure 7.22, Quattro Pro provides functions for entering data into a simple data entry form, performing queries, and sorting records.

To create a database in Quattro Pro, type in the fieldnames in the first row of the spreadsheet area that you will use for the database. (This can be the entire spreadsheet or a particular range of cells within the spreadsheet.) Enter data into the fields below each field name to create a database record. Select all the cells and then execute the Query command from the Data menu. You are then presented with a dialog box in which you can specify the Database block range. You should also initialize the fieldnames.

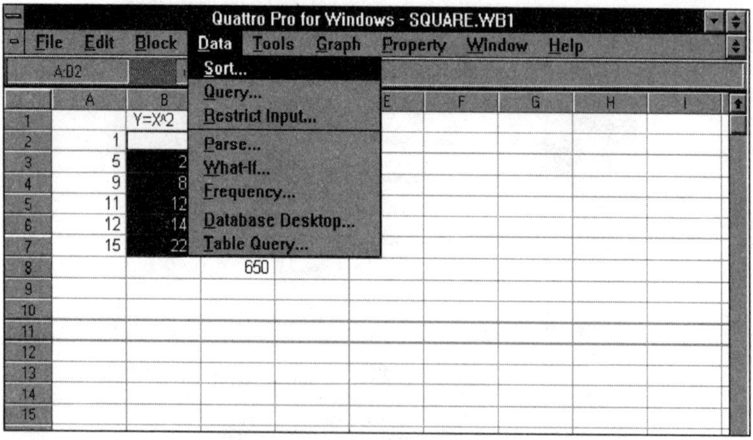

Figure 7.22 The Data menu.

An example of creating a database is shown in Figure 7.23. Here we have entered the fieldnames and adjusted the column widths using the Column Width command to accommodate the data.

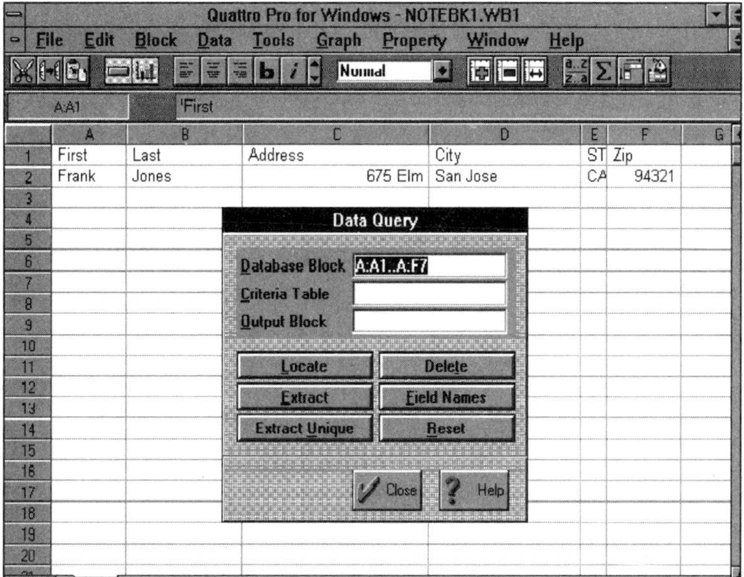

Fig 7.23 An example of a database. Use the Data Query dialog box to specify the block containing the database.

It should be noted that Quattro Pro also includes the so-called Database Desktop, which allows you to access Paradox and dBASE databases and exchange data with them directly from Quattro Pro. For more information, see the Database Desktop Guide in the Quattro Pro documentation.

Macros and Other Tools

As shown in Figure 7.24, the Tools menu provides an array of commands for manipulating data and performing calculations. Among these commands is the Macro command, which allows you to record and play command sequences. Quattro Pro includes an extensive macro language and an extensive library of functions which can be included in your spreadsheet applications. For more information, consult the "Building Spreadsheet Applications Guide" in the Quattro Pro documentation.

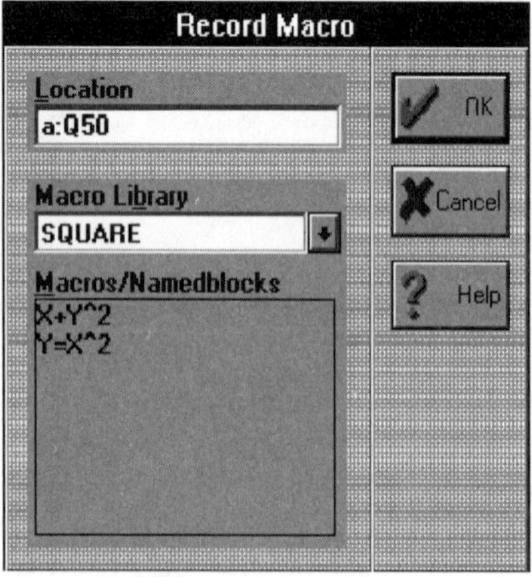

Figure 7.24 The Tools menu.

Figure 7.25 The Record Macro dialog box.

Within the scope of this book, we can briefly discuss recording your own keyboard sequences as macros. To do so, open the

Record Macro dialog box using the Macro command in the Tools menu as shown in Figure 7.25. You must specify a block in your spreadsheet where the macro will be stored. You should select a single cell that has no cells containing data below it. (Select a cell address such as A:Q50, for example.) Quattro Pro will fill additional cells as needed to store the macro commands. (If you select a specific block of cells, the macro will stop recording once the block is full.) After selecting the block and pressing Enter in the record macro dialog box, you can record the macro. Open the Macro command again to stop recording. Then move to the cell you specified for storing the macro (A:Q50, for example) and name the block using the Block Names command. For more information, see the "Building Spreadsheet Applications Guide" in the Quattro Pro documentation.

Lotus 1-2-3   8

*A concise list of Lotus 1-2-3
keystrokes begins on page 284.*

This chapter covers the basic keystrokes for Lotus 1-2-3. Although Visicalc was the first spreadsheet on the market, Lotus 1-2-3 is the program that set the standard. While 1-2-3 completely dominated the PC spreadsheet market for many years, it is now facing strong competition in the Windows arena from Microsoft Excel and Borland's Quattro Pro. Nevertheless, 1-2-3 is still the most widely used spreadsheet product in the world. It has undergone many revisions and enhancements since its introduction nearly ten years ago.

As of this writing, Lotus is preparing a new version of 1-2-3 for Windows. However, the keystrokes described here will still be applicable. In fact, most of the improvements in the new version will be of greater interest to mouse users, since they will involve features like "buttons," which are inaccessible from the keyboard.

Lotus 1-2-3 is generally a Windows-compliant application, although, like Quattro Pro, version 1.0 does not support Ctrl+X, Ctrl+C, Ctrl+V, and Ctrl+Z (for Cut, Copy, Paste, and Undo). We expect that this deficiency will be corrected in the new version of the product. But in virtually all other aspects, 1-2-3 is consistent with the Windows interface, using the Windows menu bar and supporting the Windows clipboard and windowing system. Naturally, 1-2-3 is also designed to take advantage of the mouse.

In the most recent feature wars among spreadsheet applications, the emphasis has been on mouse-driven features such as toolbars and button bars, similar to those we encountered in the chapters on the word processors. Likewise, 1-2-3 has some features that work only with the mouse. Fortunately, 1-2-3 provides equivalent keystroke functionality for virtually every mouse feature. As in the earlier chapters, however, we'll start off by examining what can't be done from the keyboard.

What You Can't Do from the Keyboard

The horizontal and vertical scroll bars do not work from the keyboard. You can duplicate the function of the scroll bars with Arrow keys and other navigation keys, as described later in this chapter.

Like Ami Pro, 1-2-3 features an optional graphical *SmartIcons bar,* which allows mouse users to point and click on icons representing frequently used commands such as opening, printing, and closing files, or activating other 1-2-3 features such as changing fonts or copying cells, for example. The SmartIcons bar includes customizable buttons so that users can add other commands or macros represented by icons. The SmartIcons bar is shown in Figure 8.1.

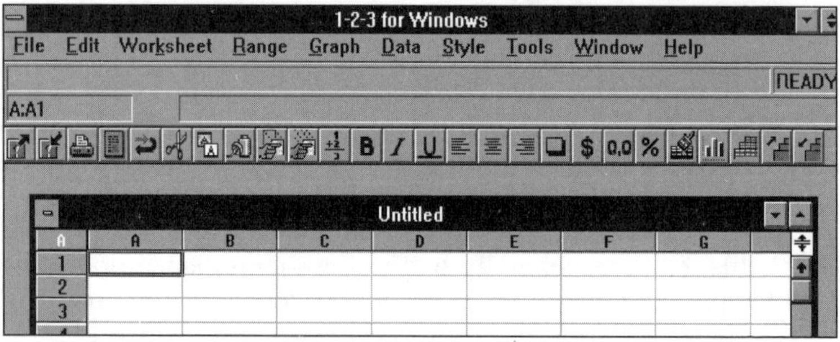

Figure 8.1 The SmartIcons bar.

Most, if not all, of the functionality of the SmartIcons can be duplicated from the keyboard using keystroke sequences or the 1-2-3 menu options. If you are strictly using the keyboard, you can reclaim some space on the screen by removing the SmartIcons. This is accomplished by hiding SmartIcons using the SmartIcons command in the Tools menu (Alt+T,I) which is covered in more detail in the next section on customizing 1-2-3.

The 1-2-3 Keyboard

The 1-2-3 keyboard generally conforms to the Windows keyboard interface. As mentioned earlier, the Ctrl+X, Ctrl+V, Ctrl+C, and Ctrl+Z functions are not yet implemented, and the product makes limited use of the function keys in comparison to Excel.

Veteran DOS 1-2-3 users will be pleased to know that the old slash key (/) still works in 1-2-3 for Windows, bringing up a window called "1-2-3 Classic" with the standard DOS 1-2-3 commands, as shown in Figure 8.2. While we think it's best to move on and learn to work with the Windows interface, if you're hopelessly stuck in your old ways, you can use the "1-2-3 Classic" commands.

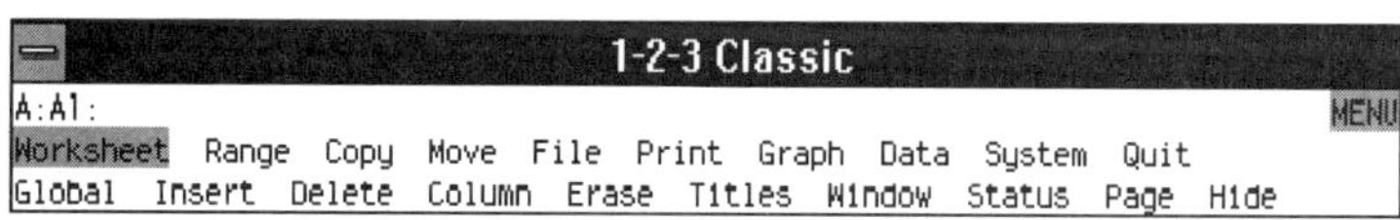

Figure 8.2 The 1-2-3 Classic window.

Customizing 1-2-3

A useful customization option in 1-2-3 is to remove the SmartIcons bar. You can do this from the Tools menu by selecting SmartIcons, as shown in Figure 8.3(a), which opens the dialog box shown in Figure 8.3(b). Then check the Hide Palette box. (Press Alt+H to do this.)

The User Setup command in the Tools menu provides options for customizing international settings such as the default currency or the date and time format, as well as settings for recalculation and options such as enabling the Undo function. The User Setup dialog box is shown in Figure 8.4. Note the International and Recalculation buttons (press Alt+I and Alt+R, respectively), which open additional dialog boxes.

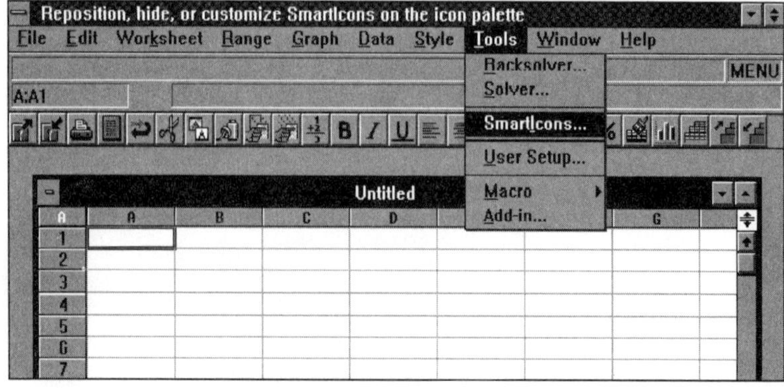

(a)

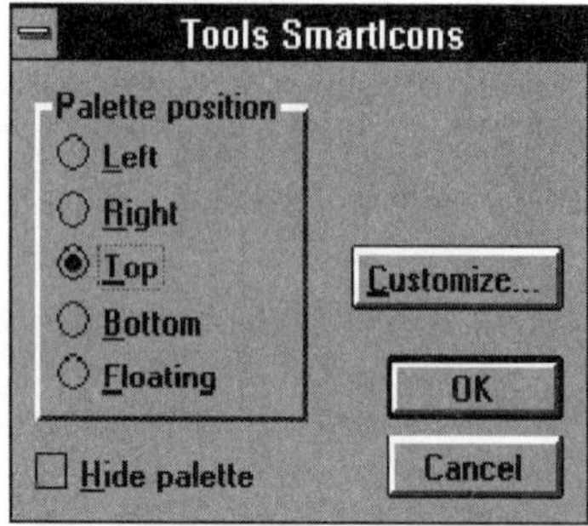

(b)

Figure 8.3(a–b) The Tools menu allows you to hide the SmartIcons bar.

Figure 8.4 The User Setup dialog box.

The Global Settings command in the Worksheet menu (Alt+K,G), shown in Fig. 8.5(a), allows you to set global worksheet formats: whether to display blanks in cells having the value zero, alignment of labels, column width, and so forth. The Global Settings dialog box is shown in Figure 8.5(b).

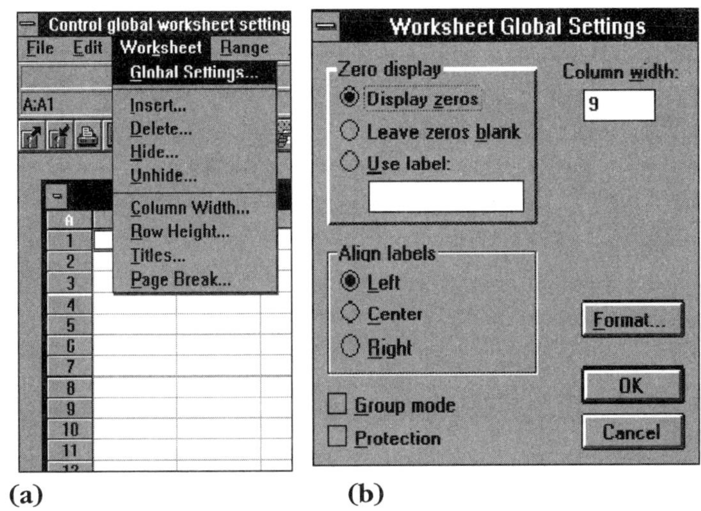

(a)   (b)

Figure 8.5(a) The Global Settings option in the Worksheet menu. (b) Settings for global worksheet formats.

You can also customize the display options in 1-2-3 such as background and foreground colors, cell borders, and so forth, by selecting the Display Options command in the Windows menu (Alt+W,D), shown in Figure 8.6(a). The Display Options dialog box is shown in Figure 8.6(b).

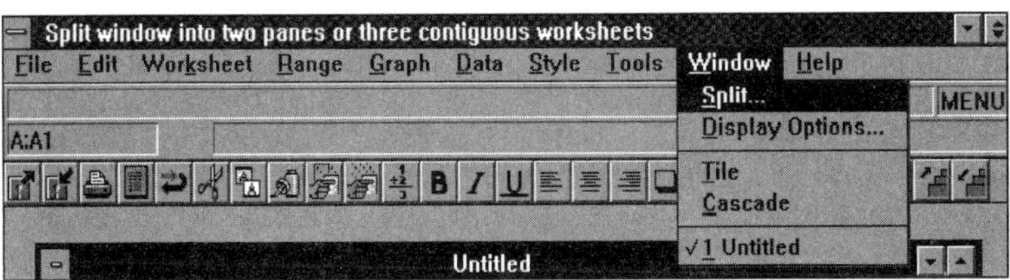

Figure 8.6(a) The Display option in the Window menu.

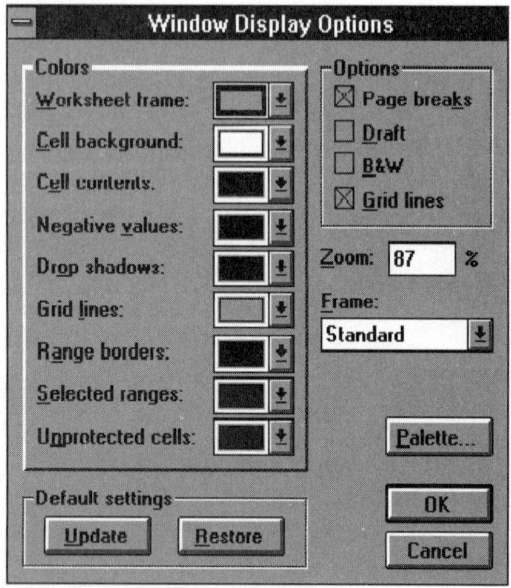

Figure 8.6(b) Settings for customizing display characteristics.

Getting Started in 1-2-3

1-2-3 behaves very much like other Windows applications, and much of the product will look familiar to you if you have mastered the basic Windows navigational and menu keystrokes discussed in Chapter 1.

A typical 1-2-3 document window is shown in Figure 8.7. You access the 1-2-3 menu bar like you would any other Windows menu bar. Pressing Alt activates the menu bar. Alt+Spacebar brings up the application Control menu, which we discussed in Chapter 1. Alt+Hyphen brings up the document Control menu shown in Figure 8.7.

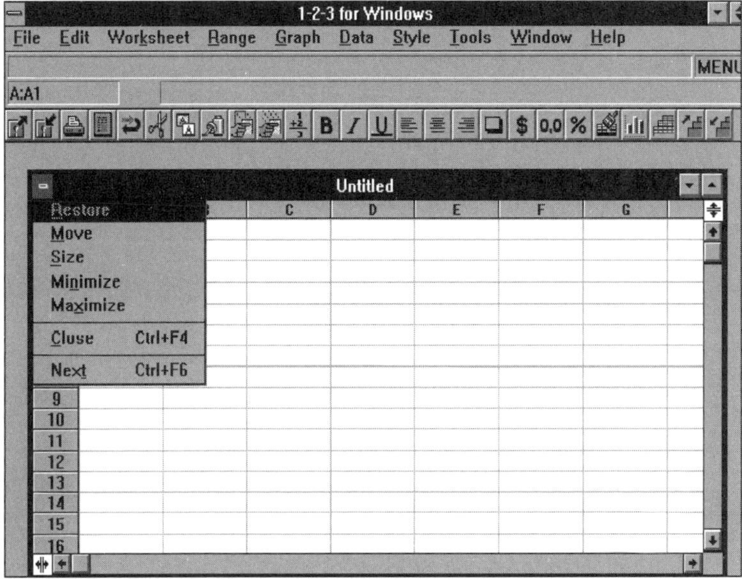

Figure 8.7 A typical 1-2-3 document window with the document Control menu open.

Note the additional option in the document Control menu called Next, which stands for next window. The Next Window option (Alt+Hyphen,T or Ctrl+F6 from the document window) switches to the next document window if you are working with multiple documents. (See the next section on working with files.)

Alt+F opens the File menu, Alt+E opens the Edit menu, and so forth. As in other Windows applications, the menu bar must be deactivated for keystrokes to take effect in the main document window. (If one of the menu bar options is highlighted, the menu bar is still active.) Press the Esc key to deactivate the menu bar.

It should be noted that 1-2-3 relies heavily on dialog boxes for implementing most menu commands. As you may recall from Chapter 1, the easiest way to move to various fields in a dialog box is by pressing Alt+ the underlined letter in the heading of the field.

Working with Files

Lotus 1-2-3 primarily uses the .WK3 file type. WK3 files can consist either of a single worksheet or multiple worksheets. Multiple worksheets stored in a single file are the equivalent of the notebook concept in Quattro Pro, in which individual worksheets are referred to as pages. While Lotus doesn't call them pages, you work with multiple worksheets the same way you work with notebook pages in Quattro Pro.

Unless you specify a file, 1-2-3 opens with a blank worksheet and is ready for you to begin entering data. As we learned in the first two chapters, you can open files associated with an application directly by selecting the file's icon in Program Manager or the filename in File Manager and pressing Enter. The associated application opens automatically to display the file. If you open 1-2-3 without specifying a file (by selecting the 1-2-3 icon or the file \123W\123W.EXE and pressing Enter), you start with a blank worksheet.

To open a file in 1-2-3, you press Alt+F to open the File menu, shown in Figure 8.8. Note that the Open command opens an existing file in a new window. If you want the file to appear in the current window, you must either use the Cut, Copy, and Paste functions to copy the data from a different window into the current window, or use the Combine From or Import From commands in the File menu.

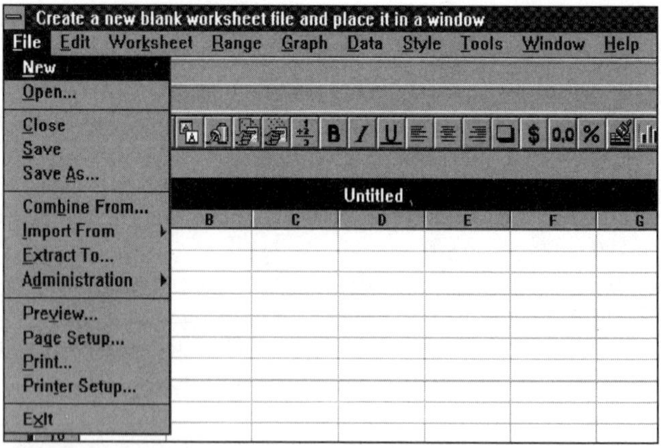

Figure 8.8 The 1-2-3 File menu.

WORKING WITH MULTIPLE FILES

You can work with multiple documents in one 1-2-3 session. However, only one document can be active at a time. To switch from one document to another, the easiest method is to press Ctrl+F6 until you reach the desired window. You can also press Alt+Hyphen to open the document Control menu and then select the Next Window option. Finally, you can open the Window menu (Alt+W), and select from the list of open documents displayed in the menu list.

Navigating the Worksheet

There are two distinct regions in a worksheet: *the contents box,* in which you perform edit operations, and the *main worksheet area,* where the cells of the worksheet are located. A typical worksheet is shown in Figure 8.9(a). The currently active cell is indicated by the shaded border around the cell. In the example in Figure 8.9(a), the currently active cell is B3. The contents box is the area immediately above the spreadsheet's title bar, indicating the currently active cell and the contents of the cell. In the example, the contents of cell B3 is the formula "A3^2." If we move to cell A3, note the corresponding change in the contents box as shown in Figure 8.9(b).

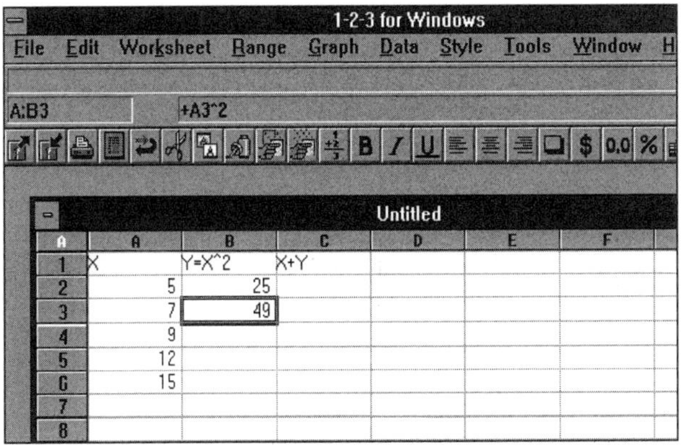

Figure 8.9(a) The active cell is highlighted.

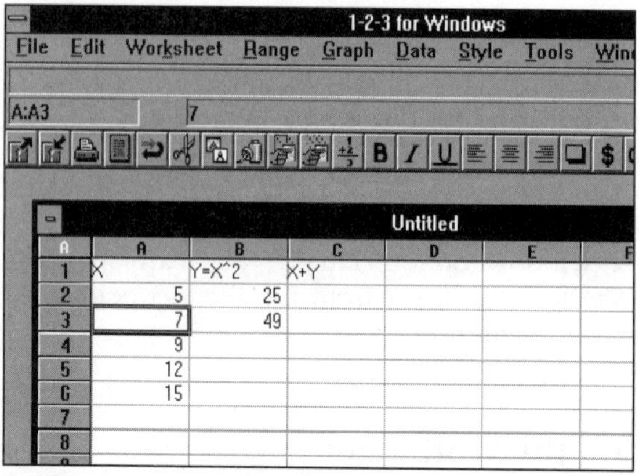

Figure 8.9(b) The cell formula, if any, is displayed in the contents box above the spreadsheet.

Directly above the contents box in the upper right corner is the mode indicator, which provides information on what commands are currently active in the spreadsheet. For example, when the mode indicator displays "Edit," that means you are in the contents box and not in the main worksheet. The mode indicator displays "Ready" when you are in the spreadsheet and can enter data.

Moving around the Worksheet

Most work can be done directly in the main worksheet area. You move from cell to cell with the Arrow keys and other navigation keys as described in the next paragraph. You enter new data by simply typing directly in the cell and then pressing the Enter key or using the navigation keys to move to the next cell. You can replace the contents of a cell simply by moving to the cell and typing over the contents of the cell. Note, however, that your typing first appears in the contents box rather than in the cell itself until you either press Enter or move to another cell. Pressing the Esc key will cancel whatever you entered into the cell, leaving the cell's original contents unchanged.

Moving from cell to cell in a spreadsheet is analogous to moving from character to character in a word processing document.

The Arrow keys move the cursor one cell at a time. Pressing Ctrl+Left Arrow or Ctrl+Right Arrow moves one screen to the left or right, respectively. Pressing Ctrl+Home brings you to the beginning of the spreadsheet. The PgUp and PgDn keys move one screen up or down. Pressing Ctrl+PgUp or Ctrl+PgDn moves one worksheet up or down.

Selecting Cells in the Worksheet

As with navigation, selecting cells is similar to selecting text. Pressing down the Shift key simultaneously with the Arrow keys or other navigation key combinations will select the cells as they are traversed. Pressing an Arrow key without the Shift key cancels the selection.

Another selection method is to press the F4 key to turn on what is called Point mode, and then simply move the navigation keys as you would normally (without holding down the Shift key). The cells that you traverse with the navigation keys are automatically selected. (Pressing Esc cancels Point mode.)

You can also select cells by reference or range name using the Go To command in the Range menu (Alt+R,G) or by pressing the F5 key from the main document window, which opens the Go To dialog box shown in Figure 8.10. The Go To dialog box displays the available cell range names. You can name ranges using the Name command in the Range menu. For more information on naming blocks, consult the 1-2-3 user's guide.

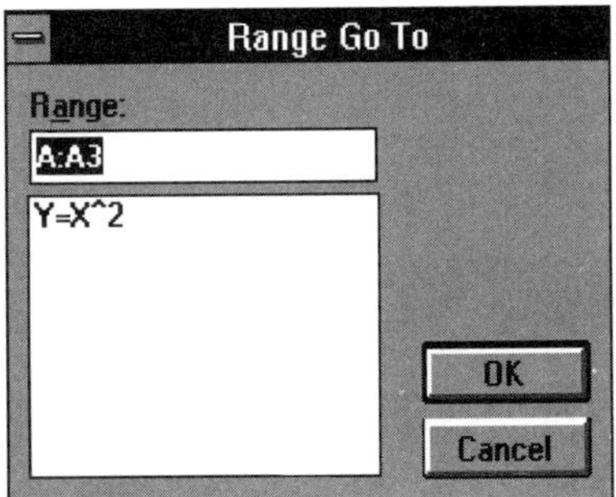

Figure 8.10 The Go To dialog box.

Editing in the Contents Box

You use the contents box to edit the contents of a cell, rather than completely replacing the contents (which you can do by typing over the existing cell contents). To use the contents box for editing, move to the desired cell and press the F2 key to activate the contents box. When the contents box is active, two boxes, called the *Enter box* and the *Cancel box,* appear in the contents box. The enter box is denoted by a check and the cancel box by an X. These boxes can be used by mouse users to complete or cancel an editing operation, simply by clicking on either box. From the keyboard, pressing Esc cancels the operation and returns you to the main cell area. Pressing the Enter key returns you to the cell with your editing changes reflected in the cell. An active contents box is shown in Figure 8.11. Note that the mode indicator at the top right of the screen displays the word "Edit" when the contents box is active.

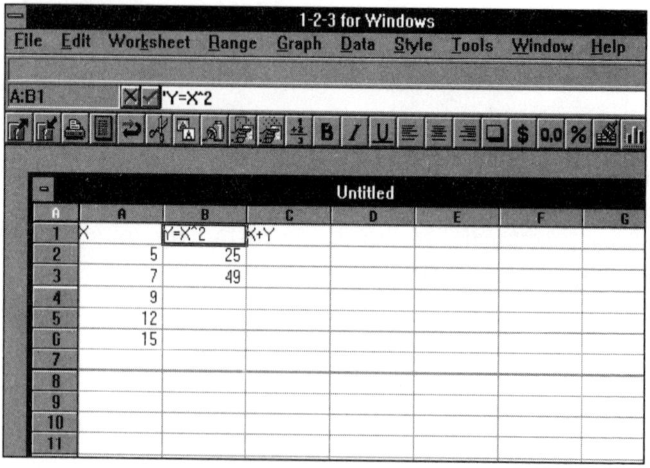

Figure 8.11 An active contents box.

Editing in the contents box is just like editing in a Windows-compliant word processor. The insertion point is a vertical bar and can be moved with the Arrow keys. Pressing Ctrl+Right Arrow or Ctrl+Left Arrow moves the insertion point one word at a time. The Home key brings you to the beginning of the cell text. The End key brings you to the end of the text. Use the Shift key with the above navigational keystrokes to select text (e.g., Shift+Ctrl+Right Arrow selects the word to the right). The Cut, Copy, and Paste commands (Shift+Del for Cut, Ctrl+Ins for Copy, Shift+Ins for Paste) all work in the contents box. The Undo function (Alt+Backspace) works after you have pressed Enter to insert the contents in the cell and then want to undo the insertion. However, to undo editing while still in the contents box, you'll have to press Esc and then F2 to start over again.

Note that Ctrl+X, Ctrl+C, Ctrl+V, and Ctrl+Z are almost certainly going to be supported in future versions of the product.

DELETING TEXT IN THE CONTENTS BOX

The Backspace key deletes the character immediately before (to the left of) the current location of the cursor. The Del key deletes the character immediately ahead (to the right) of the cursor. Pressing Ctrl+Del deletes the word to the right of the cursor, while pressing Ctrl+Backspace deletes the word to the left of the insertion point.

Working with Selected Cells

Once you have selected cells, you are obviously going to do something with them. You may want to cut, copy, and paste, perform calculations, copy formulas, create graphs, and so forth. Selected cells in 1-2-3 are called *ranges,* and most operations are performed on ranges of cells. Commands that apply to ranges can be found in all the menu selections in 1-2-3.

For example, the Style menu (Alt+S) provides commands for modifying the appearance of selected cells. The Range menu (Alt+R) provides commands for naming selected cells as ranges, changing numeric format, and so forth. The Data menu (Alt+D) provides commands for numerical analysis and for working with databases.The Worksheet menu (Alt+W) does not apply to selected cell ranges but to the entire worksheet or worksheets, providing commands for inserting and deleting worksheets, inserting titles and page breaks, setting row height and column width, and so forth.

Cut, Copy, and Paste

As mentioned earlier, 1-2-3 version 1.0 does not support the standard Ctrl+X, Ctrl+C, Ctrl+V, and Ctrl+Z keystrokes for Cut, Copy, Paste, and Undo. Instead, you use the old DOS keystrokes: Shift+Del for Cut, Ctrl+Ins for Copy, Shift+Ins for Paste, and Alt+Backspace for Undo. You can also use the Edit menu (Alt+E) to perform these operations, as shown in Figure 8.12.

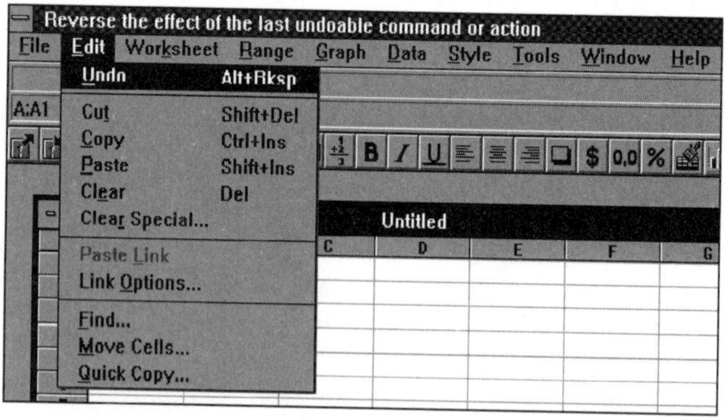

Figure 8.12 The 1-2-3 Edit menu.

Cutting the cell or range contents removes it from the cell or cells and places it in the Windows clipboard. (See Chapter 1 for more on the Windows clipboard.) If you wish to delete the contents without storing the deleted contents in the clipboard, you must use the Clear command in the Edit menu (Alt+E,E) or press the Del key.

Copying the contents of a cell places a copy in the clipboard while at the same time leaving it in the original cell location. The Copy command is particularly useful for copying formulas into additional cells, as discussed in a separate section later in this chapter. To paste the contents into a different location or into another spreadsheet, move the active cell indicator to where you wish to paste the contents, in either the current document or another one, and press Shift+Ins to paste. You can also use the Quick Copy command in the Edit menu (Alt+E,Q) to copy the selected cells to another cell address, as shown in Figure 8.13.

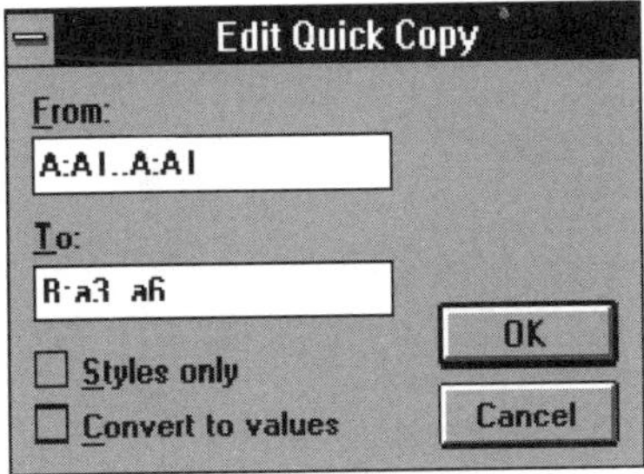

Figure 8.13 The Quick Copy command in the Edit menu.

Modifying Selected Cells with the Style Menu

The Style menu shown in Figure 8.14 provides commands for modifying the appearance of selected cells. (Press Alt+S to open the Style menu.) The Font and Alignment dialog boxes are shown in Figure 8.15(a) and 8.15(b). There are also commands for applying borders and shading to selected cells. Note the check boxes in the Font dialog box for specifying bold, italics, or underlining. In this version, there are no keyboard shortcuts for applying these attributes. To apply boldface, press Alt+B in the Font dialog box to check the Bold box.

Figure 8.14 The 1-2-3 Style menu.

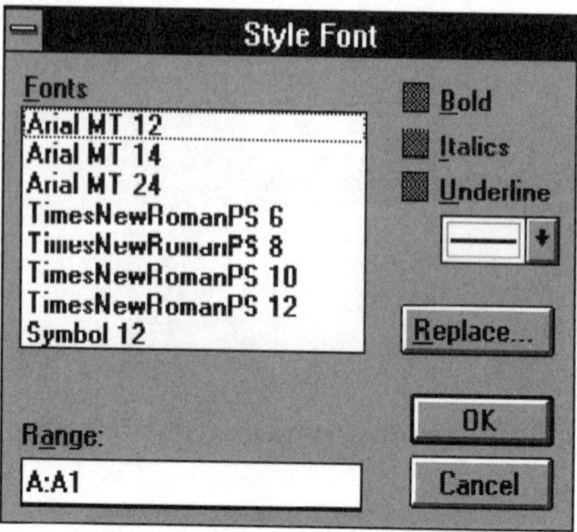

(a)

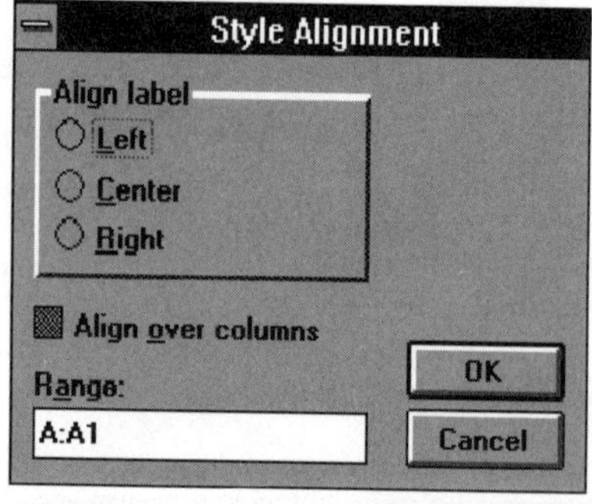

(b)

Figure 8.15(a) The Font command in the Style menu. (b) The Alignment command in the Style menu.

Setting the Column Width for Selected Cells

Although the command is in the Worksheet menu (see Fig. 8.5a), you can use the Column Width command to set the column width for selected columns rather than for the entire worksheet. The Column Width command opens the dialog box shown in Figure 8.16.

Figure 8.16 The Column Width command in the Worksheet menu.

Formulas and Calculations

Spreadsheets are most useful for performing calculations: adding up totals, multiplying cell values by other values, and so forth. And to perform calculations, you need to use formulas. Formulas must begin with a plus sign (+). For example, Figure 8.17(a) shows a simple spreadsheet that calculates the square of the value in the first column and puts that value in the second column. The third column adds the first two columns together ($y + x^2$). In cell B2, the formula is "+A2^2." As shown in Figure 8.17(b) the formula in cell C2 is "+A2+B2."

Figure 8.17(a) The active cell is represented by a formula in the contents box.

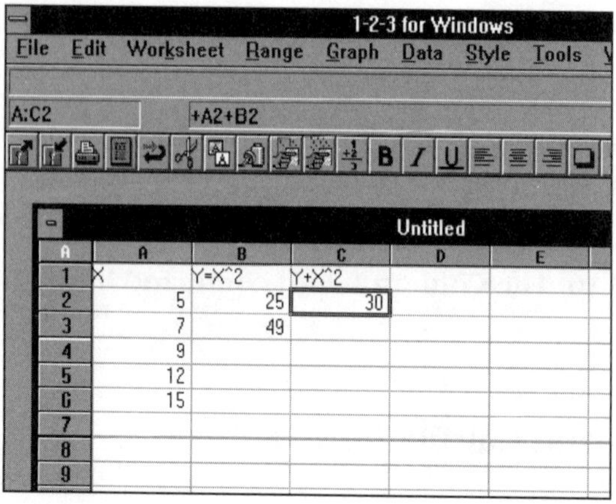

Figure 8.17(b) Formulas must start with the plus sign (+).

Copying Formulas

Now, we want to replicate these formulas in the remaining cells of the spreadsheet. There are two ways to copy formulas. One is to simply select the cell or cells in which the formula or formulas exist and then press Ctrl+Ins or Alt+E,C to copy the formula. Then select the cells in which you want this same formula or block of formulas to appear, and press Shift+Ins or Alt+E,P to paste the formula. Note that you can copy multiple formulas this way. In the example, if you select both cells B2 and C2, copy them, and then select the two columns below them, and paste, each formula will be replicated with the correct cell addresses.

Another method is to use the Quick Copy command in the Edit menu as discussed above in the section on Cut, Copy, and Paste.

Using @SUM for Totals

To calculate totals in 1-2-3, use the @SUM function in the cell in which you wish to display the total. (Mouse users have the luxury of clicking on the *SmartIcons sum icon* to do this automatically, but this feature is not available from the keyboard.) An example of using the @SUM function is shown in Figure 8.18(a). Note that if you insert additional rows in the range for which totals are calculated, these new values are automatically included and the @SUM formula is adjusted accordingly, as shown in Figure 8.18(b).

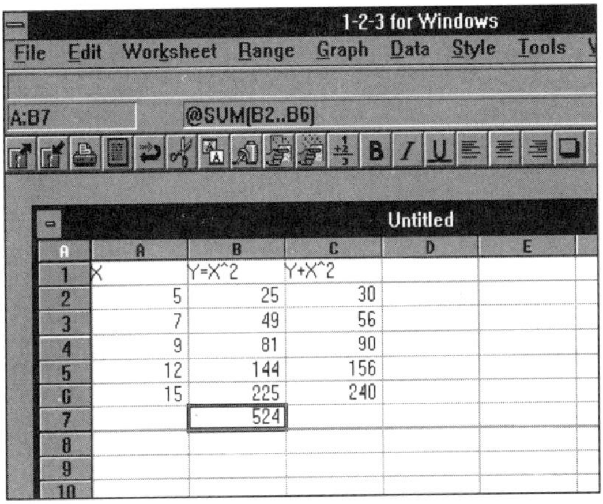

	A	B	C	D	E
1	X	Y=X^2	Y+X^2		
2	5	25	30		
3	7	49	56		
4	9	81	90		
5	12	144	156		
6	15	225	240		
7		524			
8					
9					
10					

(a)

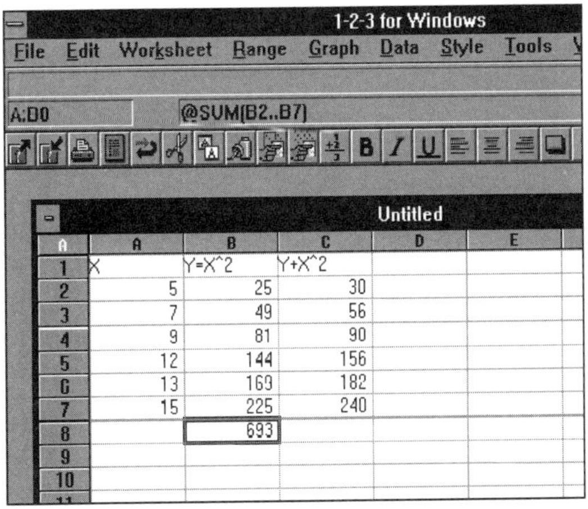

	A	B	C	D	E
1	X	Y=X^2	Y+X^2		
2	5	25	30		
3	7	49	56		
4	9	81	90		
5	12	144	156		
6	13	169	182		
7	15	225	240		
8		693			
9					
10					

(b)

Figure 8.18(a) The @SUM formula allows you to easily set up totals. (b) Note that the formula automatically adjusts the cell range if additional rows are inserted.

The Range Menu

The Range menu (Alt+R) shown in Figure 8.19 provides commands for manipulating selected cells. In fact, a single cell is also considered a range, so that you can use this menu without selecting cells.

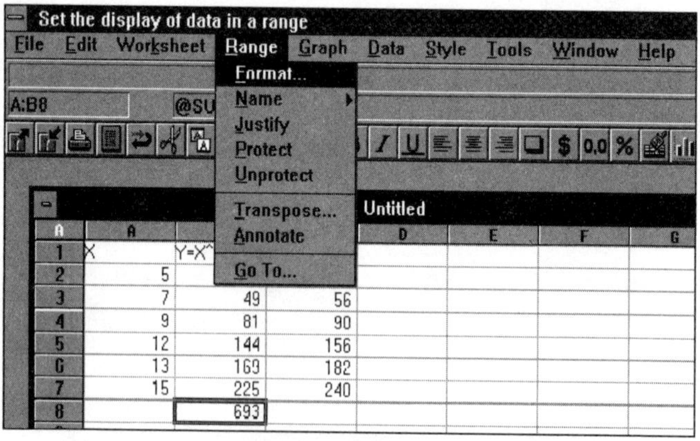

Figure 8.19 The 1-2-3 Range menu.

Use the Name command to name ranges of cells. Use the Transpose command to switch columns to rows and rows to columns. Use the Justify command to set text justification on ranges of labels (such as a row of column headings, for example). The Go To command allows you to move a specific range name or cell address as discussed earlier in the section on selecting cells.

Graphs

Keyboard users are at somewhat of a disadvantage when it comes to graphing in 1-2-3. 1-2-3 provides a SmartIcons bar specially for graphs, which is not accessible from the keyboard. The graph interface is really optimized for mouse users. Nevertheless, it is possible to create and insert graphs in your spreadsheet. Figure 8.20 shows a sample spreadsheet with an inserted line graph.

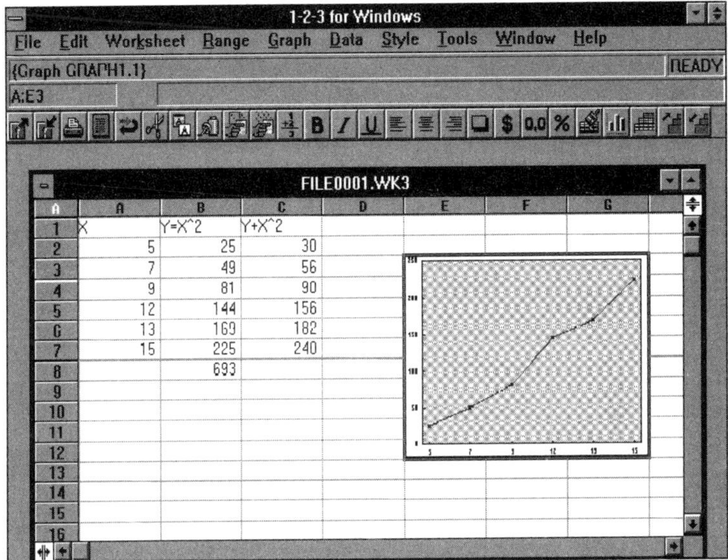

Figure 8.20 The Add to Sheet command in the Graph menu.

To create a graph, select the cell ranges that you want to graph and then press Alt+G to open the Graph menu. Select New to open the Graph New dialog box shown in Figure 8.21. Once you have created the graph, you can add it to the spreadsheet at the current cell or specified cell address using the Add to Sheet command in the Graph menu. Note that a separate menu bar opens up when you're working on a graph, with commands for graph layout, chart types, and so forth, as shown in Figure 8.22. Also note that you can also import other graphics file formats using the Import command in the Graph menu.

Figure 8.21 The Graph New dialog box.

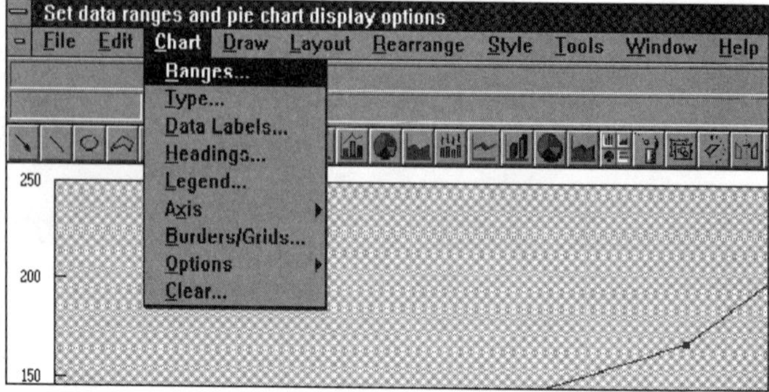

Figure 8.22 A Graph menu bar appears.

Working with Databases

While spreadsheets are mainly known for their ability to work with rows and columns of numbers, they can also be used effectively as databases if the spreadsheet application supports this function. Most full-featured spreadsheet programs, including 1-2-3, allow you to work with the spreadsheet as you would with a flat-file database, treating each cell as a database field and each row as a database record. Among other data manipulation functions provided in the Data menu (Alt+D), shown in Figure 8.23, 1-2-3 provides functions for entering data into a simple data entry form, performing queries, and sorting records.

Figure 8.23 The Data menu.

To create a database in 1-2-3, type in the fieldnames in the first row of the spreadsheet area that you will use for the database. (This can be the entire spreadsheet or a particular range of cells within the spreadsheet.) Enter data into the fields below each fieldname to create a database record. You can then select the range in which the data is entered to perform queries and data sorts. An example of creating a database is shown in Figure 8.24. Here we have entered the fieldnames and adjusted the column widths using the Column Width command to accommodate the data.

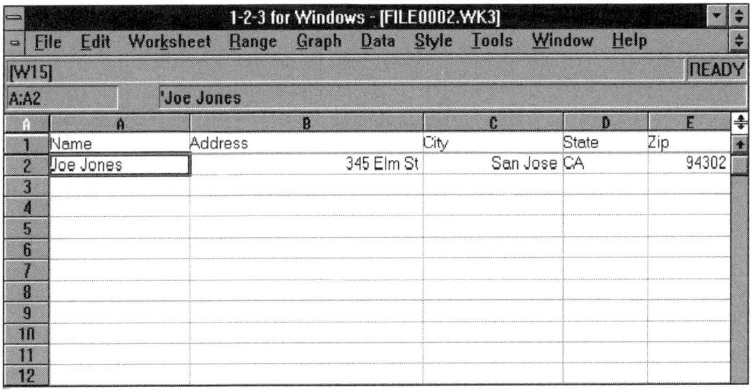

Figure 8.24 A typical database application.

It should be noted that 1-2-3 also includes the so-called *Datalens application,* which allows you to access various databases and exchange data with them directly from 1-2-3. For more information, see the Datalens documentation that comes with 1-2-3.

Macros and Other Tools

As shown in Figure 8.25, the Tools menu includes the Macro command, which allows you to record and play command sequences. 1-2-3 includes an extensive macro language and an extensive library of functions which can be included in your spreadsheet applications. For more information, consult the 1-2-3 documentation.

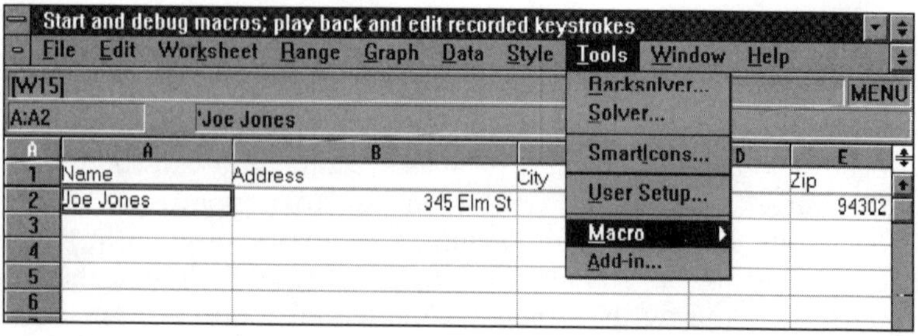

Figure 8.25 The 1-2-3 Tools menu and the Macro command.

Within the scope of this book, we can only briefly discuss recording your own keyboard sequences as macros. To do so, execute the Show Transcript option using the Macro command in the Tools menu (Alt+T+M+S) as shown in Figure 8.26. You must then make the Transcript window *active* by pressing Ctrl+F6 until the window is highlighted. Then open the Edit menu and select Clear All as shown in Figure 8.27. Note that the menu bar has a different set of options when the Transcript window is active. After clearing the window, return to your application and perform the tasks that you wish to record. These will be saved in the Transcript window. Then return to the Transcript window and select the Run command from the Macro menu. For details, see the chapter on macros in the 1-2-3 user's guide.

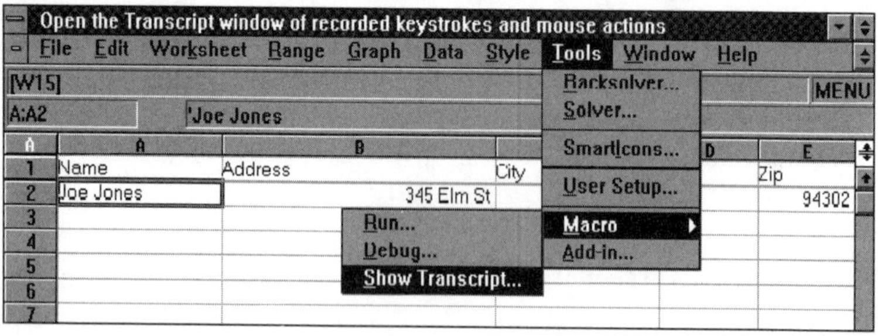

Figure 8.26 The Show Transcript command.

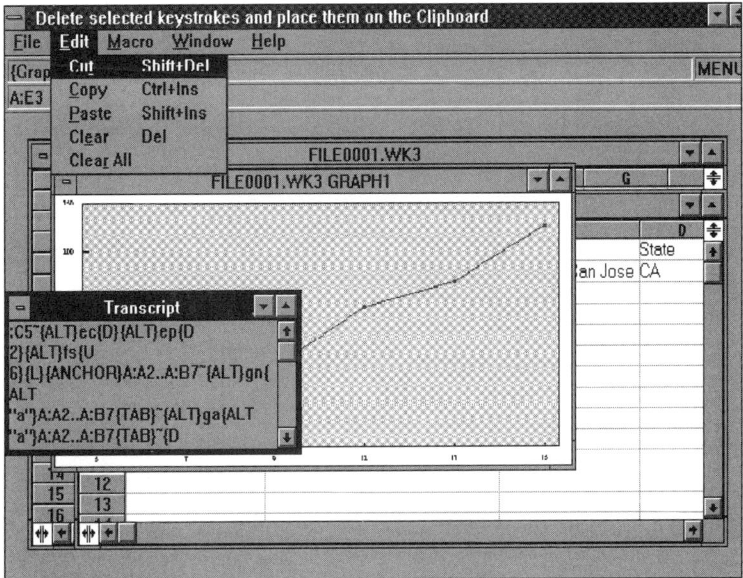

Figure 8.27 First clear the old contents of the Show Transcript window before recording.

APPENDIX: Keystroke Summary Charts

A

The tables that follow contain charts of the most common keystrokes used in Windows and the six applications discussed in this book.

The Keystroke Summary Charts are organized as follows:

WINDOWS KEYSTROKE SUMMARY CHART

General System

Help	F1 *or* Alt+H
Task List	Ctrl+Esc

Menus

Activate menu bar	Alt
Move through menu bar	Left or Right Arrow
Open highlighted menu	Enter
Cancel menu or operation	Esc
Move through menu list	Up or Down Arrow
Activate highlighted menu item	Enter
Directly open menu with underlined letter	Alt+<u>menu letter</u>
Directly activate menu item with underlined letter	Alt+<u>menu letter,item letter</u>

Document versus Application Windows

Move between group windows or icons	Ctrl+F6 *or* Ctrl+Tab
Move between icons *within* a group	Arrow
Open (run) highlighted application icon	Enter

Open highlighted document — Enter
Close (exit from) current application — Alt+F4 *or* Alt+Spacebar,C
Close current document window — Ctrl+F4 *or* Alt+Hyphen,C
Open application Control menu — Alt+Spacebar
Open document Control menu — Alt+Hyphen

Arranging Windows

Arrange windows in tile format — Shift+F4
Arrange windows in cascade format — Shift+F5
Switch DOS app between full screen and window — Alt+Enter

Switching from One Application to Another

Task List — Ctrl+Esc
Switch to next application running as icon or window — Alt+Esc
Switch back and forth between current
 and previously current applications — Alt+Tab
Switch back to previous application — Shift+Alt+Tab
Cycle through open applications — Alt+Tab+Tab

Dialog Boxes

Move forward through fields	Tab
Move backward through fields	Shift+Tab
Move to field of underlined letter	Alt+letter
Move to first item/character	Home
Move to last item/character	End
Scroll up/down one screen	PgUp/PgDn
Open drop down list	Alt+Down Arrow
Select or cancel selected item in list	Spacebar
Check or un-check check box	Spacebar
Select all items in a list	Ctrl+Slash (/)
Cancel all selections in list	Ctrl+Backslash (\)
Select first character in text box	Shift+Home
Select last character in text box	Shift+End
Execute dialog box settings	Enter
Close dialog box (same as Esc)	Alt+F4

Clipboard

Undo most recent action	Ctrl+Z (Alt+Backspace)
Cut selected text	Ctrl+X (Shift+Del)
Copy selected text	Ctrl+C (Ctrl+Ins)
Paste contents of clipboard	Ctrl+V (Shift+Ins)
Capture screen	Print Screen
Capture active window	Alt+Print Screen

Cursor Movement

Move cursor up/down one line	Up/Down Arrow
Move cursor left/right one character	Left/Right Arrow
Move cursor right one word	Ctrl+Right Arrow
Move cursor left one word	Ctrl+Left Arrow
Move cursor to beginning of line	Home
Move cursor to end of line	End
Move cursor up one screen	PgUp
Move cursor down one screen	PgDn
Move cursor to start of document	Ctrl+Home
Move cursor to end of document	Ctrl+End

WINDOWS (continued)

Text Selection

Use the above Cursor Movement keys with the addition of the Shift key. (For example, press Shift+Ctrl+Right Arrow to select the word to the right. Press Shift+Ctrl+End to select text from the current cursor position to the end of the document.)

File Manager

Move between directory tree, contents list, and drive icons	Tab *or* F6
Refresh directory window	F5
Move selection cursor within a list or between drive icons	Arrow
Move selection cursor one screen up/down	PgUp/PgDn
Move to first or last selection in a list	Home/End
Select root directory	Backslash (\)
Select next directory/file beginning with characterCharacter key	
Select next directory (up/down) at same level	Ctrl+Up Arrow/Ctrl+Down Arrow
Select adjacent files (in sequence)	Shift+Arrow
Select non-adjacent items (out-of-sequence)	Shift+F8+Spacebar
Select all items in list	Ctrl+Slash (/)
Cancel multiple selection	Ctrl+Backslash (\)

Toggle check boxes, complete out-of-sequence selections	Spacebar
Execute program or opens file	Enter
Open a new directory window	Shift+Enter
Change to drive of specified letter designation	Ctrl+*drive letter*
Change drives within drive icon panel	Spacebar

W ORDPERFECT KEYSTROKE SUMMARY CHART

General System Keys

	From Document	*From Menu*
Help	F1	Alt+H
Context Sensitive Help	Shift+F1	Alt+H
Open Application Control menu	Alt+Spacebar	
Open Document Control menu	Alt+Hyphen	
Restore Window		Alt+Hyphen,R
Move Window		Alt+Hyphen,M
Size Window		Alt+Hyphen,S
Minimize Window		Alt+Hyphen,N
Maximize Window		Alt+Hyphen,X
Close Window	Ctrl+F4	Alt+F,C
Switch to Next Document	Ctrl+F6	Alt+Hyphen,T
Exit WordPerfect	Alt+F4	Alt+F,X

Cursor Movement

Move cursor up/down one line	Up/Down Arrow
Move cursor left/right one character	Left/Right Arrow
Move cursor right one word	Ctrl+Right Arrow

Move cursor left one word	Ctrl+Left Arrow
Move cursor to beginning of line	Home
Move cursor to end of line	End
Move cursor up one screen	PgUp
Move cursor down one screen	PgDn
Move cursor up one page	Alt+PgUp
Move cursor down one page	Alt+PgDn
Move cursor to start of document	Ctrl+Home
Move cursor to end of document	Ctrl+End

Text Selection

Use the above Cursor Movement keys with the addition of the Shift key. (For example, press Shift+Ctrl+Right Arrow to select the word to the right. Press Shift+Ctrl+End to select text from the current cursor position to the end of the document.)

WORDPERFECT (continued)

File Operations (File Menu)

	From Document	From Menu
New	Shift+F4	Alt+F,N
Open	F4	Alt+F,O
Retrieve		Alt+F,R
Close	Ctrl+F4	Alt+F,C
Save	Shift+F3	Alt+F,S
Save As	F3	Alt+F,A
Print	F5	Alt+F,P
Print Preview	Shift+F5	Alt+F,V
Exit	Alt+F4	Alt+F,X

Edit Operations (Edit Menu)

	From Document	From Menu
Undo	Ctrl+Z (Alt+Backspace)	Alt+E,U
Undelete	Alt+Shift+Backspace	Alt+E,N
Cut	Ctrl+X (Shift+Del)	Alt+E,T
Copy	Ctrl+C (Ctrl+Ins)	Alt+E,C
Delete Left	Backspace	
Delete Right	Del	

Paste	Ctrl+V (Shift+Ins)	Alt+E,P
Search	F2	Alt+E,S
Replace	Ctrl+F2	Alt+E,R
Go To	Ctrl+G	Alt+E,G

View

Ruler (toggle on/off)	Alt+Shift+F3	Alt+V,R
Reveal Codes	Alt+F3	Alt+V,C
Draft Mode		Alt+V,D
Button Bar (toggle on/off)		Alt+V,B

Layout

	From Document	From Menu
Line	Shift+F9	Alt+L,L
Line Center	Shift+F7	Alt+L,L,C
Line Spacing		Alt+L,L,S
Paragraph		Alt+L,R
Page	Alt+F9	Alt+L,P
Columns	Alt+Shift+F9	Alt+L,C
Tables	Ctrl+F9	Alt+L,T
Document	Ctrl+Shift+F9	Alt+L,D
Footnote		Alt+L,F
Justification		Alt+L,J
Justification Left	Ctrl+L	Alt+L,J,L
Justification Right	Ctrl+R	Alt+L,J,R
Justification Center	Ctrl+J	Alt+L,J,C
Justification Full	Ctrl+F	Alt+L,J,F
Margins	Ctrl+F8	Alt+L,M
Styles	Alt+F8	Alt+L,S

Tools

Spell Checker	Ctrl+F1	Alt+T,S
Thesaurus	Alt+F1	Alt+T,T
Word Count		Alt+T,W
Date (insert date in text format)	Ctrl+F5	Alt+T,D,T
Date (insert date in code format)	Ctrl+Shift+F5	Alt+T,D,C
Sort	Ctrl+Shift+F12	Alt+T,R
Merge	Ctrl+F12	Alt+T,M
Mark Text	F12	Alt+T,K
Define Index, T.O.C., Lists	Shift+F12	Alt+T,F
Generate Index, T.O.C., Lists	Alt+F12	Alt+T,G

Font

Font	F9	Alt+O,O
Font Bold	Ctrl+B	Alt+O,B
Font Italic	Ctrl+I	Alt+O,I
Font Normal	Ctrl+N	Alt+O,N
Underline	Ctrl+U	Alt+O,U
Size	Ctrl+S	Alt+O,S
WP Characters (Special Char.)	Ctrl+W	Alt+O,W

WORDPERFECT (continued)

Graphics

	From Document	From Menu
Graphics Figure		Alt+G,F
Retrieve Figure	F11	Alt+G,F,R
Edit Figure	Shift+F11	Alt+G,F,E
Graphics Text Box		Alt+G,B
Text Box Create	Alt+F11	Alt+G,B,C
Text Box Edit	Alt+Shift+F11	Alt+G,B,E
Graphics Equation		Alt+G,E
Graphics Table Box		Alt+G,T
Graphics User Box		Alt+G,U
Graphics Line		Alt+G,L

Macro

	From Document	From Menu
Macro Play	Alt+F10	Alt+M,P
Macro Record	Ctrl+F10	Alt+M,R
Macro Stop	Ctrl+Shift+F10	Alt+M,S
Macro Pause		Alt+M,U
Macro Assign to Menu		Alt+M,A

Window

	From Document	From Menu
Cascade		Alt+W,C
Tile		Alt+W,T

MICROSOFT WORD KEYSTROKE SUMMARY CHART

General System Keys

	From Document	From Menu
Help	F1	Alt+H
Context Sensitive Help	Shift+F1	Alt+H
Cancel Current Command	Esc	
Open application Control menu	Alt+Spacebar	
Open document Control menu	Alt+Hyphen	
Restore Window	Ctrl+F5	Alt+Hyphen,R
Move Window	Ctrl+F7	Alt+Hyphen,M
Size Window	Ctrl+F8	Alt+Hyphen,S
Minimize Window	Ctrl+F9	Alt+Hyphen,N
Maximize Window	Ctrl+F10	Alt+Hyphen,X
Close Window	Ctrl+F4	Alt+Hyphen,C
Switch to Next Document	Ctrl+F6	Alt+Hyphen,T
Exit Word	Alt+F4	Alt+F,X

Cursor Movement

Moves cursor up/down one line	Up/Down Arrow
Moves cursor left/right one character	Left/Right Arrow

Moves cursor right one word	Ctrl+Right Arrow
Moves cursor left one word	Ctrl+Left Arrow
Moves cursor to beginning of line	Home
Moves cursor to end of line	End
Moves cursor up one screen	PgUp
Moves cursor down one screen	PgDn
Moves cursor to start of document	Ctrl+Home
Moves cursor to end of document	Ctrl+End

Text Selection

Use the above Cursor Movement keys with the addition of the Shift key. (For example, press Shift+Ctrl+Right Arrow to select the word to the right. Press Shift+Ctrl+End to select text from the current cursor position to the end of the document.) In addition, you can perform an extended selection by pressing the F8 key.

MICROSOFT WORD (continued)

File Operations (File Menu)

	From Document	From Menu
New		Alt+F,N
Open	Ctrl+F12	Alt+F,O
Close	Ctrl+F4	Alt+F,C
Save	Shift+F12	Alt+F,S
Save As	F12	Alt+F,A
Save All		Alt+F,E
Template		Alt+F,T
Print	Ctrl+Shift+F12	Alt+F,P
Print Preview		Alt+F,V
Print Setup		Alt+F,R
Exit	Alt+F4	Alt+F,X

Edit Operations (Edit Menu)

	From Document	From Menu
Undo Typing/Edit	Ctrl+Z (Alt+Backspace)	Alt+E,U
Repeat Typing/Edit	F4	Alt+E,R
Cut	Ctrl+X (Shift+Del)	Alt+E,T
Copy	Ctrl+C (Ctrl+Ins)	Alt+E,C

Paste	Ctrl+V (Shift+Ins)	Alt+E,P
Delete Left	Backspace	
Delete Right	Del	
Select All		Alt+E,A
Find		Alt+E,F
Replace		Alt+E,E
Go To	F5	Alt+E,G
Repeat Find/Go To	Shift F5	
Object		Alt+E,B

View

Normal	Alt+V,N
Outline	Alt+V,O
Page Layout	Alt+V,P
Draft Mode	Alt+V,D
Toolbar (on/off)	Alt+V,T
Ribbon (on/off)	Alt+V,B
Ruler (on/off)	Alt+V,R
Header/Footer	Alt+V,H
Close Header/Footer	Alt+Shift,C
Footnotes	Alt+V,F

MICROSOFT WORD (continued)

Insert

	From Document	From Menu
Page break	Ctrl+Enter	Alt+I,B
New Line	Shift+Enter	
Page numbers		Alt+I,U
Bookmark	Ctrl+Shift+F5	Alt+I,M
Date and Time		Alt+I,T
Symbol		Alt+I,S
File		Alt+I,L
Frame		Alt+I,F
Picture		Alt+I,P
Object		Alt+I,O

Format

	From Document	From Menu
Character		Alt+T,C
Font	Ctrl+F	Alt+T,C
Point Size	Ctrl+P	
Bold	Ctrl+B	Alt+T,C
Italic	Ctrl+I	Alt+T,C

Subscript	Ctrl+= (equal sign)	
Superscript	Ctrl++ (plus sign)	
Underline	Ctrl+U	Alt+T,C
Paragraph		Alt+T,P
Paragraph Nest	Ctrl+N	
Paragraph Un-nest	Ctrl+M	
Line Spacing	Ctrl+1,2,5 (1.5)	
Alignment		Alt+T,P
Alignment Left	Ctrl+L	
Alignment Right	Ctrl+R	
Alignment Center	Ctrl+E	
Justified Right and Left	Ctrl+J	
Tabs		Alt+T,T
Style	Ctrl+S	Alt+T,Y
Page Setup		Alt+T,U
Columns		Alt+T,O
Frame		Alt+T,F
Picture		Alt+T,P

MICROSOFT WORD (continued)

Tools

	From Document	From Menu
Spelling		Alt+O,S
Thesaurus	Shift+F7	Alt+O,T
Hyphenation		Alt+O,H
Bullets and Numbering		Alt+O,B
Create Envelope		Alt+O,E
Sorting		Alt+O,I
Record Macro		Alt+O,R
Macro		Alt+O,M
Options (customization)		Alt+O,O

Table

	From Document	From Menu
Insert Table		Alt+A,I
Delete Columns		Alt+A,D
Convert Text to Table		Alt+A,T
Select Row		Alt+A,R
Select Column		Alt+A,C
Select Table		Alt+A,A

Window

New Window	Alt+W,N
Arrange All	Alt+W,A

AMI PRO KEYSTROKE SUMMARY CHART

General System Keys

	From Document	*From Menu*
Help	F1	Alt+H
Context Sensitive Help	Shift+F1	Alt+H
Open Application Control Menu	Alt+Spacebar	
Open Document Control Menu	Alt+Hyphen	
Restore Window		Alt+Hyphen,R
Move Window		Alt+Hyphen,M
Size Window		Alt+Hyphen,S
Minimize Window		Alt+Hyphen,N
Maximize Window		Alt+Hyphen,X
Close Window	Ctrl+F4	Alt+F,C
Switch to Next Document	Ctrl+F6	Alt+Hyphen,T
Exit Ami Pro	Alt+F4	Alt+F,X

Cursor Movement

Moves cursor up/down one line	Up/Down Arrow
Moves cursor left/right one character	Left/Right Arrow
Moves cursor right one word	Ctrl+Right Arrow

Moves cursor left one word	Ctrl+Left Arrow
Moves cursor to beginning of line	Home
Moves cursor to end of line	End
Moves cursor up one screen	PgUp
Moves cursor down one screen	PgDn
Moves cursor up one page	Ctrl+PgUp
Moves cursor down one page	Ctrl+PgDn
Moves cursor to start of document	Ctrl+Home
Moves cursor to end of document	Ctrl+End

Text Selection

Use the above Cursor Movement keys with the addition of the Shift key. (For example, press Shift+Ctrl+Right Arrow to select the word to the right. Press Shift+Ctrl+End to select text from the current cursor position to the end of the document.)

AMI PRO (continued)

File Operations (File Menu)

	From Document	From Menu
.New		Alt+F,N
Open	Ctrl+O	Alt+F,O
Retrieve		Alt+F,R
Close	Ctrl+F4	Alt+F,C
Save	Ctrl+S	Alt+F,S
Save As		Alt+F,A
Revert to Saved		Alt+F,R
Import Picture		Alt+F,I
Master Document		Alt+F,E
Merge		Alt+F,G
Print	Ctrl+P	Alt+F,P
Exit	Alt+F4	Alt+F,X

Edit Operations (Edit Menu)

Undo	Ctrl+Z (Alt+Backspace)	Alt+E,U
Cut	Ctrl+X (Shift+Del)	Alt+E,T
Copy	Ctrl+C (Ctrl+Ins)	Alt+E,C
Paste	Ctrl+V (Shift+Ins)	Alt+E,P
Delete Left	Backspace	
Delete Right	Del	
Delete Next Word	Ctrl+Del	
Delete Previous Word	Ctrl+Backspace	
Find & Replace	Ctrl+F	Alt+E,R
Go To	Ctrl+G	Alt+E,G
Go To Next Item	Ctrl+H	
Insert		Alt+E,I
Power Fields		Alt+E,F

View

Full Page	Ctrl+D	Alt+V,F
Custom		Alt+V,C
Standard		Alt+V,S
Layout Mode		Alt+V,L
Draft Mode	Ctrl+M	Alt+V,D

AMI PRO (continued)

View   *continued*

	From Document	From Menu
Show/Hide SmartIcons	Ctrl+Q	Alt+V,I
Show/Hide Clean Screen		Alt+V,N
Show/Hide Ruler		Alt+V,R
View Preferences		Alt+V,P

Text

	From Document	From Menu
Font		Alt+T,F
Normal	Ctrl+N	Alt+T,N
Bold	Ctrl+B	Alt+T,B
Italic	Ctrl+I	Alt+T,I
Underline	Ctrl+U	Alt+T,U
Word Underline	Ctrl+W	Alt+T,W
Alignment		Alt+T,A
Justification Left	Ctrl+L	Alt+T,A,L
Justification Right	Ctrl+R	Alt+T,A,R
Justification Center	Ctrl+J	Alt+T,A,C
Justification Full	Ctrl+F	Alt+T,A,J

Indention		Alt+T,D
Spacing		Alt+T,S
Fast Format	Ctrl+T	Alt+T,T

Style

Create Style		Alt+S,C
Modify Style	Ctrl+A	Alt+S,M
Define Style		Alt+S,D
Select a Style	Ctrl+Y	Alt+S,S

Page

Header/Footer		Alt+P,H
Insert Page Layout		Alt+P,I
Modify Page Layout		Alt+P,M
Ruler		Alt+P,R
Page Numbering		Alt+P,P
Breaks		Alt+P,B

AMI PRO (continued)

Frame

	From Document	From Menu
Create Frame		Alt+F,C
Modify Frame Layout		Alt+F,M
Graphics Scaling		Alt+F,S

Tools

	From Document	From Menu
Spell Check		Alt+L,S
Tables		Alt+L,B
Footnotes		Alt+L,F
Sort		Alt+L,O
SmartIcons (Customizing)		Alt+L,I
User Setup		Alt+L,U
Macros		Alt+L,M
Quick Record		Alt+L,M,Q
Quick Playback		Alt+L,M,U

Window

New Window	Alt+W,N
Cascade	Alt+W,C
Tile	Alt+W,T

MICROSOFT EXCEL KEYSTROKE SUMMARY CHART

General System Keys

	From Document	From Menu
Help	F1	Alt+H
Context Sensitive Help	Shift+F1	Alt+H
Activate Edit Mode	F2	
Cancel Current Command	Esc	
Open application Control menu	Alt+Spacebar	
Open document Control menu	Alt+Hyphen	
Restore Window	Ctrl+F5	Alt+Hyphen,R
Move Window	Ctrl+F7	Alt+Hyphen,M
Size Window	Ctrl+F8	Alt+Hyphen,S
Minimize Window	Ctrl+F9	Alt+Hyphen,N
Maximize Window	Ctrl+F10	Alt+Hyphen,X
Close Window	Ctrl+F4	Alt+Hyphen,C
Switch to Next Document	Ctrl+F6	Alt+Hyphen,T
Exit Excel	Alt+F4	Alt+F,X

Cursor Movement in the Formula Bar

Insert a carriage return	Alt+Enter
Move cursor up/down one line	Up/Down Arrow
Move cursor left/right one character	Left/Right Arrow
Move cursor right one word	Ctrl+Right Arrow
Move cursor left one word	Ctrl+Left Arrow
Move cursor to beginning of text	Home
Move cursor to end of text	End
Enter data and exits formula bar	Enter

Text Selection in the Formula Bar

Use the above Cursor Movement keys with the addition of the Shift key. (For example, press Shift+Ctrl+Right Arrow to select the word to the right. Press Shift+Ctrl+End to select text from the current cursor position to the end of the text.)

Cursor Movement in the Worksheet

Enter data into current cell and moves up/down to next cell	Up/Down Arrow
Move cursor up/down one cell	Up/Down Arrow
Move cursor left/right one cell	Left/Right Arrow

MICROSOFT EXCEL (continued)

Cursor Movement in the Worksheet   *continued*

Move cursor right to end of block	Ctrl+Right Arrow
Move cursor left end of block	Ctrl+Left Arrow
Move cursor down to end of block	Ctrl+Down Arrow
Move cursor up to end of block	Ctrl+Up Arrow
Move cursor to beginning of row	Home
Move cursor to end of row	End
Move cursor up one screen	PgUp
Move cursor down one screen	PgDn
Move cursor left one screen	Ctrl+PgUp
Move cursor right one screen	Ctrl+PgDn
Move cursor to start of worksheet	Ctrl+Home
Move cursor to end of worksheet	Ctrl+End

Cell Selection

Use the above Cursor Movement keys with the addition of the Shift key as follows:

Select up/down one cell	Shift+Up/Down Arrow
Select left/right one cell	Shift+Left/Right Arrow
Select right to end of block	Shift+Ctrl+Right Arrow

Select left end of block	Shift+Ctrl+Left Arrow
Select down to end of block	Shift+Ctrl+Down Arrow
Select up to end of block	Shift+Ctrl+Up Arrow
Select to beginning of row	Shift+Home
Select to end of row	Shift+End
Select up one screen	Shift+PgUp
Select down one screen	Shift+PgDn
Select left one screen	Shift+Ctrl+PgUp
Select right one screen	Shift+Ctrl+PgDn
Select to start of worksheet	Shift+Ctrl+Home
Select to end of worksheet	Shift+Ctrl+End
Select entire row	Shift+Spacebar
Select entire column	Ctrl+Spacebar
Extended Selection	F8
Non-adjacent extended selection	Shift+F8

File Operations (File Menu)

	From Document	From Menu
New		Alt+F,N
Open	Ctrl+F12	Alt+F,O
Close	Ctrl+F4	Alt+F,C
Save	Shift+F12	Alt+F,S

File Operations (File Menu)   *continued*

	From Document	From Menu
Save As	F12	Alt+F,A
Delete Document		Alt+F,D
Print	Ctrl+Shift+F12	Alt+F,P
Print Preview		Alt+F,V
Exit	Alt+F4	Alt+F,X

Edit Operations (Edit Menu)

	From Document	From Menu
Undo	Ctrl+Z (Alt+Backspace)	Alt+E,U
Cut	Ctrl+X (Shift+Del)	Alt+E,T
Copy	Ctrl+C (Ctrl+Ins)	Alt+E,C
Paste	Ctrl+V (Shift+Ins)	Alt+E,P
Delete Selection		Alt+E,D
Insert row, column, or selection		Alt+E,I
Insert object		Alt+E,O
Fill Right	Ctrl+R	Alt+E,H
Fill Down	Ctrl+D	Alt+E,W

Formula

Paste Name		Alt+R,P
Paste Function		Alt+R,T
Define Name		Alt+R,D
Create Names		Alt+R,C
Goto	F5	Alt+R,G
Find	Shift+F5	Alt+R,F
Find Next Cell	F7	
Find Previous Cell	Shift+F7	
Replace		Alt+R,E
Select Special		Alt+R,S
Insert Autosum	Alt+= (equal sign)	

Format

Number Formats		Alt+T,N
Date Format	Ctrl+Shift+#	Alt+T,N
Time Format	Ctrl+Shift+@	Alt+T,N
Currency Format	Ctrl+Shift+$	Alt+T,N
Alignment		Alt+T,A
Font	Ctrl+F	Alt+T,F
Bold	Ctrl+B	Alt+T,F

MICROSOFT EXCEL (continued)

Format   *continued*

	From Document	From Menu
Italic	Ctrl+I	Alt+T,F
Underline	Ctrl+U	Alt+T,F
Border		Alt+T,B
Patterns		Alt+T,P
Column Width		Alt+T,C
Justify		Alt+T,J

Data (Database Commands)

	From Menu
Form	Alt+D,O
Find	Alt+D,F
Extract	Alt+D,E
Delete	Alt+D,D
Set Database	Alt+D,B
Sort	Alt+D,S
Table	Alt+D,T
Consolidate	Alt+D,N

Options

Set Print Area	Alt+O,A
Set Page Break	Alt+O,B
Display (customize)	Alt+O,D
Toolbars (customize, add, remove)	Alt+O,O
Workspace (customize)	Alt+O,W
Add-ins (integrating)	Alt+O,I

Macro

Macro Run	Alt+M,R
Macro Record	Alt+M,C
Macro Start Recorder	Alt+M,S
Macro Resume	Alt+M,E
Macro Assign to Object	Alt+M,O

Window

New Window	Alt+W,N
Hide	Alt+W,H
Un-hide	Alt+W,U
Split	Alt+W,S

BORLAND QUATTRO PRO KEYSTROKE SUMMARY CHART

General System Keys

	From Document	From Menu
Help	F1	Alt+H
Context Sensitive Help	Shift+F1	Alt+H
Activate Edit Mode	F2	
Cancel Current Command	Esc	
Open Application Control Menu	Alt+Spacebar	
Open Document Control Menu	Alt+Hyphen	
Restore Window		Alt+Hyphen,R
Move Window		Alt+Hyphen,M
Size Window		Alt+Hyphen,S
Minimize Window		Alt+Hyphen,N
Maximize Window		Alt+Hyphen,X
Close Window	Ctrl+F4	Alt+Hyphen,C
Switch to Next Document	Ctrl+F6	Alt+Hyphen,T
Exit Quattro Pro	Alt+F4	Alt+F,X

Cursor Movement in the Input Line

Enter data into current cell and moves up/down to next cell	Up/Down Arrow
Enter data and exits input line	Enter
Move cursor left/right one character	Left/Right Arrow
Move cursor right one word.	Ctrl+Right Arrow
Move cursor left one word	Ctrl+Left Arrow
Move cursor to beginning of text	Home
Move cursor to end of text	End

(*Note*: The above keystrokes assume that the DOS Keyboard Compatibility option is not selected. If using the DOS Compatibility option, Ctrl+Left Arrow or Ctrl+Right Arrow moves five characters instead of one word. See Chapter 7 for more details).

Text Selection in the Input Line

Use the above Cursor Movement keys with the addition of the Shift key. (For example, press Shift+Ctrl+Right Arrow to select the word to the right. Press Shift+Ctrl+End to select text from the current cursor position to the end of the text.)

Cursor Movement in the Worksheet

Move cursor up/down one cell	Up/Down Arrow
Move cursor left/right one cell	Left/Right Arrow
Move cursor right one screen	Ctrl+Right Arrow *or* Tab
Move cursor left one screen	Ctrl+Left Arrow *or* Shift+Tab
Move to upper left cell of current page	Home
Move to upper left cell of first page	Ctrl+Home
Move cursor to end of row	End
Move cursor up one screen	PgUp
Move cursor down one screen	PgDn
Move cursor backward one page	Ctrl+PgUp
Move cursor forward one page	Ctrl+PgDn

Cell Selection

Use the above Cursor Movement keys with the addition of the Shift key. For example, to select from the current cell to the beginning of the page, press Shift+Home. Press Shift+Down Arrow to select cells in the current column below the current cell. Press Shift+F7 to perform extended selection.

File Operations (File Menu)

	From Document	From Menu
New		Alt+F,N
Open		Alt+F,O
Close	Ctrl+F4	Alt+F,C
Close All		Alt+F,E
Save		Alt+F,S
Save As		Alt+F,A
Save All		Alt+F,L
Retrieve		Alt+F,R
Print		Alt+F,P
Print Preview		Alt+F,V
Page Setup		Alt+F,T
Named Settings		Alt+F,M
Workspace		Alt+F,W
Exit	Alt+F4	Alt+F,X

Edit Operations (Edit Menu)

	From Document	From Menu
Undo		Alt+E,U
Cut	Shift+Del	Alt+E,T
Copy	Ctrl+Ins	Alt+E,C

Edit Operations (Edit Menu)   *continued*

	From Document	From Menu
Paste	Shift+Ins	Alt+E,P
Paste Special		Alt+E,I
Delete Cell Contents	Del	
Clear		Alt+E,A
Goto	F5	Alt+E,G
Search and Replace		Alt+E,S
Define Style		Alt+E,D
Insert Object		Alt+E,O

Block

	From Document	From Menu
Move		Alt+B,M
Copy		Alt+B,C
Insert		Alt+B,I
Delete		Alt+B,D
Fill		Alt+B,F
Names		Alt+B,N
Insert Break		Alt+B,B

Data

Sort		Alt+D,S
Query		Alt+D,Q
Restrict Input		Alt+D,R
What-If		Alt+D,W
Table Query		Alt+D,T

Tools

Macro		Alt+T,M
Macro Execute	Alt+F2	Alt+T,M,X
Macro Record		Alt+T,M,R
Define Group		Alt+T,G
Combine		Alt+T,C
Extract		Alt+T,E
Import		Alt+T,I

BORLAND QUATTRO PRO (continued)

Graph

	From Document	From Menu
Type		Alt+G,Y
New		Alt+G,N
Edit		Alt+G,E
Insert		Alt+G,I
Delete		Alt+G,D
Copy		Alt+G,C
View	F11	Alt+G,V

Property (Object Inspectors)

	From Document	From Menu
Current Object	F12	Alt+P,C
Application	Alt+F12	Alt+P,A
Active Notebook	Shift+F12	Alt+P,N
Active Page		Alt+P,P
Move between OI Dialog Box Options	Ctrl+PgUp/PgDn	

Window

New View	Alt+W,N
Tile	Alt+W,T
Cascade	Alt+W,C
Hide	Alt+W,H
Panes	Alt+W,P

LOTUS 1-2-3 KEYSTROKE SUMMARY CHART

General System Keys

	From Document	From Menu
Help	F1	Alt+H
Context Sensitive Help	Shift+F1	Alt+H
Activates Edit Mode	F2	
Cancel Current Command	Esc	
Open Application Control Menu	Alt+Spacebar	
Open Document Control Menu	Alt+Hyphen	
Restore Window		Alt+Hyphen,R
Move Window		Alt+Hyphen,M
Size Window		Alt+Hyphen,S
Minimize Window		Alt+Hyphen,N
Maximize Window		Alt+Hyphen,X
Close Window	Ctrl+F4	Alt+Hyphen,C
Switch to Next Document	Ctrl+F6	Alt+Hyphen,T
Exit Excel	Alt+F4	Alt+F,X

Cursor Movement in the Contents Box

Enter data into current cell and moves up/down to next cell	Up/Down Arrow
Enter data and exit input line	Enter
Move cursor up/down one line	Up/Down Arrow
Move cursor left/right one character	Left/Right Arrow
Move cursor right one word.	Ctrl+Right Arrow
Move cursor left one word	Ctrl+Left Arrow
Move cursor to beginning of text	Home
Move cursor to end of text	End
Enter data and exit contents box	Enter

Text Selection in the Contents Box

Use the above Cursor Movement keys with the addition of the Shift key. (For example, press Shift+Ctrl+Right Arrow to select the word to the right. Press Shift+Ctrl+End to select text from the current cursor position to the end of the text.)

Cursor Movement in the Worksheet

Move cursor up/down one cell	Up/Down Arrow
Move cursor left/right one cell	Left/Right Arrow

Cursor Movement in the Worksheet *continued*

Move cursor right one screen	Ctrl+Right Arrow *or* Tab
Move cursor left one screen	Ctrl+Left Arrow *or* Shift+Tab
Move cursor to cell A1	Home
Move horizontally to end or beginning of data	End+Left/Right Arrow
Move vertically to end or beginning of data	End+Up/Down Arrow
Move to bottom right of active data area	End Home
Move cursor up one screen	PgUp
Move cursor down one screen	PgDn
Move cursor to next worksheet	Ctrl+PgUp
Move cursor to previous worksheet	Ctrl+PgDn
Move cursor to start of first worksheet	Ctrl+Home

Cell Selection

Use the above Cursor Movement keys with the addition of the Shift key. For example, to select from the current cell to cell A1, press Shift+Home. Press Shift+Down Arrow to select cells in the current column below the current cell.

File Operations (File Menu)

	From Document	From Menu
New		Alt+F,N
Open		Alt+F,O
Close	Ctrl+F4	Alt+F,C
Save		Alt+F,S
Save As		Alt+F,A
Combine From		Alt+F,B
Import From		Alt+F,I
Print		Alt+F,P
Print Preview		Alt+F,V
Exit	Alt+F4	Alt+F,X

Edit Operations (Edit Menu)

Undo	Alt+Backspace	Alt+E,U
Cut	Shift+Del	Alt+E,T
Copy	Ctrl+Ins	Alt+E,C
Paste	Shift+Ins	Alt+E,P
Clear	Del	Alt+E,E
Clear Special		Alt+E,R
Find		Alt+E,F

Edit Operations (Edit Menu) *continued*

	From Document	From Menu
Move Cells		Alt+E,M
Quick Copy		Alt+E,Q
Insert object		Alt+E,O

Worksheet

	From Document	From Menu
Global Settings		Alt+K,G
Insert		Alt+K,I
Delete		Alt+K,D
Hide		Alt+K,H
Un-hide		Alt+K,U
Column Width		Alt+K,C
Titles		Alt+K,T
Page Break		Alt+K,P

Range

Format	Alt+R,F
Name	Alt+R,N
Justify	Alt+R,J
Protect	Alt+R,P
Un-protect	Alt+R,U
Transpose	Alt+R,T
Go To	Alt+R,G

Graph

New	Alt+G,M
View	Alt+G,V
Add to Sheet	Alt+G,A
Name	Alt+G,M
Import	Alt+G,I
Size	Alt+G,S
Refresh	Alt+G,F
Go To	Alt+G,G

LOTUS 1-2-3 (continued)

Data

	From Document	From Menu
Fill		Alt+D,F
Sort		Alt+D,S
What-If-Table		Alt+D,T
Parse		Alt+D,P
Query		Alt+D,Q
Connect to External		Alt+D,C
External Options		Alt+D,E

Style

	From Document	From Menu
Font		Alt+S,F
Alignment		Alt+S,A
Border		Alt+S,B
Shading		Alt+S,S
Name		Alt+S,N

Tools

Backsolver	Alt+T,B
SmartIcons	Alt+T,I
User Setup	Alt+T,U
Macro	Alt+T,M
Add-In	Alt+T,A

Window

Tile	Alt+W,T
Cascade	Alt+W,C
Display Options	Alt+W,D
Split	Alt+W,S

Index

The Index for this book is divided into seven sections, starting with a general Windows section covering the foreword and the first two chapters, followed by sections for each individual application in alphabetical order: Ami Pro, Excel, Lotus 1-2-3, Quattro Pro, Word, and WordPerfect.

Ami Pro

Excel

Lotus 1-2-3

Quattro Pro

Word

WordPerfect